W9-AMU-228

Your Struggling Child

Robert F. Newby, Ph.D.,

with Carol A. Turkington

A LYNN SONBERG BOOK

Collins

An Imprint of *HarperCollins*Publishers

Your Struggling Child

A Guide to Diagnosing,

Understanding, and

Advocating for Your

Child with Learning,

Behavior, or Emotional

Problems

HarperCollins books may be purchased for educational, business, or sales
promotional use. For information, please write: Special Markets Department,
HarperCollins Publishers, 10 East 53rd Street, New York, NY 10022.

FIRST EDITION

Designed by Kate Nichols

Printed on acid-free paper

Library of Congress Cataloging-in-Publication Data
Newby, Robert F.
    Your struggling child : a guide to diagnosing, understanding, and advocating for
your child with learning, behavior, or emotional problems / Robert F. Newby with
Carol A. Turkington.
        p.   cm.
    Includes bibliographical references and index.
    ISBN-10: 0-06-073522-8
    ISBN-13: 978-0-06-073522-7
    1. Learning disabilities.   2. Problem children.   I. Turkington, Carol A.
II. Title.
RJ496.L4N49   2005
618.92'85889—dc22

                                                                    2005052523

06 07 08 09 10 /RRD 10 9 8 7 6 5 4 3 2 1

THIS BOOK contains advice and information relating to health care. It is not intended to replace medical advice and should be used to supplement rather than replace regular care by your doctor. It is recommended that you seek your physician's advice before embarking on any medical program or treatment.

All efforts have been made to ensure the accuracy of the information contained in this book as of the date published. The authors and the publisher expressly disclaim responsibility for any adverse effects arising from the use or application of the information contained herein.

The names and identifying characteristics of parents and children featured throughout this book have been changed to protect their privacy.

To all the dedicated parents

Contents

Acknowledgments

EVERY DAY I see parents and children who are struggling at home and at school because of learning, emotional, or behavior problems. I know what frightens kids and parents, and I know their most pressing concerns. I have attempted to distill my experience as a clinician to the task of writing this book and have tried to organize it in a way that will be useful to parents who are just starting the journey of discovering and thoroughly investigating their children's difficulties. The advice and information I have gathered is based on my own experience with literally thousands of parents and children and also presents the research and thoughtful ideas of others working and publishing in the field.

Several teachers with whom I've had the honor to work deserve special credit in this effort, including Chuck Matthews, Connie Clune, Russell Barkley, Carl Whitaker, Ilana Hadar, Lynn Blackburn, B. Kent Houston, and Chuck Hallenbeck. My faculty colleagues and residents in the Neuropsychology Division at the Medical College of Wisconsin have provided valuable input, particularly the current developmental neuropsychology members: Tanya Brown, Lisa Conant, Mariellen Fischer, Grace Fong, Amy Heffelfinger, Jennifer Koop, and Elizabeth Nelson. It's truly a privilege to work with such a strong community of clinicians and scholars. This book also owes a great deal to Carol Turkington, who worked indefatigably with me in crafting the text, as well as to Lynn Sonberg and Toni Sciarra, for their astute editorial guidance. I also deeply appreciate the support of family and friends, particularly the partnership of my wife, Donna.

And most of all, thanks to the thousands of parents and children who have shared their struggles and joys in the neuropsychological evaluations we have conducted together. You'll read about some of them in the pages that follow. We've been careful to mask the identities of the children whose stories we tell in this book by giving them different names, and also by often shifting other important personal information such as age, grade, parents' occupations, or gender. Some of the cases we describe blend the stories of more than one child from my clinical practice, and others have been shared with me by colleagues. It's important to emphasize, however, that all our case material presented here is real and, in that way, is very much like what you may be facing with your child.

Robert F. Newby, Ph.D.

Preface

EACH YEAR, as the mountain forests come alive again with spring, my wife and I take a walk in the woods. (Those of you who have read Bill Bryson's humorous and insightful book by that title, *A Walk in the Woods*, will recognize the reference. If you haven't read the book, I would heartily recommend it as a metaphor for the decision to become a parent.) We take our two dogs, load up our backpacks, and spend a week or so hiking a small section of the Appalachian Trail, choosing a different section each year.

To some extent, this popular trail, which stretches continuously over two thousand miles from Georgia to Maine, is easy to follow. All you have to do is keep your eye out for the white marks on the trees, about the size of an index card, that the trailblazers have painted regularly along the way. It's just like parenting: Your child wakes up every morning and tries to communicate to you what he or she needs, day after day, for thousands of miles. You just keep on walking with them.

But there's a problem. If your child's development, behavior, emotions, or learning skills aren't going well, you need a lot more information in addition to the fact that he or she wakes up every day. In the same way,

Donna and I find that we like to have more than the white marks on the trees as we hike. So what do we do?

We get a map.

This helps us with all sorts of issues, such as how steep the trail will be over the next few miles, where to find water along the way, and where we cross roads (so we can put the leashes on the dogs to keep them from running into traffic).

One year on our hike, we decided to save a few dollars and skip the map. Bad idea! It's not that we got lost. After all, the white marks on the trees kept going on and on, just as your children wake up every day and try to tell you what they need. But without the map, we didn't know what to expect. We got quite a shock when suddenly facing a steep hill . . . wondering how long the swamp would continue . . . wondering where the next watering hole might be, because we only knew what we could see a few hundred feet around us in the woods. We couldn't really plan when to rest or where we might set up our tent for the night. Now, we *do* enjoy surprises, but my wife will tell you that I got crabby at times, and all four of us got unnecessarily thirsty and exhausted.

If you're reading this book, you're probably concerned about your child's bumps, valleys, and swamps. Do you feel as if you're hiking in the rugged mountains without a map? Is the fact that you *chose* to be a parent—just as Donna and I *choose* to hike each year—not completely enough when it comes to figuring out where you're headed?

Get a map.

Here's how.

Your Struggling Child

1

Helping You Better Understand Your Child

Y OU SENSE that your child has a problem. Maybe Jack's a whiz in math, but by second grade he's still not reading. Mary has a phenomenal vocabulary for a fourth grader, but she's still having trouble tying her shoes. Jody is a helpful eighth grader around the house, with lots of friends—but he's constantly sitting in the principal's office. At seventeen, Sally still can't pay attention long enough to finish her homework, so she's getting frustrated and discouraged. Or maybe you have a teenager who seemed to do fine in elementary school, but now that he's facing more challenging work in high school, he's starting to have problems and you're wondering if he has an undiagnosed learning disability.

You know *something* seems to be wrong—but what? So many times parents have told me, *I just had a feeling that something wasn't right.* All too often, parents with these vague concerns don't know what to do with their intuitive feelings. In some mild cases, a teacher may not mention your child's problems at all. At other times, a teacher may notice something going on at school that doesn't happen at home, and suddenly you get a surprise call from a teacher because your child's progress isn't what it should be. Here you were thinking everything was going well, and suddenly you've got a teacher with another point of view entirely.

If this sounds like your situation, take heart! Your feelings of confusion or uncertainty are really quite common, but so often unaddressed. The problem is that many behavioral or learning issues aren't obvious or straightforward. It's hard for parents to figure out if their child's skills or behavior are simply at the far end of "normal," or if the child really has a problem. And if your child *does* need help—where do you start?

That was the dilemma for Sandra, a single mom who was worried about her only child, seven-year-old Celeste. "When Celeste was in kindergarten and first grade, she seemed fine," her mom reported. She made friends, enjoyed school, and was reading above grade level. But by the end of first grade, something had changed. Her teacher noticed that Celeste had started to withdraw and stare blankly out the window. She wouldn't eat lunch with her friends. By the third grade the problems had only gotten worse.

"After a month of school that fall," her mother reported, "her teacher called and said something had to be done." Celeste was acting spacey and was barely speaking in class. When the teacher asked her what was wrong, she'd just shrug. "I noticed these changes at home, too," Sandra said, "but I didn't know what to do or where to turn."

Was Celeste just bored? Unchallenged? Slow? Could she have a brain disease?

The Guilt Game

Sandra's story isn't unique. In fact, lots of parents sense something isn't quite right with their child about the same time that the child starts to have problems at school. Often, this begins in late preschool or in the early elementary grades. When you see your child struggle, it's easy to feel guilty or worried. Parents ask themselves, "Did we do something wrong? Are my child's problems my fault?"

It can be even more upsetting if you think there's a problem, but the school either doesn't recognize a problem or shrugs off your valid concerns. At that point, you're left with a haunting dilemma: *Is it me? Is my child actually okay? Am I just overreacting? Maybe the school knows best . . .*

Between the confusion about what *might* be wrong and not knowing where to go for help or whom to ask, it's not surprising that you feel lost, anxious, and frustrated. At this very moment, millions of children across the United States are falling behind in school or acting out impulsively at home. Some of these kids don't have any friends. They don't get along with their brothers and sisters. They may be troubled by dramatic mood swings; perhaps they're hostile, hyperactive, listless, apathetic, easily distracted, withdrawn, antisocial, or destructive. And their parents are frustrated and afraid because they feel they've lost control and they don't know how to find out what's wrong. They don't know where to turn for help, how to get a diagnosis, what treatments are available, or how to cope with their child's challenging behaviors and moods. They don't know whether their child's struggles are normal or abnormal.

Why I Wrote This Book

If this sounds like what's going on with your family, don't worry—there's hope! That's why I've written this book—to help you find the answers to all the heartrending questions that many other parents just like you have asked me over the years:

> *What's wrong with my child?*
> *Will my child make it through school?*
> *Will my child ever be normal?*

All these questions were on Sandra's mind after she had spoken to Celeste's teacher. Something was definitely going on with this student, the teacher insisted. So Sandra took Celeste to her pediatrician, and then to another pediatrician, and then to a child psychologist—but none of them seemed to understand her daughter's problems. One recommended that Celeste start taking antidepressant medication after a mere five-minute interview. "She might be depressed," the doctor suggested, but Sandra resisted the idea of medicating her child before she really knew what the problem was.

Sandra had a growing intuition that this problem wouldn't go away on its own, but she needed more information. Eventually, Celeste was referred to our clinic for an evaluation.

A Typical Day at the Neuropsychology Clinic

After Sandra made the first appointment to meet with me, the clinic sent her two sets of behavior-rating questionnaires—one for her and the other for Celeste's teacher. On the morning of her appointment, I sat down with Sandra and assured her we'd try to figure out what was going on with Celeste. I explained that we'd look for certain specific problems, but that we weren't simply going to put Sandra's parenting style under a microscope. Right away, she felt less confused and guilty.

I explained to her that no matter what sorts of issues a child is facing, you *can* help your child—today, right now. The first thing you need to do is figure out if there really *is* a problem—and if so, what that problem might be. After our initial discussion, I called Celeste into the room and explained in "kid language" what to expect. I told her that at this clinic, we're just "talking doctors," so there wouldn't be any shots. I explained that we'd ask her some questions, play word games, check out her memory, maybe do some work on a computer, and work on some school things. We'd also talk about school, family, and friends.

Then one of our testing assistants (they're called psychometrists) took Celeste down the hall while I interviewed Sandra in more detail. During this interview, I collected more background information, looked at the behavior questionnaires, and checked the records she'd brought. I'd use all of these things to help me pinpoint Celeste's problems.

Meanwhile, Celeste was busy with various tests. During one break, I "interviewed" her by playing and talking together about her ideas, feelings, reactions to school, and so on. (If there's more testing planned for the afternoon, we give the child a good lunch break with their parents. If the child tires out before we've completed the testing, we just stop for that day and continue another time.) In Celeste's case, we were able to complete and score all the tests that same morning. After lunch, I sat down with Sandra to discuss the results.

I explained to Sandra that it seemed Celeste had some learning gaps that meant she'd need some extra help, but the gaps weren't serious enough to have been caused by learning disabilities. We also discovered that Celeste's problems were indeed complicated by mild depression. We gave Sandra a written report to share with Celeste's pediatrician, teachers, tutor, and the counselor we arranged for Celeste. I explained to Sandra that if the other professionals had more questions, we'd be available to talk on the phone or go to the school and chat with the school staff.

Will My Child Need a Neuropsychological Exam?

At this point, you may be wondering whether a neuropsychological exam makes sense for *your* child. The answer depends on your child's particular problems. There are many kinds of highly qualified professionals who can do excellent evaluations, depending on what your child needs. Neuropsychologists are trained to study how the brain affects human behavior, and how to evaluate children with learning, brain function, and behavior problems. Other professionals also can evaluate the types of problems I discuss in this book, with some important differences. For instance, psychiatrists don't directly administer IQ and standardized tests. In Celeste's case, an evaluation by a psychiatrist would have shed light on her mood problems, but might have overlooked her learning gaps. On the other hand, special education teachers and school psychologists could have assessed her academic skills, but they wouldn't have been trained to fully evaluate her depression.

Whatever kind of professional you start with, you may need to get a referral to other specialists if more detail is needed in a particular area. We'll be comparing the different types of experts you may want to consider in chapter 4, and we'll discuss testing in much more detail in chapter 5. At that point, you should have a pretty clear idea of what type of professional would best be able to help identify your child's problems.

The First Step: Overview
of Problem Areas

Many parents are so confused by their child's conflicting symptoms that they don't know where to begin. That's why I'd like to start with a brief overview of the characteristics of the broad categories of problems I'll be talking about in this book. I'm giving you this information now to help you start thinking about which particular problems your child may have. The categories I'll discuss include:

- learning difficulties
- attention-deficit/hyperactivity disorder and other disruptive behaviors
- autistic spectrum patterns
- anxiety and traumatic reactions
- mood problems (including depression)

By carefully reading about the main symptoms in each category, you can get a general idea of what may be going on with your child. Or you might begin to suspect there isn't anything going wrong at all—perhaps your child is just going through a phase!

That's where this book is unique. I'll start at your point of uncertainty and confusion and doubt, then lead you, step by step, on a journey to discover the what, why, how, where, and when that's associated with your child's struggles. When you finish this book, you'll have a much clearer idea about how to find out what's going on with your child, and how to work with professionals to get the best diagnosis and treatment for your child.

The most important thing to do first is to understand the *main problems* that your child has. I call these key problems "core deficits"—they're the most obvious symptoms. Once you identify these main symptoms, a confusing picture can become much clearer.

Labels Are Tools, Not Chains

Now, one thing I've learned over the years is that parents (and often professionals) are afraid that putting a label on a child can be harmful. Not so!

First, a label or a diagnosis isn't important by itself. It simply provides a kind of shorthand to help summarize what's triggering your child's everyday problems. The more accurate the diagnosis, the easier it will be to find a treatment that works. Once you have a reliable diagnosis, you can start learning the best way to help your child. Labels can give everybody a place to start the healing—a road map to help you find your way through a confusing maze of symptoms.

A diagnosis or a label also tells us about a child's recurring patterns—but it isn't designed to tell you everything you need to know about your child. That's why experts these days try to avoid terms such as *the difficult child* or *the learning disabled child*—because such a label can't capture all the important aspects of a person.

First and foremost, a child is his own person. But he's also somebody's son, someone else's grandchild, sibling, or nephew. He's also a student in somebody's classroom, a kid on the playground, in a group of friends, doing a particular job, participating in an organization such as a club or sports team. Last, but not least, he's a kid with a learning disability . . . or depression . . . or an attention problem.

You also need to keep in mind that your child's problems may seem to be quite different in various settings. Has your child ever had a teacher who complained about some problem when last year's teacher handled the same situation with aplomb? There can be real differences in how a child functions in different situations.

So why use labels or diagnoses at all? Because they help condense a vast amount of scientific knowledge and professional wisdom into a manageable shorthand. The problems one child has are very much like the problems other children have. If we can identify these patterns, we won't have to start from scratch each time when we're trying to solve problems. Many of the diagnoses don't just label a pattern, but also reveal something important about the possible causes of the problems. The diagnosis often implies how a child's problems are likely to develop, including what treatments might work best. To best help your child, you need a map, not just an endless detailed list of your child's struggles, conflicts, inadequacies, and sufferings. You deserve as concise a map as we can draw.

Individual Problem Areas

Now I'd like to briefly discuss the five main types of learning, behavioral, and emotional problems that I'm going to discuss in this book. (You can read more details about each of these specific disorders in chapters 6 through 10.) As I'm sure you already know, living with a child who has problems with learning, behavior, or mood control can be really stressful. By learning about some of the main features of these different problems, you're taking a step toward feeling less frustrated and out of control.

Learning Difficulties: Thinking, Academics, Language, Speech, and Motor Skills

There are all sorts of different learning problems, because the capacity to learn involves most of the skills or abilities that we want children to develop. It's important to understand, however, that not all learning *problems* are learning *disabilities*. Many children are simply slow to develop certain skills. Because children show natural differences in their rate of development, sometimes what seems to be a learning disability may simply be a mild delay in acquiring certain skills.

For example, Sam was a fifteen-year-old freshman who had started to struggle in some of his classes. His parents weren't sure if this was just a minor developmental glitch that would work itself out, or something more lasting and serious. They knew he was trying hard to get good grades, but they didn't have a clear sense of how much they should expect him to catch up, or how soon. He was having trouble with reading, spelling, memorization, and attention. His parents wondered if his problems might be related to the transition from a supportive middle school to his first year at a challenging high school.

Ever since elementary school, Sam had struggled with reading, spelling, and written language. He'd been getting extra help and phonics practice at a tutoring center several times a week for the past year, and he seemed to gain confidence from the one-to-one instruction. Yet he still needed hours to finish his homework and often needed coaching from his parents.

Sam's parents wisely decided to try to find out if Sam had some type of specific problem that hadn't been identified. First, they asked their local public school district to test his intelligence, academic skills, and a few important mental-processing skills. While his academic delays weren't serious enough to qualify for special education, the evaluation team did identify a few key problem areas. Sam's parents then brought him to us at the clinic to assess his attention, memory skills, and "executive mental functions," such as planning and organization.

The combined results: Sam had above-average intelligence, but scored in the "low-average" range for word-recognition accuracy, reading comprehension, math calculation, math reasoning, spelling, and sentence composition. He showed mildly below-average *speed* in reading and math tasks, along with a particular pattern of strengths and weaknesses in mental-processing skills that suggested a borderline learning disability in reading speed or fluency. The evaluation results really helped his parents focus on what they could do to help Sam reach his potential, because we clarified his *pattern* of strengths and weaknesses.

As a result of our evaluation, Sam transferred to a smaller private high school where his parents thought he'd get more attention for his learning problems. His parents also worked with an independent tutor outside of school to focus on the best ways to enhance his reading efficiency.

As Sam's parents discovered, a child with learning difficulties may have problems receiving, organizing, understanding, remembering, or offering information. Although we don't know exactly what causes learning disorders, they are often linked to heredity, problems in brain development during pregnancy, brain damage, or a mismatch between the kind of instruction he gets and what his learning strengths and weaknesses are.

The different types of learning problems I'll discuss include troubles with reading, math, and written language; speech and language difficulties; fine-motor coordination problems, and below-average intelligence. Here's a brief list of the different categories:

- *Developmental dyslexia* (also called reading disability): This involves inaccurate or slow word recognition. Most children with dyslexia also have poor spelling and phonics skills. This is the most common type of learning difficulty and often leads to problems in closely related areas such as reading comprehension or written expression.

- *Nonverbal learning disability:* This problem is a less common syndrome including problems in visual-spatial processing, eye-hand coordination, attention, abstract reasoning, problem solving, perception of emotions, and social communication. Academic problems in math, reading comprehension, and the fine-motor part of written language are common. Basic oral language skills, rote verbal memory, reading word recognition, and spelling are usually relatively strong.

- *Phonological disorder and speech dysfluency:* These are fancy words for speech problems. Kids with this problem substitute sounds, stutter, or don't use speech sounds that you'd expect for the child's age and dialect.

- *Receptive and/or expressive language disorders:* These problems affect the way a child understands or produces language in one or more common patterns. Some kids don't completely understand what others say to them, even though they may seem to understand. Others have trouble organizing their speech into conventional grammar. Some don't understand word meanings. A few can't communicate clearly with other people because they don't receive or produce language well enough.

- *Developmental coordination disorder:* This is a broad term that is sometimes applied either to movements using large muscles, such as walking (called gross motor skills), or to movements using smaller muscles, such as writing (fine motor skills). The fine motor area is more often linked to learning disorders. There are many different patterns of coordination disorders, so that some children with some reasonably developed fine motor skills can build skillfully with blocks, even though their drawing and writing are poor.

- *Mental retardation or cognitive disabilities:* These problems are diagnosed when a child shows significant delays in most key areas of development, including intelligence, self-care or social relationships, and academic skills. There's also a gray area I call below average intelligence. Intelligence is really a continuum of abilities: low average, an IQ score of 80 to 89; borderline mentally retarded, 70 to 79; mild retardation, 55 to 69; moderate mental retardation, 40 to 54; and severe to profound mental retardation, below that. A child is considered to have mental retardation if IQ is below 70 to 75 and there are significant problems in at least two "adaptive skill areas," such as schoolwork or self-care.

Different experts often use different labels for the problems I've outlined above. For example, some professionals speak of "dyscalculia" for some types of math problems, "dysgraphia" for some types of writing problems, or "developmental aphasia" for some types of language problems. One particularly important alternative way of grouping and labeling learning problems comes from the federal government, which requires all states to use certain terms in determining if a child qualifies for special education assistance. Unfortunately, these terms don't necessarily match the latest scientific research, but we have to follow these categories by law to get kids the services they need.

Extra Help for Learning Difficulties

In the United States, seven legally defined types of *learning disabilities* qualify for special education services. To receive these services, a child must show significant discrepancies between learning *potential* (as indicated by IQ tests) and academic *performance* (as indicated by achievement tests) in at least one of the following areas:

- oral expression
- listening comprehension

- written expression
- basic reading skill
- reading comprehension
- mathematics calculation
- mathematics reasoning

(There are other special education categories for impairments of speech and language skills, motor coordination, mental retardation, and other problems.) What's important for you to know at this point is that each of these official categories requires a severe enough problem with a *particular, well-defined pattern* so that the public school district experts would decide your child needs special education services.

Fortunately, most schools also have other programs for extra help when children have learning problems that aren't severe enough for special education. In addition, parents often get other help for their kids outside school.

Attention-Deficit/Hyperactivity Disorder and Other Disruptive Behavior Patterns

Sergi was referred for an evaluation by his brother's psychologist, who suspected that Sergi might have attention-deficit/hyperactivity disorder (ADHD). He'd been adopted from an understaffed orphanage in Romania at eighteen months of age, and his parents assumed his bursts of uncontrolled behavior were due to a lack of social stimulation during his infancy. Life in the orphanage hadn't been easy, and he'd lain untouched in a crib for long months. Although he'd been a healthy baby and toddler, by the time he started kindergarten Sergi was shouting in the lunchroom, running wildly up and down stairs at school, and knocking into his classmates.

If you have a child like Sergi, you might sympathize with his parents' reluctance to get him a formal ADHD evaluation during preschool. They hoped that in time, and with the positive atmosphere in his kindergarten classroom, he'd outgrow his behavior problems. He didn't seem to be anxious, depressed, or aggressive, and he was described by all his teachers as "happy-go-lucky." Because Sergi was sociable and good at making friends, his teachers didn't think he was autistic, but he did spend a lot of time alone—and he could be selfish sometimes. If another child had a toy he wanted, he'd just grab it without thinking to ask first. His parents wondered if he had some other kind of problem going on, such as sensory processing issues—a concept they'd heard about from an occupational therapist.

In our evaluation, we carefully reviewed questionnaires completed by his parents and teachers, as well as report cards from school. During testing in the clinic, we saw that Sergi was indeed friendly and talkative. As testing began, he was curious about his performance. He'd ask, "How many did I get right?" But he gave up easily if he thought a test was boring, and he needed lots of encouragement to keep going once he got bogged down. He'd often jump up and walk around the room, impulsively grabbing objects from the table, and he was easily distracted by objects around the room.

Our tests clearly reflected his underlying problems with sustained attention and impulsivity. We confirmed a diagnosis of mild ADHD. Once his parents knew what they were dealing with, they began learning how best to help Sergi. They joined a parent-training group in our clinic, and they discussed possible medications with their pediatrician. They were sad to learn that his behavior control problems wouldn't probably go away as he approached adolescence, but they were relieved to understand what they were dealing with and were encouraged with the results of the medication and the behavior techniques they learned in the training group.

Like Sergi, many children who have attention disorders are easily distracted and seem to daydream a lot. Children with ADHD typically have problems with *sustained attention* (working or playing for a period of time) and controlling their impulses, planning, stopping and thinking before acting, and considering the consequences of their actions—what experts call *behavioral inhibition*. Some kids with ADHD have problems with only one of these two areas, but many others struggle with both. Most also have a number of other related problems: They may have a tough time meeting the demands of school, or they may seem accident prone. These kids also have a hard time sitting still, waiting to be called on before giving answers, and waiting to take turns. They may interrupt too much, run into traffic, or do other things they've been taught not to do. In short—these kids just act without thinking.

Because they usually have problems with following rules, excessive motion, and explosive energy, younger children with ADHD often get into trouble with parents, teachers, and peers. By adolescence, this physical hyperactivity often subsides into fidgeting and restlessness, but the problems with inattention and impulsivity usually continue into adulthood. Here's something to keep in mind: While ADHD and learning disabilities often occur together, *they aren't the same*.

- *ADHD:* Kids with ADHD have trouble paying attention, they act or blurt out answers without thinking, and they can't seem to control their behavior.

- *Learning disabilities:* Kids with learning difficulties have trouble receiving, organizing, understanding, remembering, and producing information.

Researchers estimate that between 5 and 20 percent of all school-aged children in the United States have learning disabilities, depending on exactly how the diagnosis is made. Of those, up to a third also have ADHD. Although ADHD is fairly common, it can be difficult to diagnose and even harder to understand. Once viewed as just a childhood disorder primarily involving hyperactivity and the inability to pay attention, ADHD is now recognized as a lifelong condition.

Other disruptive behavior disorders—called oppositional-defiant disorder and conduct disorder—involve more serious problems with defiance and aggression for at least six months (and usually many years).

- *Oppositional-defiant disorder:* Kids with this problem experience repeated severe problems with negative behavior such as temper outbursts, arguing, or deliberately annoying others.

- *Conduct disorder:* Kids with this problem are aggressive with people or animals, violate the rights of others, destroy property, lie, steal, and break all kinds of rules.

Autistic Spectrum Disorders

Jeanne was a fourth grader who had appeared completely normal for the first two years of her life. In preschool, she began to have trouble understanding what others were saying and struggled to organize her own speech. By kindergarten she needed speech/language therapy. At this point, her parents had a heart-to-heart talk with Jeanne's pediatrician, who thought she might have ADHD because of her lifelong history of short attention, impulsivity, and restlessness. Her parents weren't so sure, because her behavior seemed so different from that of her cousin Jimmy, who took medication to control his ADHD. When Jeanne's teachers suggested that she repeat kindergarten because she was immature, her parents accepted the recommendation. It didn't help.

When she entered elementary school, Jeanne really began to have trouble with her schoolwork. She spent most of first and second grade getting extra instruction in the school's resource room. As years passed, she made improvements in many of her academic skills, and by fourth grade, she was switched back to a regular reading group. About a year ago, her parents reluctantly accepted the pediatrician's recommendation for medication, which has improved her attention problems tremendously.

Even though Jeanne seemed to be making real progress, her parents were still worried. Jeanne had never had a close friend. They were even more worried about some of her unusual behaviors. Jeanne would constantly mimic movie scripts, talk to herself, and dream away the day in a ritual fantasy world. Her parents took her for a psychiatric evaluation, which suggested a possible anxiety disorder—but a two-week trial of the antidepressant Zoloft made her more aggressive, so they stopped the medication.

When Jeanne's parents brought her to us, we carefully reviewed her complex background and gave her a brief, carefully selected set of neuropsychological tests. Some of her previous diagnoses were correct, but the particular combination of all her problems indicated she was on the mild end of the autistic spectrum: a condition called pervasive developmental disorder—not otherwise specified (PDD-NOS). Now that we understood more clearly what her problem was, her school program could be modified to emphasize communication and social skills training. Her parents returned to the clinic for several follow-up consultations on how to help her make friends and get along with others, as well as continuing their ongoing work with her other problems.

The autistic spectrum disorders (also known as pervasive developmental disorders) are characterized by:

- delayed development of social skills
- limited communication
- unusual or stereotyped behavior

The primary problem for a child on the autistic spectrum is relating to others. They often have difficulty communicating, and they may play in an unusual way with toys—flicking, shaking, spinning, or lining them up. Children with this category of problems also may lack curiosity about their environment or have trouble with changes in routines.

Of course, all children can sometimes behave oddly or may seem shy much of the time without having an autistic disorder. The difference is the *consistency* of the unusual behavior. This condition affects just about every part of a child's life, including a lack of social interaction and problems with nonverbal behavior.

At the moment, we recognize three separate types of autistic spectrum disorders, although many professionals believe these types overlap so much that they really represent one disorder with different degrees of severity. The three main types include:

- *Autism:* This condition seriously affects verbal and nonverbal communication as well as social, thinking, and behavioral skills.

- *Asperger's syndrome:* This milder condition refers to children with social deficits and certain types of unusual behavior patterns, without significant impairment in overall intelligence or basic language skills. Sometimes, Asperger's syndrome is compared to or even equated with other conditions, including high-functioning autism or nonverbal learning disabilities, but not all professionals agree that these are the same disorder.

- *Pervasive developmental disorder—not otherwise specified:* This category includes children with a few autistic symptoms but who don't fit completely into either of the two categories above.

A quite rare diagnosis in this area—Rett syndrome—will be discussed in chapter 11.

Anxiety and Traumatic Disorders

Anxiety is a feeling of apprehension, fear, or worry that isn't always connected to a specific threat. All children experience anxiety sometimes. For example, from about eight months of age through the preschool years, healthy youngsters may get anxious when separated from mom and dad. Young children may have short-lived fears of the dark, storms, animals, or strangers. Anxiety becomes a problem when it interrupts a child's normal activities. A seventeen-year-old girl who sometimes worries whether her biology grades are good enough for vet school is experiencing normal anxiety. The anxiety goes beyond normal if she persistently avoids going to school because she is panicking about her grades.

Anxiety disorders are among the most common type of mental health problem for children and adolescents, affecting as many as 10 percent of

Learning Disorders or ADHD vs. Anxiety

Children with learning disorders often have problems with anxiety, especially in connection with schoolwork. Reading aloud, taking timed tests, or trying to start a writing assignment may all trigger anxiety and cause even more problems. An anxious child may freeze up in one of these situations. Others may get restless or agitated.

Sometimes it can be hard to tell the difference between anxiety and ADHD. An inability to focus may often lead to anxiety, and anxiety itself can make it hard for a child to pay attention to a task. In some cases, a child has both ADHD and significant anxiety symptoms. It's also possible for a child with anxiety to be misdiagnosed as having ADHD.

young people. Studies suggest that kids are more likely to have an anxiety disorder if their parents have anxiety or mood problems.

Generalized Anxiety Disorder

Children with generalized anxiety disorder (previously called over-anxious disorder of childhood) have recurring fears and worries they can't control. They worry unnecessarily about almost anything—school, sports, being late, even natural disasters. They may be restless, irritable, tense, or easily tired and may have trouble concentrating or sleeping. Children with this pattern are sometimes overly eager to please others or may be perfectionists, dissatisfied with their less-than-perfect performance.

Separation Anxiety Disorder

Children with separation anxiety disorder are so anxious about being away from home that their social or school function is affected. These kids feel a great need to stay close to their parents. When they're apart, children with this pattern may worry excessively about their parents' whereabouts or safety. When they're together, they may cling to parents, resist going to school, or be afraid to go to sleep. Repeated nightmares about separation, or physical symptoms such as stomachaches and headaches, also are common.

Social Phobia

Anxiety about certain social situations often appears in the midteens; it less frequently affects younger children. Kids with this pattern have a consistent fear of particular social or performance situations, such as speaking in class or eating in public. They're always afraid of being embarrassed in these situations. This fear is often accompanied by physical symptoms such as sweating, blushing, a pounding heart, shortness of breath, or muscle tenseness. Young people with this disorder typically respond to these feelings by avoiding the frightening situation, such as staying home from school or not going to parties.

Specific Phobias

Children with specific phobias suffer from an intense, unrealistic fear of a specific object or situation, such as spiders, dogs, or heights. The fear is usually inappropriate to the situation, and the child usually knows that the fear is irrational. Kids with phobias often avoid whatever common, everyday situation is linked to their fear. The most common specific phobia in the general population is fear of animals, particularly dogs, snakes, insects, and mice.

Obsessive-Compulsive Disorder

Children with this problem have frequent and uncontrollable thoughts (obsessions) and feel they must perform rituals (compulsions) to cope with the thoughts. In this condition a child often repeats behaviors as a way of avoiding an imagined consequence. For example, a child who's afraid of germs might constantly wash his hands. Other common compulsions include counting, repeating words silently, and rechecking completed tasks. The obsessions and compulsions may take up a lot of time and make a child feel anxious. This pattern appears more often in adolescence.

Post-traumatic Stress Disorder (PTSD)

Children who experience a physical or emotional trauma such as witnessing a shooting, surviving abuse, or being in a bad car accident may develop PTSD. Young people are often more easily traumatized than adults, so that an event that may not be traumatic to an adult (such as a turbulent plane ride) might be really upsetting to a child. As a result of the trauma, a child may reexperience the event through nightmares, constant thoughts about what happened, or by reenacting the event while playing. Children with this pattern can experience symptoms of general anxiety, including trouble sleeping and eating or being irritable. Many children may exhibit other physical symptoms as well, such as being easily startled.

Depression and Other Mood Problems

Karen was a normal, well-adjusted teenager until her mother unexpectedly died when Karen was in tenth grade. As Karen's sadness deepened, her father became concerned and took all his children for grief counseling with a group of other families. Karen's younger brother and sister coped well with their loss, but Karen had a rougher time. Her father was particularly alarmed when she stopped talking to him the way she used to do. He wasn't sure if she was just going through a teenage stage, or if she was withdrawing in some maladaptive way.

When Karen's boyfriend pressured her into having sex for the first time during this emotionally vulnerable period, adding to her turmoil, she started cutting her arms in a desperate attempt to find emotional relief. Her father wisely took her for individual counseling, but she didn't get much better. Antidepressants only helped a little, and she was briefly hospitalized twice. By the time Karen was referred for a neuropsychological evaluation, she was clearly having a major depressive episode.

Fortunately, the thorough neuropsychological assessment helped us rule out some other problems that were suspected, including both ADHD and learning disabilities. Karen's mild memory problems during testing seemed to be related to her serious depression and lack of confidence. Her father decided to take Karen for more frequent therapy sessions and get a second opinion on medication treatment from a different psychiatrist.

Many people don't realize that it's possible for young children—even preschoolers—to be clinically depressed. A depressed child may feel sad, hopeless, tired, agitated, or have low self-esteem, which can have a devastating impact on school performance, friendships, and family relationships. Of course, a simple case of "the blues" can be completely normal, especially if there's good reason (such as the loss of a pet or a loved one). But unexplained low mood or depression that continues for weeks or months is not normal. Because it's not unusual for children with learning problems to feel a loss of self-confidence or even despair, and because kids with other problems such as ADHD are also often depressed, it's essential that persistent symptoms of depression be evaluated.

International Rates

How often do we see these different problems in Western countries such as the United States, Canada, the United Kingdom, Australia, and New Zealand? You can find general figures related to the United States in chapters 6 through 11 on the specific disorders. But be aware that different methodologies are used in different countries, so it isn't possible to compare rates with complete accuracy.

Both parents and professionals in the different countries and cultures interpret and report symptoms with different levels of sensitivity or concern, making comparisons suspect. When reasonably similar comparison methods have been used with some of these disorders (especially ADHD), roughly similar *prevalence* rates have been found, even if rates of *diagnosis* differ. The *prevalence* rate means how often a condition appears within a group of people. However, the same condition may not be *diagnosed* as often as it could be for a variety of reasons.

Overlapping Conditions

If you've made it this far, you can see that there's a significant overlap of symptoms not only within one category of problems, but among categories as well. In fact, many children with learning, behavioral, or emotional problems typically have more than one condition. The good news is that many available treatments can be used for several different areas.

Charles and Maria knew their seven-year-old son, Jason, had behavioral problems, but they hadn't realized that he was also struggling with dyslexia, an associated learning disability in math calculations, and depression as well. "He'd been labeled as having ADHD, and we were told he had to take medication, but he hasn't been evaluated for learning disorders," Maria said. "We never knew he could have more than one problem at the same time. Why didn't anyone tell us about these tests before now?"

Once Jason's parents arranged for an evaluation of his learning difficulties at school, they discovered his significant trouble with reading and math, and they were able to get him into the right programs to help him. His academic progress has made a difference in his behavior, and his depression has lifted. Between the specialized help Jason receives at school and the family therapy sessions they all attend, the whole family is now feeling much happier and more connected.

As Jason's parents learned, the journey toward a happier, more fulfilled child can be long and often frustrating, involving both wise clinical judgment by his therapists and careful measurement of his learning skills by special education staff at school. But the rewards for Jason and his parents were enormously satisfying: they were able to identify his problems with a helpful "map," work out a solution, and move on with their lives. Jason today is not only a successful student but a happy child, self-confident and secure. They've all learned the valuable lesson that identifying and facing problems is worth all the time, trouble, and effort involved.

In the Next Chapter . . .

Now that you have a good general idea of the types of problems that I'll be discussing in this book, it's time to start the journey toward figuring out exactly what's going on with your child. In the next chapter, you'll learn how to take notes and keep records of your child's behavior or problems. I'll give you some hints about how to watch your child's behavior, and how to group any learning, behavioral, emotional, and social symptoms into meaningful clusters. This will help you focus on the particular problems your child may have.

2

Charting the Problem:
Notes, Checklists, and
Behavior Diaries

I N THE FIRST CHAPTER you learned a bit about all the categories
of possible problems a child could have. Now it's time to start thinking
about what's going on with your own child.

Of course, before you figure out how to solve a problem, you have to
be quite clear about what that problem *is*. One of the best ways is to
record all of your child's symptoms using checklists and diaries. It's a great
way to map out what's really happening with your child. Completing at
least a few of these checklists and diaries will help bring into focus exactly
what your child is doing—or not doing—that worries you. You don't have
to complete all of these exercises, and you'll probably find some of these
methods more useful than others. But most parents I work with find that
doing this bit of sleuthing really pays off.

It sure did for Carla. As with many parents, her realization that her
child might be having problems came as an unpleasant shock. Carla was a
smart, caring mother who thought her daughter, Emma, was getting along
just fine in third grade except for some continuing mild problems with
reading. So she was startled when Emma's teacher began to send home
notes every week complaining about her restlessness and behavior prob-

lems. None of Emma's other teachers had ever complained about her behavior before! And what was this about tantrums and aggression? Carla never noticed anything like this at home.

Emma's problems were especially pronounced during reading. Her teacher complained that during read-aloud time, Emma would stare out the window, fidget with her desk, or draw pictures. Sometimes she'd pester the children nearby, kicking and poking the boy who sat in front of her. Even silent reading sometimes triggered bouts of anxiety, tears, or frustration, since Emma knew she was going to be the last one to finish.

Worried about what was going on with Emma, Carla called and made an appointment at our clinic. We sent her some detailed questionnaires for her and the teacher to complete that asked lots of specific questions about Emma's behavior, when it occurred, and what seemed to trigger the problems of anxiety, inattention, and misbehavior.

You can see a brief example of the questionnaires we sent Carla in the boxes below. Getting questionnaires from both parents and teachers can be really helpful, because different adults tend to see things a bit differently. In addition, kids can behave very differently at home than at school. In the examples below, I'm only offering a few sample questions to give you a brief example.

Parent Form

Item	Emma's Mom's Response
Acts too young for his/her age	Not true
Fails to finish things he/she starts	Somewhat or sometimes true
Daydreams or gets lost in his/her thoughts	Not true
Has difficulty learning	Somewhat or sometimes true

Copyright © 2001, T. Achenbach, ASEBA, University of Vermont, 1 South Prospect St., Burlington, VT 05401-3456, www.ASEBA.org.

Teacher Form

Item	Emma's Teacher's Response
Acts too young for his/her age	Somewhat or sometimes true
Fails to finish things he/she starts	Very true or often true
Daydreams or gets lost in his/her thoughts	Very true or often true
Has difficulty learning	Somewhat or sometimes true

Copyright © 2001, T. Achenbach, ASEBA, University of Vermont, 1 South Prospect St., Burlington, VT 05401-3456, www.ASEBA.org.

As Carla sat in my office during our first meeting, I sensed both her anger and frustration. She wasn't seeing any of these problems at home, she insisted, handing over the completed questionnaires. But as the two of us looked through the teacher's comments, we realized the teacher was obviously seeing very different behavior at school than Carla noticed at home. It soon became obvious what was going on: Emma was being asked to handle much more complex tasks at school than she was during homework time in the evening. This was why her teacher saw more signs of inattention and restlessness. Moreover, the specific examples the teacher recorded clearly illustrated what Emma was doing.

"Emma can't stop bothering the boy in front of her during reading," the teacher wrote. "She looks out the window and stares into space during silent reading. Today, when called on to read, Emma slammed her desk shut and knocked all her papers onto the floor."

When Carla saw—in black and white—the concrete examples of Emma's behavior, she was able to have an open, productive conference with Emma's teacher, even before the testing evaluation was completed. For Emma's mother, completing and thinking through the checklists was just what she needed to get a handle on her daughter's behavior.

What Concerns You Most?

Clarifying your child's specific behavior and learning patterns is a critical part of your first meeting with your child's teacher or with an independent professional. That's why you should think about your child's symptoms *ahead of time*—then write them down. You want to define your suspicions in a specific way.

Take a few minutes right now to think about all of your child's problems that you've been worrying about. Include everything! Too often, parents focus only on the most urgent problems. What I'd like you to do is to think of everything that seems to be a problem so you can get the clearest possible picture of what's going on.

Now, briefly jot down some answers to the following questions, and then discuss your notes with your spouse or another caregiver—anybody who knows your child really well:

1. What worries you most about your child's skills or abilities? (For example, are you worried about her fine motor skills, such as drawing, printing, or cursive writing? Does she seem to have problems expressing herself in writing and speaking? Did your son learn to walk or talk later than the other kids? Do you think he's got problems with counting or reading skills?) Be specific! How old was your child when these problems first appeared?

2. What concerns you most right now about your child's behavior, such as her ability to listen, willingness to sit still, friendliness, ability to follow commands, self-control? Does she get teased by others? How old was your child when these problems first appeared?

3. What worries you most about the way your child handles emotions? For example, how does he deal with disappointment or handle fears or sad feelings? Is your child self-confident? Does she have temper tantrums? At what age did these problems first appear?

What Are the Important Positives in Your Child's Life?

Kids are more than just a collection of problems. To get an idea of the "whole" child, I'd like you to focus for a moment on your child's characteristics from a positive point of view. Answer the following questions as clearly as you can:

1. List your child's most positive points, coping skills, strongest talents or abilities, and so on.

2. Note a few of the most important positive influences (people, activities, and so on) in your child's life—now and in the past.

3. What do you think are the key characteristics of some recent teachers or some recent school years that have been more successful for your child than other teachers or other years?

What Are Your Main Questions?

Next, think about the answers to the questions you've just written down. What are the most important things you want to understand? Make a short list (five items or fewer) of what you'd most like to find out about your child. For example, here are a few questions several different parents have asked me recently:

- I've been told my child has ADHD, and I'm looking for a second opinion.
- My child doesn't like to be hugged. Is he autistic?
- How can I best help my child in math now and in the future?
- How much of my child's behavior problem is due to learning disabilities, and how much could be related to emotional problems?

Keep in mind that the above examples illustrate questions different parents might have for four different children. The questions that *you* list about your child may be much more focused on fewer areas. Okay, now list your questions.

Your Child's Specific Symptoms: Introducing Checklists

Now it's time to consider the details about what your child is doing—or not doing—that worries you. Sometimes it's hard for parents to notice every little problem their child has. You wouldn't believe how many times I've had parents come in and describe all the developmental delays, learning struggles, or behaviors that worry them—only to have them call me up right afterward because they've forgotten to tell me other key points. That's why it's a good idea to sit down and complete a checklist about your child's symptoms before you make an appointment with any professional. I've provided some sample lists below that you can use to check off problems your child may be having.

These checklists can help you narrow and focus your attention on the issues that are really a problem for your child. At this point you aren't looking for a *diagnosis*—just trying to be specific about what problems you notice your child has.

These checklists are such a good idea that many experts routinely use published professional versions, just as we do at our clinic. These professional questionnaires may have titles such as Child Behavior Checklist or ADHD Rating Scale IV (two common examples). If you're asked to fill out any of these professional checklists, *make sure you do so as thoughtfully and thoroughly as you can!* These checklists can really help make your child's evaluation more efficient. If your specialist or school doesn't ask you to complete a questionnaire about your child's patterns before the first office visit, you can take the pages I've provided below with you to your first appointment. The checklists I've adapted for this book are more general than the lengthy ones your specialist may give you, but they'll help you focus in on your child's symptoms.

Some Checklist Tips

When filling out questionnaires or checklists (either the lists below or the ones your specialist sends you), take your time and think about your child's behavior. Some checklists may be easier for you than others. You might want to discuss your answers with your spouse or other family members. To make sure you're accurately noting symptoms, sit quietly and watch your child for a few minutes here and there, or for an hour or so if you have the time. Most of us are so busy these days, we don't always spend time just watching our kids as they go about daily life. Try observing your child doing homework, reading a book, or playing with friends.

You may find these lists tedious, but they can really help identify particular problems. Working on the lists also forces you to really look at your child's specific behaviors. Don't be surprised if you notice patterns you never noticed before!

These lists assess problems your child may have with schoolwork, speech/language development, motor skills, activity level, social skills, attention and memory, sensory development, anxiety, mood, and other behavior. But they aren't intended to cover every possible problem that you might observe, so feel free to jot down additional items where you think they might fit. There may be some overlap from one list to the next. Whether you work with the lists below or a checklist provided by an evaluator (or both), don't fret if only a few items apply to your child's situation. Just indicate that a particular category or item isn't a problem and go on to the next. Try to specify whether your child has this problem or not, and how often it occurs (sometimes, often, most of the time, always).

THE CHECKLISTS

Academic Skills

Does your child have problems with . . .

- ❏ ordering (listing the ABCs, months of the year . . .)?
- ❏ learning the alphabet or letter sounds?
- ❏ phonics skills or sounding out words?
- ❏ reading too slow or too fast?
- ❏ understanding or remembering what was read?
- ❏ learning math facts and remembering math processes?
- ❏ figuring out mental math or math word problems?
- ❏ applying previously learned math skills?
- ❏ math anxiety?

❏ spelling and written expression?

❏ writing with enough detail?

❏ taking too long to complete work?

❏ preparing for and taking tests?

❏ certain kinds of test items, such as multiple-choice questions or essays?

Speech/Language

Does your child . . .

❏ have a significant delay in language (such as not using single words by age two or speaking phrases by age three)?

❏ use gestures or pointing instead of words?

❏ repeat words or phrases in place of normal language?

❏ substitute sounds?

❏ lack normal fluency in speaking?

❏ stutter or repeat sounds?

❏ have trouble speaking coherently?

❏ not seem to understand what he or she hears?

❏ show poor comprehension?

❏ have trouble grasping abstract concepts?

Motor Skills

Does your child . . .

❏ have trouble building with LEGO or other toys?

❏ hold a pencil tightly or awkwardly?

❏ draw poorly?

❏ have poor handwriting?

❏ have trouble copying accurately?

❏ experience left-right confusion?

❏ find school tiring?

❏ have uneven gross/fine motor skills (may not want to throw a ball but can stack blocks)?

❏ show problems in gross motor skills, such as walking, running, hopping, skipping, throwing, and catching?

Self-Control and Goal-Directed Behavior

Does your child . . .

- ❑ fidget, climb, or run more than other kids the same age?
- ❑ seem extremely overactive or underactive?
- ❑ talk too much?
- ❑ have tantrums for no apparent reason?
- ❑ misplace or lose things?
- ❑ interrupt often?
- ❑ have trouble taking turns?
- ❑ blurt out answers?
- ❑ act before thinking?
- ❑ engage in high-risk activities?
- ❑ seem disorganized?
- ❑ have trouble with time management?

Social Skills

Does your child . . .

- ❑ have trouble making friends or mixing with others?
- ❑ prefer to be alone?
- ❑ seem uninterested in sharing enjoyment, interests, or achievements with other people?
- ❑ make little or no eye contact?
- ❑ not want to cuddle or act cuddly?
- ❑ have trouble expressing needs?
- ❑ have an aloof manner?
- ❑ laugh or giggle inappropriately?

Attention/Memory

Does your child . . .

- ❑ have problems paying attention?
- ❑ follow instructions inconsistently?
- ❑ have a short attention span?

❑ not focus during class or homework?
❑ forget things?

Sensory Development

Does your child . . .

❑ not react to verbal cues, or act as if he or she doesn't hear?
❑ squint or complain about not seeing clearly?
❑ have trouble concentrating on one particular kind of input, such as sights or sounds?
❑ seem to be insensitive or overly sensitive to pain?
❑ seem easily overwhelmed by noise?
❑ insist on wearing loose, comfortable clothing?

Repetitive or Stereotyped Behaviors

Does your child . . .

❑ resist changes in routine and insist on sameness?
❑ have problems looking people in the eyes or expressing emotions with facial expressions?
❑ have an inappropriate attachment to objects?
❑ have overwhelming, abnormally intense preoccupations with one area of interest (such as train schedules or stop signs)?
❑ insist on following specific routines or rituals?
❑ have repetitive mannerisms such as hand or finger flapping or twisting?
❑ seem preoccupied with parts of objects, such as the wheels on a toy truck?
❑ play in odd ways, spinning or twisting objects?
❑ have no real fear of dangerous situations?

Feelings

Does your child . . .

❑ worry so much about events or activities that it causes problems in school or with friends?

❑ refuse to leave the house or go to sleep alone or sleep away from home?

❑ have repeated nightmares?

❑ feel anxious in social situations or when speaking in public?

❑ have deep sadness or crying spells?

❑ have chronic insomnia or excessive sleepiness?

❑ have outbursts of shouting and anger?

❑ no longer enjoy hobbies and favorite activities?

❑ feel worthless, unattractive, or guilty?

❑ have concentration problems or muddy, foggy thoughts?

❑ have suicidal thoughts?

❑ worry about being contaminated by germs or dirt?

❑ worry about hurting others?

❑ have repeated doubts about whether having done something correctly (such as locking the door or turning off the stove)?

❑ feel an extreme need for exactness or symmetry?

❑ wash, clean, check, count, or hoard excessively?

Post-Traumatic Stress

If your child experienced or witnessed a traumatic event, does he . . .

❑ worry, relive, or have bad dreams about the event?

❑ avoid thoughts, conversations, people, places, or feelings that remind him of the event?

❑ have trouble remembering some important part of the event?

❑ feel emotionally "numb," irritable, angry, or have trouble concentrating?

❑ feel there's no point in planning for the future?

❑ feel jumpy, easily startle?

What's Going On in Your Child's Environment?

You're probably quite aware that what goes on at your child's school and in your family directly influences your child—just as your child influences all of the different ways each of you interact with one another. That's why it's important to have a clear picture of important things that are going on in these situations—even if some of it isn't within your control. I'd like you to list any concerns you might have. Write down:

- any major family changes, such as moves, separation or divorce, sibling moving out, and so forth
- problems with family finances
- problems or dissatisfaction at work for you or your spouse
- significant health problems for any family member (including your child)
- learning, emotional, or behavioral problems of other family members, including both parents and siblings
- tension or conflict between parents
- staff shortages or changes in school staff
- teaching strategies that don't seem to be well matched to the child
- programs at school you wish your child could get into
- whether your child is moving from one school to a different school

Creating a Behavior Diary to Pinpoint Problems

If your child has trouble following requests, commands, routines, or rules, you'll find it helpful to create a special type of diary detailing exactly what happens when you ask your child to do something or follow a rule. This kind of written observation can be really helpful when you meet with professionals for a diagnosis and treatment.

What you'll be doing is creating what I call a behavior diary that highlights specific problems. Each time you ask your child to do something, you'll record a "behavior sequence"—a fancy name for writing down who says what, who does what, what happens next, the result of that action, and so on.

This kind of diary was really helpful for George's mother, who used a behavior diary to record the sequence of events when George was watching TV and his mother asked him to do his homework. Here's what happened:

Mom: "It's time to do your homework."
George: (Ignores her, keeps watching TV)
Mom repeats the command, louder: "It's time to do your homework!"
George: "Okay." (Doesn't move, keeps watching TV)
Mom: "You'll have to go to bed early if you don't come right now and do your homework."
George: (Gets up and starts jumping on the couch)
Mom: *"Stop jumping!"*
George: (Stops jumping, leans over and pokes his sister)
Mom: "Go to your room!"
George: (Goes to his room and plays with a computer game. Mom sends him to bed a half hour early, at which point he has completed only a small part of his homework.)

Outcome: Bad behavior gets worse, homework doesn't get done. Sound familiar? This behavior diary could just as easily describe your child's reluctance in picking up her room, taking out the trash, setting the table, coming in late from a date, or the countless other tasks or rules that you and your child argue about.

Here's what George's behavior diary would look like:

BEHAVIOR DIARY					
Date and Time	Parent Making Request	Request	Child's Reaction	Parent Tries to Manage Situation	Outcome
Monday 5 p.m.	Mom	"It's time to do your homework."	Silence	Repeat louder: "It's time to do your homework!"	
			"Okay." (Doesn't move)	Threat: "You'll go to bed early if you don't come now!"	
			Jumps on couch	Yells: "Stop!"	
			Pokes sister	"Go to your room!"	Played in room, did little homework

As you can see from the diary in this example, George's misbehavior is allowing him to get out of doing something that he doesn't want to do. It's not that George deliberately planned it that way, and he may not even have realized that's the consequence of his behavior. But writing down the sequence in a behavior diary like this can help you understand what's reinforcing your child's behavior, or why your child is doing certain things that you don't want him to do.

John was the father of seventeen-year-old Pete, who'd slipped into the habit of sleeping in and getting to school late about twice a week. I'd recommended to John that he start keeping a behavior diary, beginning with one specific command: "Get out of bed." The next morning after meeting with me, John went into Pete's bedroom and asked him to get up. Pete ignored him.

John went right out to the kitchen and sat down with the behavior diary, filling out the form right away so he wouldn't forget details. He wrote "Ignored me" under the "Child's Reaction" section of the diary. As he sat writing at the kitchen table, Pete stuck his head into the kitchen.

"What are you doing?" Pete asked his dad.

"My homework for the parent training class," his dad answered. "Dr. Newby wants me to write down what I tell you to do, what your reaction is, and then what happens after that."

"Hmpf!" his son snorted, and left the room.

When John and Pete came in for their next appointment two weeks later, they reported a dramatic improvement. After that first day, each line of the behavior diary started with the request "Get out of bed" and each child's reaction read, "Did."

Why the sudden turnaround? It's quite simple: When a child knows he's being observed and his responses are being recorded, that alone may be enough to get him to change his behavior. It sure did in Pete's case! When Pete realized his dad was writing down every single time he didn't get up when asked, he had quite an incentive for getting up. Don't hold your breath that it will work in your case—but it just might!

Here's a blank diary form for you to copy and fill out. Jot down the series of tasks and events that make up a typical day in your child's life to get some perspective on what points are most important or cause the most problems. I usually tell parents to choose one particular command or family rule to plot in the diary over a number of days, to help them see more than one example of any patterns. It's simpler that way.

You need to be specific and accurate (but not tediously neat or detailed) in listing who says what and in what order. As John did, it helps to write everything down right after an incident, rather than waiting until later. For most parents, writing this type of diary even just a few times helps them to think differently about their child's behavior.

You can then take this chart along to your interview with a mental health professional (who may either be impressed with your motivation or suspect you of being compulsive!). Then you can review the chart together and figure out how what you do affects your child's behavior. This sort of behavior diary can help you think about how to change what you do instead of falling into the same old patterns that don't work. By working with a professional using the behavior charts, you'll be able to see how you can solve your child's problems as you work on a treatment plan together.

SAMPLE BEHAVIOR DIARY FORM					
Date and Time	Parent Making Request	Request	Child's Reaction	Parent Tries to Manage Situation	Outcome

What You've Already Tried

Now that you've listed your child's specific problems, it's a good idea to think about what you've already done to solve your child's problems, and how effective that was. These are all questions that a professional should ask you when you go for your first appointment, so it'll help to be prepared! Basically, there are three questions you should ask yourself for each problem you've identified:

1. How have I tried to solve the problem, and did it work?
2. What has the school tried, and did that work?
3. What have other professionals suggested, and did that work?

It's not so hard. For example, Laura was a divorced mom having trouble with her middle-school daughter, Jen, whose grades were starting to slip. Here's how she filled out the "What I Tried . . ." outline:

WHAT I TRIED . . .

The problem: Jen's grades dropped from mostly B's in elementary school to mostly C's and D's in the first year of middle school.

1. *How have I tried to solve the problem/did it work?*
   - Talked about how important it is to succeed in school—Jen listened but didn't change what she was doing.
   - Offered a trip if all her grades were B or above for a semester—grades dropped in second week.
   - Grounded when homework was missing—worked for two weeks and then stopped working.
   - Yelled—didn't help, just let me blow off steam.
   - Said she'd have to live with her dad—she ignored me!

2. *What the school tried/did it work?*
   - Teachers tried sending home weekly reports about missing work—helped a lot, until teachers got inconsistent in sending reports home.

- Two teachers invited Jen in for extra help before school—she didn't go, but in fairness she probably didn't need to, since she's smart and understands the material pretty well.

3. *What other professionals tried/did it work?*
- Tried family counseling during the last two months of sixth grade—helped for a while, and she really liked the counselor, then her work got spotty again during seventh grade, but we never made an appointment to go back because I was too busy with work.

Okay, now it's your turn. Briefly answer these same three questions:

1. How have I tried to solve the problem, and did it work?
2. What has the school tried, and did that work?
3. What have other professionals suggested, and did that work?

You'll probably find that it's most helpful to jot down your first answers to these questions quickly, then come back to them later, to see if you want to add anything. Be as specific as you can.

In the Next Chapter . . .

You can't solve a problem if you don't know exactly what you're dealing with, so you've taken an important first step in helping your child. You've spent some time thinking about exactly what's worrying you, what your child is and isn't doing, and how you've tried to solve the problem and how it worked (or didn't work). You've filled out symptom lists and behavior diaries.

For many parents and in most cases, the next logical step is to check in with your child's school to start working on key problems. In the next chapter, you'll learn that whatever challenges your child may be facing— learning problems, behavior issues, or mental health concerns—it's critical for you to establish and maintain a good working relationship with the experts in your child's school. Read on to find out how!

3

How to Work with
Your Child's School

JANET'S DAUGHTER was struggling with reading in the fourth grade, but the school didn't seem to notice a problem—and when Janet brought it to their attention, they didn't seem too concerned. "They just said some kids are slower than others," Janet complained. "But I want a better answer than that. Can't we *do* something to help her?"

I've heard so many parents with the same concerns. Maybe you've been struggling with how to work with your child's school to figure out if there's a problem with your child, too. Whatever challenges your child may be facing—but *especially* if the problems affect school performance—it's absolutely crucial for you to establish and maintain a good working relationship with the experts in your child's school. Yet I often find that parents simply don't know about the options at school—and schools don't always do a thorough job of explaining these options to parents.

All too often, schools and parents get into finger-pointing blame games in these situations. That's what happened to Harry, an eleventh grader whose school performance was suddenly taking a nosedive. Harry was failing one course after another, while his parents and teachers blamed each other for his struggles. His distraught parents accused the school of not doing a good enough job of educating their son, while several of Harry's teachers complained that his parents weren't providing enough follow-through at home.

In another situation, Mary's mother repeatedly lashed out at the special education staff for not discovering her daughter's reading disability before she had reached fourth grade barely able to get through a sentence. The teachers privately complained that they just didn't think Mary's parents took the time to work with her at home.

Whatever the source of the problem, blaming each other isn't the best way to reach a solution. It can take some really dedicated effort to tease out the source of the problems and then come up with a solution. While most of the learning problems that I discuss in chapter 6 will appear fairly early in a child's school career—by kindergarten, first or second grade—other types of learning difficulties may not get noticed until later in elementary school or even high school, when the curriculum becomes far more complex.

In this chapter, I'll discuss the kinds of programs your school system probably uses to identify and help kids with educational challenges, and how you and your child's school can work together to develop a plan that will help your child succeed. So many times, I see kids who were sent to me for more detailed assessment after undergoing some testing at school—children like Jason, who was an appealing six-year-old with a real knack for conversation. Most of the parents I see in this situation, like Jason's folks, don't have a major problem with the school district's assessments. They're just looking for another viewpoint on the school's evaluations. In Jason's case, his school had discovered some mild learning difficulties, inattention, and impulsivity. We agreed with their findings, and we were happy to work with the school district to help Jason succeed. Later in this chapter, you'll read more about how we worked with Jason during several evaluations over the years.

The Best Place to Start

If you've been thinking that your child might have some type of learning problem, the best place to start is with your child's teacher. After all, the teacher's the one who sees your child every day and spends the most time working with him. The teacher can be a terrific resource when it comes to working out strategies to deal with any problems you've uncovered.

The teacher was the first person Sharon's parents consulted when the eighth grader's grades suddenly started to slip. Sharon had always been a conscientious student—in fact, you could say she was almost obsessive about her schoolwork. In the past, she'd spend hours redoing her assignments, erasing and re-erasing until the entire thing needed to be redone. That's why her parents were startled when Sharon suddenly didn't seem to care about her grades at all. She began to spend her time giggling with her friends at school and chatting with friends on the Internet at night.

"Should we take Sharon for testing?" her worried parents asked the middle-school reading specialist. "She used to like to read, but now all she wants to do is chat on the computer with her friends. We can't even *suggest* that she redo an assignment because it's not neat enough. If we ask her to do something over, she just shrugs and rolls her eyes. Sometimes she flatly refuses."

No wonder her parents were worried! Sharon was the oldest child in her family and had always been so responsible and hardworking. This sudden decline in her work seemed completely out of character. But Sharon's teacher had seen hundreds of other middle schoolers pick their way through the emotional minefield of sixth, seventh, and eighth grades, just as Sharon was doing. Her teacher understood that Sharon's attitude change looked like a healthy sign that the young teen might be separating a bit from her parents' need for control.

"She *is* a bright child," the teacher reassured Sharon's parents. "She's still doing very well in discussions and in the work that she completes in class." Her teacher suggested they learn to relax their control a bit, allowing Sharon more responsibility for her assignments. As they backed off, her attitude and classwork improved—just as the teacher had predicted.

Of course, you know your child better than anyone else. But it's also true that your child's teacher may have taught hundreds of other kids your child's age—and that can provide a different perspective. What seems scary or alarming to you may just be a normal developmental stage. And you know, there's a vast difference between the demands placed on your child at school and at home. The fact is, many children just act differently at school. What may seem to be unusual behavior to you, with an intimate knowledge of the few kids in your own family, may appear completely normal to the teacher, who's worked with hundreds of kids over the years. Embrace the teacher's rich experience—it can be an invaluable help as you try to discover what's going on with your child.

Your child's teacher can tell you how well your child behaves in class, and how he interacts with others. The teacher can report whether your child is daydreaming, fidgeting, or having trouble staying focused. She may notice unhappiness or an inability to make friends. If the teacher does think there's a problem, she may suggest you contact the school's guidance counselor to discuss the situation. Guidance counselors have also been educated as teachers, and they're usually trained in student services and in test interpretation as well. The counselor can help you review your child's school records and may uncover a possible learning problem.

Putting Heads Together

Okay, let's say that you, the teacher, and maybe the guidance counselor agree that some problem's affecting your child's function at school. Perhaps your son is struggling with reading, and he's starting to lag behind his classmates. Maybe your daughter can't seem to sit still and focus on her classwork.

At this point, your child's teacher may recommend that you meet with your school's "child study team" to look more closely at your child's situation. (Some schools call this team a "student intervention team," "student assistance group," "pupil assistance committee," or some other name—but they're all the same thing.) You may never have heard of a child study team, but every public school is required to have one.

The school-based child study team usually meets regularly to address the concerns of teachers or parents about students who are struggling in school, within the regular education program. It's the first step when a kid is having trouble in school—*before* a formal evaluation to see if a child needs special education. It's the child study team who can help identify children who need extra support, recommend what help the school might offer, and advise if testing or outside evaluation might be needed. The

Private Schools and Special Education Law

Private schools (both independent schools and religious schools) that don't accept any federal money aren't bound by special education laws and are *not* required to provide special testing or help to their students who may have learning problems. In fact, because of limited resources, many independent schools carefully screen out students with learning problems as part of their admission testing.

If your child attends a private school and qualifies under the law for special help, she can get help from your *public* school district, which must by law also provide evaluation services to her. However, the courts have reached different conclusions in different states about exactly how and where the public school district must provide these services to private school students, and when or if intervention services are needed.

team, which typically includes teachers, an administrator, and the child's parents, reviews information about the child from parents, school records, administrators, counselors, and teachers. Sometimes this group also includes the child in meetings.

A team like this can conduct interviews with you and your child, have the child observed closely in the classroom by teachers and/or specialists such as the school psychologist, and review all the child's educational records. If a school-related problem is suspected, team members might suggest a first round of testing in any of several areas:

- intelligence
- academic skills such as phonics analysis, reading word identification, reading speed or fluency, reading comprehension, math calculations, math reasoning, spelling, or written expression
- information processing skills such as phonological processing, attention, or general verbal reasoning

If you've been worried about your child, you may feel relieved when you hear that the school is calling in the child study team—at last, the school is "finally doing something!" But a few parents get worried or even feel suspicious of the school's motives, as did seventeen-year-old Mark's parents when their son's school wanted to call in the study team. Mark's parents worried that the school wanted to ship him off to remedial classes with the "losers," rather than inspire him to achieve the strong academic potential they were sure he possessed. All parents want to know that their child is doing well and is successful in school, so it's not surprising if you have conflicting feelings about needing special help. But really, you and the school all want the same thing—for your child to be successful in school. Try to focus on that ultimate goal as you work toward solving some of your child's issues.

If your school has not yet assembled this kind of team for some reason, don't despair! You can bring one together to address the needs of your child. Simply ask for a meeting that includes you, the principal, the classroom teacher, and other staff members, such as the guidance counselor or a reading teacher.

Once the Study Team's Results Are In

Reports of any work by team members should be written and discussed with you. These reports sometimes have names like "nonexceptional education evaluations." Once reviews, observations, and testing are completed, the team should then come up with some ways to help your child do better.

You can expect the team to recommend some things the classroom teacher can do to help with your child's specific educational needs. In Mark's case, teachers prepared weekly lists of completed and missing assignments for his parents to review. Carol was given extra reading instruction every day. Your child's teacher might simplify the course work, give your child extra practice on a lesson, or try peer tutoring or computer-assisted instruction. Teachers might try offering audiovisual aids, a calculator for math, a computer for word processing, a tape recorder to help with note-taking or memory problems. Some teachers ask a student to check in at the end of each day to make sure assignments are written accurately in a notebook. The teacher might try giving your child weekly assignment sheets, shorter assignments, or extra time to complete assignments.

She might try seating your child up front where he can't be distracted, or offering breaks during the day. If testing is a problem, the teacher might offer oral testing, extra notice of a test, or detailed study guides.

The team may also assign tasks to you to help your child, using a variety of strategies. For example, the team at Mark's school asked his mom to check his homework every night to make sure it was complete. Carol's dad was asked to help work with her on vocabulary lists for twenty minutes a week.

After everyone has been working for a few weeks on these new strategies, you may want to schedule another meeting to review the results. Most of the time, you'll be pleased to see your child making progress—but if that hasn't happened, the team should discuss other ideas that might improve the situation.

If a few more weeks go by and your child *still* isn't improving despite this extra help, you—or the whole team—may decide to ask for a special education evaluation (sometimes called a Multidisciplinary Team Evaluation or an Individualized Education Program Evaluation, depending on your state's legal terms).

Special Education Evaluation

A formal special education evaluation will determine if your child's problems are significant enough to qualify for special education services. You'll

---

Wisconsin Department of Public Instruction

www.dpi.state.wi.us/dlsea/een/index.html

This is the special education Web site of the Wisconsin Department of Public Instruction. We're pretty lucky in our state to have relatively good special education laws and services in general, so this gives you a good example. *Find the similar site for your own state,* as each state interprets the broad federal law for specifics, and legal case law ends up having local, regional, or national implications for further interpretations of nuances or conflicts.

have to have this evaluation to determine if your child qualifies for special education placement.

The evaluation will include a detailed description of the problems your child encounters every day, samples of daily work, and examples of what accommodations did and didn't work. The team can also consider other information you've gathered, such as health screenings to rule out physical problems, or independent evaluations by private specialists. Depending on your child's problems, the special education evaluation may involve school psychologists, special education teachers, speech/language therapists or other therapists, audiologists, and vision or hearing education teachers. Health professionals such as nurses can be called, but physicians are rarely directly included.

It's important for you to understand that there are legal guidelines and requirements to ensure your child gets a good education, no matter what his problems may be. Three main federal laws govern special education:

- the Education for All Handicapped Children Act of 1975
- the Education of the Handicapped Act Amendments of 1986
- the Individuals with Disabilities Education Act (IDEA) of 1977, which was updated in 2004

These laws say educators must identify children with learning disabilities (and certain other disabilities) so they can receive the best possible education. These laws and other civil rights laws have opened access to more than 6 million children who might otherwise not have received the support programs and services they need to be successful, and they continue to hold great promise for millions more.

As you may already have discovered, however, identifying these learning disabilities and other special education needs isn't always easy. To be legally placed in "special education," your child must fit the criteria for one of the thirteen handicaps as outlined in IDEA:

- autism
- deaf-blindness
- deafness
- hearing impairment

- mental retardation (sometimes called cognitive disability)
- multiple disabilities
- orthopedic impairment
- other health impairment limiting strength, vitality, or alertness
- serious emotional disturbance (sometimes called emotional-behavioral disability)
- specific learning disability
- speech or language impairment
- traumatic brain injury
- visual impairment, including blindness

The laws also say you have the right to submit to the evaluation team independent evaluations by experts outside school. However, keep in mind that your child isn't automatically eligible for special education just because an independent evaluation report says your child should be eligible, or that he needs special education. It's up to your child's school evaluation team to consider your independent evaluation along with current academic assessments, report cards, teacher input, student work samples, previous education or behavior interventions, and parent input. Then the team must make its own decision.

The Big Meeting

Meeting with the special education team can be a daunting experience for most parents. That's how it felt for Carol's mom. She had never been so nervous as the day she walked into the school building for the evaluation, even though as a dedicated volunteer she was familiar with the place.

You may feel as if it's "us against them," but I've found that the vast majority of special education staff members really do have your child's interests in mind. Most school staffers are sensitive—after all, they chose to work with children as their profession! Most will respect your point of view. Nevertheless, I know that sitting in a room with a lot of experts reviewing your child's evaluations can feel like a pretty intense "report card" session!

Learning about testing can be confusing to you, so make sure you review chapter 5 in this book carefully before you go to the meeting. Once you're there, be sure to ask questions and get their written reports to take home. When the time comes in the meeting for you to say whether you agree with the school's conclusions and recommendations, don't be afraid to say, "I'm not sure yet. I need some more time to think and sort it out. When can we meet again to put a decision together?" Keep in mind that as a parent, you're an *official* member of the team and have every right to participate in the team's decisions. You're not just an outsider who has to accept whatever the school says, like a plaintiff awaiting a verdict from the jury.

Perhaps you all agree that your child needs help and exactly what that help will include—if so, great! But if not, you should sign the official forms establishing whether your child is eligible for special education services *only* when you're convinced that the picture makes sense.

Individualized Education Program (IEP)

Let's say your team finds that your child is eligible for special education. The next step, then, is for your school district to provide an Individualized Education Program that governs just about all areas of your child's educational program. The IEP is required by law, and it can be used as a management tool, an evaluation device, and a communication method. It's important to keep in mind that as a parent, you do have input into the IEP planning, and you should certainly be involved to make sure your child gets the best help possible.

So what does a typical IEP look like? First, it includes your child's current level of performance, plus annual goals. The IEP may also spell out a variety of extra services (such as occupational therapy) that your child will receive (including how often and from whom). Finally, the IEP will outline your child's areas of impairment from the list of thirteen federal categories that I provided earlier in this chapter.

Remember Jason, whom you met at the beginning of this chapter? His parents had brought him to our clinic for more neuropsychological testing to evaluate his learning disabilities as a way of coming up with more ideas for his IEP. Because they wanted to pursue all possible ways to help their son, Jason's parents had first enrolled him in an intensive private tutoring program during second grade and the following summer, in addition to the learning disabilities instruction that he received at school. Next, his father had taken a course in a reading instruction method called Orton-Gillingham and had given Jason extra work at home several times a week during third grade. His mother studied books and Web site resources on how to write the best Individualized Education Program. Then, she and Jason's dad worked with the school to add more details to Jason's third-grade IEP.

Here's a sample of what a reasonable, thorough IEP might look like. Keep in mind that each child has distinct patterns and needs, so your child's IEP might cover different areas.

JASON'S IEP

Age: 8 **Grade:** 3

Strengths: Jason is very verbal and socially engaging. He shows strong verbal reasoning skills.

Present level of educational performance, including how the student's disability affects involvement and progress in the general curriculum: Jason's reading level is approaching mid-first-grade level. His anxiousness, impulsivity, and urge to read fast reduce his word reading accuracy below this level at many times. He often attempts to read words based on what would make sense in the sentence or story line, using few phonetic cues, despite receiving a heavy emphasis on phonics in recent instruction. When Jason is directed to look back at the word he read incorrectly, he can often independently decode it by applying his phonetic skills. He is still at the point where he needs to be reminded to read slowly enough to utilize his known word-attack skills. Jason often adds or omits words while reading. This pattern and his delay in immediate recognition of words reduces his reading rate or fluency. Jason has acquired the main phonetic skills to decode, so more extensive work on the above behaviors and on integrating reading strategies is recommended. His general comprehension abilities are grade-appropriate and are a strength. More opportunities to address and share story understanding and critical thinking would boost his self-confidence in the classroom.

The above problems are also evident in Jason's writing, which is at about the early-first-grade level overall. He makes many spelling errors. He does not consistently apply his known skills to writing. Some of these errors may be due to his anxiousness or not taking the time to think about accuracy. He can often correct his errors or at least produce phonetically correct spellings when he is encouraged to try again.

Similar application weaknesses are evident with math-related skills, as well. However, these errors have decreased over time, and few modifications are necessary when performing math tasks. He is demonstrating good problem-solving skills and has a high accuracy rate with grade-level material.

Annual goals and objectives:

- Jason will increase his reading level to a high-second-grade level, as measured by informal reading benchmark testing and the district's assessments. Fluency in oral reading will be excluded from scoring, but will be assessed for his teacher's benefit.
- Jason will improve his writing to the level 4, as measured by writing samples and the district's assessments.
- Jason will perform with 90 percent average accuracy on unit tests in the general math curriculum.

Procedures for measuring the student's progress toward the annual goals: Daily observations, anecdotal records, benchmarks (listed below), routine district assessments, daily work.

Procedures for informing parents of the student's progress toward the annual goals and the extent to which that progress is sufficient to enable the student to achieve the goals by the end of the year: Report cards, routine parent/teacher conferences, annual IEP meetings, and at least monthly phone calls or notes to home.

Benchmarks or short-term objectives necessary to allow the student to progress in the general curriculum, and to meet other educational needs that result from the student's disability: Jason will:

- read and spell single-syllable and multisyllable words and words with prefixes, suffixes, and the following phonetic elements: *art, ear, ly, tion, ore, ent, ai, le, are.*
- read a story or passage at his instructional level at seventy words per minute.
- correctly spell all the words from the district's first-grade core list and 75 percent of the words from the second-grade core list.
- apply learned nonphonetic words and spell phonetically correct while writing a paragraph.
- write a paragraph in sequential order including a topic sentence and at least two detail sentences.
- write sentences with correct use of capital letters and ending punctuation marks, as well as proper letter formation and word spacing.
- demonstrate beginning familiarity with the use of a computer-based graphic organizer for writing.
- complete the regular math curriculum with modifications, assistance to stay on task, individual explanation of tasks, and use of visual supports and manipulatives.
- demonstrate skill mastery and solve problems dealing with addition and subtraction of numbers up to three digits, single-digit multiplication, elapsed time in hours, and making change up to $1.

PROGRAM SUMMARY

Date of IEP meetings to determine special education and related services needs: 9/10/04

Projected beginning and ending dates of IEP services and modifications in effect during the school year calendar: 9/13/04–9/12/05

Physical education: Regular (not specially designed at this time)

Vocational education: Regular (not specially designed at this time)

Special education:

Frequency/Amount	Location	Duration
40–50% special education, including support from special education staff while participating in regular math	Regular ed room	9 months
10% time to collaborate with regular teachers and parents, make modifications, and help with organizational skills	Writing workshop Resource room	3 days 9 months

Related services needed to benefit from special education listed above:

Related Services:

	Frequency/Amount	Location	Duration
	None needed at this time		

Assistive technology
Audiology
Counseling
Educational interpreting
Medical services for diagnosis
   and evaluation
Occupational therapy
Orientation and mobility
   (vision impairment only)
Physical therapy
Psychological services
Recreation
Rehabilitation and counseling services
School health services
School social work services
Speech and language
Transportation

At age nine and a half, Jason returned to our clinic; in addition to seeking an evaluation of his learning disabilities, his parents wanted further evaluation of his mild inattention and impulsivity, which turned out to reflect *tendencies* toward ADHD rather than a full ADHD diagnosis.

As a result of the many interventions he received, including those in his IEP, Jason's reading disability improved steadily during his elementary years, to the point that many of the extra instructional approaches and accommodations listed above were no longer necessary in middle school.

How to Work Effectively with the School

Working with your child's teacher and the school's teams can be a great way to get a handle on your child's problems. I know it's not always easy to take off work to attend sessions at the school, but the more you participate, the better off your child will be. Be sure to bring along to every meeting any questions, suggestions, or notes from others about your child.

Remember that you're not trying to win a popularity contest, but you're not trying to "prove" the school's wrong, either. What's most important is that *your child succeeds*. Try to think of school meetings not as a battleground, but as a collaboration. You're all on the same side—your child's side. Try to stay away from black-white, either-or thinking and arguing.

Once your child's programs get going, set up regular ways to communicate with the teacher that you can both live with, as often as necessary. Some parents have found it helpful for their child to bring home a notebook each week with teacher notes detailing his progress; others prefer a structured behavior report card brought home daily. If you're computer savvy, biweekly e-mails between teacher and home can work well.

When there are disagreements, try your best to work things out directly with the professionals involved on the front line, such as the classroom teacher or speech therapist, before going over her head with a complaint to the principal or other supervisor. Check out all the different options for help that are available in your child's school, rather than grabbing on to one particular strategy. If your child has only mild problems, be open to extra help that can be provided in a flexible regular education curriculum without formal special education enrollment.

That's what worked throughout middle school for Krystina, whose family moved to Wisconsin from the Czech Republic when she was eleven years old. Although all the family members gradually learned English, it took Krystina more time than the rest—probably because she still had mild leftover effects from language delay in her native tongue during early childhood. Because of that early language delay and a behavior pattern that looked like ADHD, she'd been held back for two years in her previous Czech school. But when she got to this country, the new U.S. school wanted her to move back up the two grades, into an age-matched sixth-grade placement. Somewhat surprisingly to her parents, she did reasonably well there, due to the flexible program and the extra support her teachers and some support staff in the regular education area gave her, even though she didn't qualify for formal special education at that time. As time went on, Krystina slowly improved in both English and academic skills, but the gap between her and her classmates was widening, and her ADHD behavior persisted.

When she went to high school, the kind of extra support that had helped her through middle school wasn't available, and—not surprisingly—her schoolwork and her behavior deteriorated. In late fall, her parents asked for an evaluation for special education services, and the Individualized Education Program team met to discuss the options. Some team members insisted that most of her struggles were still related to her move to the new country and adjustment to a new language, and they didn't feel that she fit into any special education category.

Things might have gone downhill from there, but her parents appealed to our clinic for help. With our careful presentation of detailed neuropsychological data, together with patient explanations and advocacy on our part, we were able to convince the team that she had a variety of preexisting developmental weaknesses that were making Krystina fall further behind and get more frustrated. Ultimately, her parents and I prevailed, and the school agreed that she qualified for special ed help.

Once her IEP was in place, she immediately started receiving more intensive instruction, accommodations in her regular classes, and modified work expectations that were more realistic in light of her present skills. Her parents also agreed with us and took Krystina for psychotherapy and a psychiatric medication consultation. Today, Krystina is thriving, and her parents feel good about the way they were able to help their daughter with the long adjustment to her new life in a new country. With a little persistence backed up by some solid professional expertise, the family was able to convince the school of what Krystina needed.

If the Team Says No . . .

We were lucky that Krystina's school accepted our advice and eventually agreed with our assessment. But in many cases, a particular child's needs don't meet the specific legal criteria that the school district must follow. If your school's team decides that your child isn't eligible for special education services, they may refer him back to the regular education child study team to help the classroom teacher with appropriate classroom interventions. This is what ended up happening to Mark, the seventeen-year-old we mentioned earlier in this chapter, much to his parents' frustration. They felt defensive about Mark's lack of motivation during his senior year, and they didn't trust some of the regular classroom teachers to follow through with the kinds of regular education interventions and accommodations that we recommended.

Fortunately, Mark's skilled principal took the leadership role in that disagreement, so that the family and the teachers were able to slowly begin to cooperate over several months of regular meetings. Mark got extra mentoring from two teachers who were able to connect well with him. He agreed to collect a weekly list of missing homework from each of his teachers, and he got a lot more motivated during track season when his coach insisted he complete his work before he could participate in meets. He also complied with his mom's nightly homework check. The result: His grades rose to their previous level. It sure was a lot of work by several key adults in his life—but it was better than flunking spring semester and not graduating.

As you can see, things worked out well for Krystina and Mark. But sometimes, no matter how hard you try, you might hit a brick wall with your school district. What happens if your child's school doesn't even agree that your child needs to be tested? What do you do if the school doesn't think test results indicate a problem? If you've talked to the school about your child's problems, but you don't get much satisfaction, or the school flat-out doesn't want to admit there *is* a problem—when do you seek help outside the school?

The answer is simple: *whenever you want.* Some parents I've known think their child's school district is just wonderful. Others don't trust a word their principal says. Although I always like to see parents and schools working together to do everything they can to help a child, different schools have different levels of inclination or resources. Some are helpful and some just aren't.

You'll want to walk into meetings with your school assuming that your trust is justified. But let's face it—nobody and no system is perfect. At times you need to go above the authority of the class teacher, or even beyond the school's officially appointed evaluators.

If the IEP team refuses eligibility, it must give you prior written notice explaining the district's decision. Keep in mind, even if your independent evaluator says your child needs special help, if the school district disagrees, *they are not legally required to provide that help,* unless and until you pursue a successful appeal.

Also keep in mind that school districts, like all organizations, are concerned with the bottom line. Because of both money problems and laws governing their evaluations, the school's decision about what can be identified as a learning disability may be far more strict than an outside evaluator's. Remember, the more children the district identifies with problems, the more they'll have to pay for special education services.

Of course, in many situations the classroom teachers alone, or the teachers plus a non–special education support-staff member, end up working well, even without a formal IEP, but in other situations, it's not enough. Sometimes, the more assertive you are in asking for help, the more the school will figure that it's probably less trouble for them to reopen the IEP process—or to go ahead and do an IEP team evaluation if it hasn't been done—than to keep arguing or face legal action.

However, sometimes you'll need to respectfully move beyond your child's teachers and school district to get further testing outside of school, even if experts you've consulted at school believe your child just isn't motivated or will "grow out of" learning lags. You're perfectly within your rights to set up an appointment with an outside psychologist or clinic and have your child independently evaluated at any time. (You'll learn more about the types of specialists you might need to consult in the next chapter.) But be aware, if your school doesn't think your child needs the additional testing and you consult an outside evaluator anyway, the school does not usually have to pay for this testing. If the outside evaluator sees a problem and recommends treatment but the school doesn't agree, the school isn't required to provide free help. In this situation, you can seek treatment with outside professionals at your own expense, or you can appeal the decision through channels that every state's public school system is required to provide (you might want to have an attorney for this, but you aren't required to have one).

In the Next Chapter . . .

In this chapter, I've explained how you can best work with your school to try to figure out exactly what's going on with your child. It makes sense to start with the school in an effort to solve these kinds of problems. But in other cases—such as with depression, anxiety, or other mental health issues—it may make more sense to have your child evaluated privately, outside the school. That can be the most direct route to figuring out exactly what's going on in some cases, and how best to design a program to solve your child's struggles. Even after an enlightening evaluation at school, some children's problems are just too complicated to be handled exclusively at school—and in this case, you'll need more professional help.

In these situations, you'll need to consider bringing other experts on board. But what experts should you choose? In the next chapter, I'll discuss the different types of specialists who may be involved in helping a child with learning, behavioral, and/or mood problems, and which expert works best with each problem.

4

Getting an Outside Opinion: Teaming Up with Professionals

I F YOUR CHILD is struggling to learn to read or just can't seem to master elementary math, it makes sense to start with the school in your quest to find out what's going wrong. But many times, parents realize they need to look beyond the school for help, and choose to consult a clinic or a private professional.

There are many reasons why you might consider getting an independent evaluation for your child. If you don't really agree with what the school is saying, you may want someone else's opinion. Sometimes the school insists their testing hasn't found any problem with your child that would require special education services—yet you just *know* that something isn't right with your child. Or perhaps you suspect that your child's problems are more complex than the school can handle alone. Some parents simply prefer to keep their child's problems private and opt for an independent evaluator rather than asking the school to test. In still other cases, a child may have significant psychiatric problems, such as mood or anxiety issues, that the school simply isn't equipped to handle. In any of these situations, private professionals may be the answer.

In my experience, the best solution is usually a combination approach in which both the school *and* outside experts work together. Even a child with a straightforward learning disability who is in an appropriate special education program at school may make even better progress by adding some extra out-of-school help, such as a particularly strong after-school tutoring program. On the other hand, there's no denying that a multidisciplinary team in one setting is convenient; the team members probably know each other and work well together. Still, even multidisciplinary teams in single settings can get stuck in limited points of view, and this type of treatment can get expensive. In the end, most of the kids I see need multidisciplinary help in some way, but you don't have to *begin* with a multidisciplinary evaluation under one roof. For many families, using both in-school and out-of-school resources ends up as the best choice.

For example, this combination worked well for Susan, who received speech therapy at school supplemented by a summer speech/language program at a nearby university clinic staffed by grad students. Charlie benefited from good instruction for his dyslexia at school, which was closely coordinated with extra reinforcement by a private tutor on Saturdays.

Single Evaluator or a Team Approach?

If your school has suggested that you consult an outside professional—or you've sidestepped the school and want to consult your own independent evaluator—your next task is to choose an expert. Should you select an independent psychologist, psychiatrist, or learning specialist—or a clinic with a team of experts?

Sometimes the answer is simple. For example, if your child just seems to be depressed or has a problem learning to read but is otherwise reasonably happy and well adjusted, one evaluator may be all you need. But the truth is, many children *don't* have just one problem. They often have a bunch of overlapping issues.

For instance, a child with a reading disorder may also be depressed. A child suspected of mild autism may also have learning difficulties, fine motor problems affecting his ability to write, language delays, and maybe some attention issues. A child with cerebral palsy may also be anxious and worried and have a problem paying attention. In these cases, several different professionals may be needed. Ultimately, the more problems you think your child may have, or the more complex those problems may be, the more likely it is that you'll be working with a number of different professionals.

For most of the problems I discuss in this book, it makes sense to start with a carefully chosen single-source evaluator, who can usually give you a good overview of your child's problems. I usually tell parents to start with just one really well-qualified person to get a single broad view. Without being arrogant about my own profession, it's fair to say that a good-quality *doctoral-level professional* (such as a child psychologist, child psychiatrist, or pediatric neuropsychologist) will generally have the largest breadth of experience and knowledge. One expert can give you one coherent picture, which can be a godsend. A panel of experts sometimes ends up offering overdetailed or conflicting opinions!

However, if your child has several different problems or complex issues, you may eventually find you need a multidisciplinary approach. But that doesn't mean all the experts need to be located under one roof. What's important is that the professionals are able to work well together. For instance, one of my recent young patients had started treatment with a therapist at a good mental health clinic across town and came to our clinic for a neuropsychological evaluation. She's also been seeing an excellent speech pathologist at her school for the past year. A child like this can be helped enormously by this sort of multidisciplinary team in different locations, as long as everybody talks to each other and shares information.

Finding an Evaluator

So how do you *find* an evaluator? There are lots of ways to choose an expert. Fortunately, almost any of you reading this book can go to your public library, get on the Internet, and find information from a variety of sources to help you find someone, somewhere, who can evaluate your child competently. But you'll often find that the best way to locate an evaluator is through word of mouth. Ask your child's pediatrician or other doctor, teachers you might know, day care operators, or your own friends and family. People whose kids have had similar problems can be an excellent resource.

That's how Rhonda found a terrific evaluator for her daughter, Giselle. Giselle was a happy, engaging child with lots of friends and an easygoing nature. But by second grade, her reading problems really seemed to be slowing her down. After a brief test, her school insisted Giselle didn't have a reading disability, but Rhonda was sure something was going on that the school had overlooked. She wanted to take her daughter for an independent evaluation—but how did she know who would be reputable?

Rhonda started the search by picking up the phone and asking her pediatrician to suggest a few names. A teacher she knew in a neighboring school district provided another name, and a few friends whose kids also had been tested for reading disabilities gave Rhonda some recommendations as well. When several different people mentioned the same individual, Rhonda called and made an appointment.

To find the best person to do an evaluation, you'll want to do your homework. Ideally, you're looking for someone who's helpful, broad-minded, thinks scientifically, and has a good reputation in your community. Whether the evaluator is in a clinic, hospital, or independent practice, his or her professional quality and reputation is the most critical factor in deciding where to go. As a medical school faculty member, it would be easy for me to say that a clinic based in a university or medical school would probably have the best service—but that wouldn't be fair to all the skilled professionals working in other types of settings. Of course, a person's reputation is based on personal and professional opinions, not just objective evidence. You could end up getting an unlucky, unhelpful evaluation from someone with a good reputation, but such an evaluation is much less likely than if you choose someone randomly out of the phone book!

In virtually every evaluation we do at our clinic, we recommend another professional for follow-up treatment—that's one of our roles. Most important, we know a lot about the different types of resources for kids, and we can help parents look for those experts. That's exactly what we did for Jenny's parents, who came to us for suggestions on someone to help their daughter. Jenny was a brilliant young lady who had started feeling depressed as she entered adolescence. Everybody knows the teen years can be rough, but on top of her rocky early adolescence, Jenny's parents were getting a divorce. Jenny's two brothers both had ADHD, and her parents always regarded her as the family's "normal" child. When Jenny took an overdose of her father's medication and landed in the hospital, her parents finally admitted that their "normal" child needed psychotherapy. That's where we came in.

Jenny's parents started by asking for referrals from other professionals they knew and trusted, including me (since I'd evaluated her brothers), her father's psychologist, and the psychiatrist who prescribed her brothers' medication. Her parents listened to each of us as we recommended colleagues we thought might be a good match for Jenny's needs. After a positive recommendation from me, her parents zeroed in on a new colleague in my department who was able to start therapy sessions right away. Within a few therapy sessions, my colleague quickly diagnosed Jenny's depression; then, with the help of antidepressant medication and individual therapy, Jenny gradually returned to her former more upbeat self.

Luckily for her, Jenny's case was fairly straightforward. Many other situations are far more complex. That was the situation with Deb, who had mild motor tremors due to a brain condition, moderate learning delays in many areas, and severe ADHD. She was also enormously frustrated, as were her parents. An audiologist had felt there was an auditory processing disorder, and she seemed to improve when she used recommended headphones in class connected to a microphone worn by her teacher. However, it wasn't clear whether this device worked because it improved her attention and focus, or because it actually helped her hear and understand better. Did she have a hearing problem or an attention issue? The answer was critical, since Deb was beginning to resist wearing the headphones. She didn't want to look "weird" in front of her classmates.

Deb's problems in drawing, writing, mispronunciations, and behavior control were beginning to interfere with everything from her daily classwork to social acceptance. Her parents arranged for many different kinds of intensive extra instruction for her academic delays at her small, accommodating private school, but she was falling further and further behind with each year.

Deb's developmental pediatrician had tried a number of different medications for ADHD, but they didn't help much. One of the drugs gave her tics and had to be discontinued. Both her family and the school staff were experts in behavior management strategies for her ADHD, and she even had a private aide for many hours of the school day—but it still wasn't enough to help focus her attention.

As you can imagine, over the years Deb and her family had worked with many different professionals, some more useful than others. What her parents finally realized was that they needed to find the right combination of disciplines and insightful experts who could help their daughter progress despite her complex situation.

When this family came to us, we conducted a detailed neuropsychological exam that gathered information about her medical and physical problems as well as her psychological and learning issues. We referred the family to a talented neurologist, who was able to help the family understand Deb's many problems and prescribe a helpful combination of medications to help her focus. The family moved Deb to a public school that had an experienced learning-problems team who helped her set appropriate goals. With the right combination of special help, she slowly began to improve in reading, math, and writing. After a year, she was spending half of her day in a regular classroom with her peers, augmented with special help outside of school in certain subjects.

Experts A to Z

As you begin asking others for recommendations or referrals for an evaluation for your child, you're going to discover that many kinds of professionals may be involved in helping a child with learning, behavioral, and emotional problems. Trying to figure out which expert to choose can be a real challenge! I'll provide an overview of the different types of experts and which type of professional may be best suited to help your child.

Pediatrician

If you're like most parents, the search for help may have begun with your child's pediatrician. It's often a good idea to start here because you'll want to rule out any general physical problems that could be causing your child's problems. A thorough general physical exam and consultation with a doctor who's known your child for a long time is sometimes the first step on the road to getting help. If your child's basic health appears okay, the pediatrician can then refer you to one of several types of specialists for more specific testing: a child psychologist, a child psychiatrist, or a pediatric neuropsychologist. I've discovered that most parents find it challenging to understand the differences among these three specialties. The most important thing to keep in mind is this: you want to make sure to see someone who has a lot of professional experience *with children*, not just with adults.

Child Psychologist

A child psychologist is a mental health expert who specializes in the diagnosis and treatment of children's behavioral or emotional problems. If your child's problems seem mainly behavioral or emotional (maybe your son throws temper tantrums, or your daughter is depressed or anxious), a psychologist could be a good choice for evaluation and treatment. Psychologists can use a range of tests, including IQ, achievement, and personality tests, to diagnose and treat patients. This means that many learning difficulties can be understood using psychologists' methods.

A child psychologist usually has a doctorate (Ph.D., Psy.D., or Ed.D.) from a university or professional school. This type of program requires at least four years of graduate school and a year of supervised internship. Most states also require an additional year of supervised experience for a professional license in this area. Generally, a child psychologist in clinical practice will have a degree in "clinical psychology" or "counseling psychology."

A child psychologist understands emotions and behavior from a scientific angle and helps children understand, explain, and change behavior. Many child psychologists have received extra specialty training in such areas as family psychotherapy, child abuse, school problems, eating disorders, or neuropsychology. Because child psychology is such a broad field, it's important for you to find out if the psychologist you're considering has good training and experience in the particular kinds of problems that concern you.

Specially trained and certified psychologists in New Mexico and Louisiana can prescribe medication; in other states, psychologists can't prescribe medication, so they work with a physician if medication is needed. As this book went to press, seven other states were considering similar legislation to allow prescribing privileges—Georgia, Hawaii, Illinois, Missouri, Wyoming, Tennessee, and Oregon.

Child Psychiatrist

A child psychiatrist is a medical doctor who specializes in the diagnosis and treatment of disorders of thinking, feeling, or behavior that affect children, adolescents, and their families. Child psychiatrists can prescribe medication and therefore often work together with psychologists in managing drug treatments. More serious mental illnesses, such as bipolar disorder or childhood schizophrenia, would most likely include a psychiatrist on the treatment team.

Child psychiatrists must complete four years of medical or osteopathic school (earning an M.D. or O.D.). Then they spend at least three years of residency training in medicine, neurology, and general psychiatry with adults, followed by another two years of training in psychiatric work with children, adolescents, and their families in an accredited residency in child and adolescent psychiatry. After completing medical school, graduates must pass a licensing test given by the board of medical examiners for the state where they want to work. To get board certified, psychiatrists then must take and pass the certifying examination given by the Board of Psychiatry and Neurology. (To be board certified in child and adolescent psychiatry, a candidate must first be board certified in general psychiatry.)

Neuropsychologist

A pediatrician, medical specialist such as a neurologist, or school specialist might suggest a referral to a neuropsychologist (my specialty) for an evaluation. I often work closely with schools and medical doctors, as well as with family members of the child. This is especially likely if your child's abilities are complicated or difficult to assess, if there are thinking problems or behavior patterns that might be closely linked to disrupted brain function, or if your child might have some kind of actual brain damage. Neuropsychologists are trained to think about the link between brain function and behavior.

The more a problem has to do with a child's capacity to learn or master skills, or appears to be linked to a problem with brain function, the more you'll need a neuropsychologist. If your child has a neurological problem such as epilepsy or brain injury, or you've worked on your checklists and behavior diaries in chapter 2 and it appears that things seem to be lining up on the autistic-spectrum, ADHD, or learning-disabilities areas, a neuropsychologist may to be useful to you.

On the other hand, if your child's problem is social and emotional (perhaps Sammy has trouble getting along with others), or oppositional (Tracy argues with you all the time), the less you'd need a neuropsychologist. If the answers to the questions in chapter 2 seem to suggest emotional problems such as depression or anxiety, you're more likely to benefit from a child psychologist.

Clinical neuropsychologists start off with a doctoral degree (Ph.D., Psy.D., or Ed.D.) from a university or professional school, usually with the same kind of experience that a clinical psychologist needs, but sometimes in different areas of psychology such as "school" or "counseling." Along the way, they've gotten specialized education in neuropsychology and neuroscience, generally including at least two years of postdoctoral training in a clinical setting, and have often passed a national board certification exam. Holding an ABCN/ABPP Diploma in Clinical Neuropsychology is the clearest evidence of competence as a clinical neuropsychologist.

Educational/School Psychologists

These experts specialize in assessment and consultation relating to educational issues, including testing for learning disabilities and other school problems. There is some overlap with what neuropsychologists do, but one common difference is that these specialists usually work in a school setting. Educational psychologists and school psychologists (who may have either a master's degree or a doctorate) use a range of assessment tools, including intelligence and academic achievement testing. Special educational needs, learning difficulties, dyslexia, behavior problems, and gifted children all fall within the scope of their expertise, drawing on a knowledge of child psychology, child development, and education.

Experts with these specialties use lots of techniques to put together a picture of the child's strengths and weaknesses, and to identify what is affecting the child's learning and behavior. Individual tests of intelligence give a profile of the child's verbal and nonverbal thinking skills and may identify specific areas of strength and weakness. Tests of reading, spelling, and numbers are used to measure the child's achievement. These experts also observe children in class, interview teachers and parents, and use personality tests to check out social and emotional health.

School psychologists often spend most of their time addressing issues that affect a child's school performance. They can also have training in counseling and crisis intervention and are sometimes involved in one-on-one counseling and in group counseling. A school psychologist is usually a member of the team at school that determines if a student is eligible for special education services.

School Psychologist vs. Guidance Counselor

There are a couple of differences between a *school psychologist* and a *guidance counselor*. At the moment, there's an ongoing debate about the training a person must have to be a school psychologist. At the very least, most states require a specialist degree (that is, a master's degree plus thirty graduate hours) to be certified as a school psychologist. Certification allows the person to work in a public school setting, but it's not enough in most states to qualify for a license for private practice. In most states, licensure for private practice in psychology (including school psychology) requires a doctorate, with training in mental health, child development, learning, and motivation.

Guidance counselors have earned a bachelor's degree, and some have a master's degree, but they're not broadly trained to administer or interpret psychological and social-emotional tests, nor can they make diagnoses of handicapping conditions as required by federal law. Many counselors spend their school day doing individual or group counseling, and handling guidance programs.

Developmental and Behavioral Pediatrician

You may find that the person who ends up leading your child's team in a multidisciplinary clinic is a pediatrician with training in development and behavior, with interests ranging from cerebral palsy to mental retardation to autistic spectrum disorders. Sometimes called simply a developmental pediatrician, this doctor will carefully examine your child to see if there are any physical problems, but will also pay lots of attention to your child's nervous system—including speech, social skills, and behavior, as well as physical strength and coordination. This specialist often works closely with geneticists, neurologists, or physiatrists to coordinate programs for children with complex or severe developmental disabilities. These physicians have an M.D. or O.D., have completed a pediatric residency, and usually have additional fellowship training.

Speech/Language Pathologist

This expert specializes in the assessment and treatment of speech, language, communication, and voice disorders. Also known as a speech pathologist or a speech therapist, the speech/language pathologist evaluates and treats kids with communication problems associated with learning disability, hearing loss, brain injury, emotional problems, or developmental delays. They may treat those who stutter or who have voice or articulation problems along with problems with more complex language skills such as comprehension and expression. Some speech pathologists also work with what are called oral-motor issues (such as swallowing problems).

Speech/language pathologists perform tests and make recommendations for treatment, which might include a program of exercises to improve language ability or speech, along with support from the child's family and friends. Sometimes the pathologist will prescribe special listening devices or computer programs.

These specialists must have a master's degree in speech/language pathology, more than three hundred hours of supervised clinical experience, and must have passed a certifying exam. Those who meet the strict requirements of the American Speech-Language and Hearing Association are awarded a certificate of clinical competence.

Occupational Therapist

This individual works with kids who have movement or sensory problems caused by disease, injury, or developmental delay to improve daily living skills. They also help kids learn how to perform lots of fine motor activities, such as using a computer or improving handwriting. They may prescribe physical exercises to increase strength, hand-eye coordination, and dexterity, or paper-and-pencil exercises to improve penmanship. Some occupational therapists also specialize in sensory integration problems (see chapter 11).

To be licensed, OTs must have a bachelor's degree in occupational therapy from an accredited educational program and pass a national certification exam. Those who pass the test are called registered occupational therapists. Six months of supervised fieldwork is also required.

Physical Therapist

This health care professional is trained to evaluate and improve a child's movement and function, usually focusing on large-muscle strength, flexibility, coordination, balance, endurance, walking ability, and mobility. As part of the rehabilitative process, physical therapy helps children meet the mobility and functional challenges in their family, school, and social lives. Physical therapists can evaluate and improve range of motion and function, teach kids how to manage physical disabilities, recommend exercises to maintain flexibility, and teach kids how to use assistive devices, braces, or other aids. A PT must have at least a master's degree; a growing number of programs offer the doctor of physical therapy (DPT) degree. After graduation, candidates must pass a national exam; other requirements for physical therapists vary by state.

Special Education Teacher

You may find yourself working with a special education teacher as a private tutor, or in your child's school. Such a teacher must have at least a bachelor's degree with a major in special education, plus student teaching experience—but lots of special education teachers also have a master's degree. During the past decade, many training programs have begun to combine training in several of the main special education categories, but most special education teachers focus on certain age groups, such as elementary, middle, and high school, adult, early childhood (three to roughly six years old), or the very important area of birth to three.

These professionals are often the people who spend the most time with your child and, along with regular classroom teachers, provide valuable observations. They devise unique tools and techniques to meet the particular needs of your child, in addition to working with the school to provide Individualized Education Programs for their students.

Many different types of disabilities can qualify a child for special education programs, including specific learning disabilities, speech or language impairments, mental retardation, emotional disturbance, multiple disabilities, and hearing or vision problems. Early identification of a child with any of these needs is an important part of a special education teacher's job, because early intervention is essential in educating these children.

General Learning Centers

In addition to the specialists described above, some families consider taking their children to general after-school learning centers that provide extra tutoring individually or in small groups. While some of the staff in these centers can be quite skilled at teaching and supporting your child, I've found that the initial evaluations they provide can be frustrating.

First, most of these centers simply can't hire staff with the training to consider the broad range of problems that I cover in this book, so important things can get missed. Their tests are often brief and may be outdated. Some centers promise that your child's skills will become "normal" after a certain number of hours of tutoring, which may not be realistic and can raise false hopes. If you want to use a learning center for the important *teaching* step in which they can be quite strong, I'd suggest you first get a more sophisticated evaluation from one of the more specialized professionals listed above.

Keep Things in Perspective

Your evaluator should consider your child's home and school situations, because different schools have different levels of expectations and teaching approaches. For example, your child's "average" test results might mean he'd have trouble in a challenging parochial, private, or public suburban school, but not in a less stringent public school. Because legal disability standards now compare a child's performance to the "average child" rather than expectations at a particular school, it's important for evaluators not to overdiagnose disabilities when a problem is too mild to be considered below average—even if the child is struggling to succeed in a demanding situation.

Second Opinions

When it comes to getting an evaluation, things aren't usually straightforward. On the one hand, your evaluator has had lots of training—but you know that test scores aren't perfect, and not all experts use the same diagnostic criteria. That's why I'd suggest a second opinion if you still have some important questions after your first evaluation. It's not always easy to judge beforehand what type of expert is the best choice.

While a second opinion can be time-consuming, costly, and frustrating, keep in mind how important it is for you to have a solid map of your child's problems as you plan your treatment strategy.

Treatment: An A-to-Z Overview

Choosing the type of professional to evaluate your child is only part of your task. You'll also want to keep in mind the kind of treatment your child might need, based on what the experts recommend. Remember that the type of expert you choose will probably have a direct effect on the type of treatment that's recommended.

For example, a psychiatrist might be more likely to recommend medication than most psychologists, since most psychologists can't yet legally

Check Out the Research

Many times in this book I recommend that you make sure diagnoses or treatments are backed by sound research. I suggest you ask other experts you trust—or do your own research by reading good books or reputable Web sites—to discover how strong the science is behind the information an expert is telling you. Of course, many decisions you need to make are too complicated to be able to research easily, so don't expect to research every bit of advice you get. Just try to be aware when you're making a decision that may not be based completely or only on science.

prescribe medication and are usually more oriented toward behavioral or talk therapy. Beyond the basic distinction of medication vs. psychotherapy, many different mental health experts have different theories on *types* of psychotherapy and treatments—so it helps to have a general idea of what's out there.

Psychosocial Therapies

For most of the emotional and behavioral problems in this book (except for ADHD, severe mood disorders, and psychotic disorders such as schizophrenia), I believe that family therapy, behavioral therapy, play therapy, or other psychological treatment should be the first step—before trying medication. This broad category of treatment—called psychosocial therapy—involves talking, practicing skills, and changing relationships.

This is the kind of treatment that really helped Lisa, an extremely bright ten-year-old who was chronically bored and understimulated at school. Some of her teachers were sure she must have ADHD, and they consistently overlooked her strong potential. As a result, Lisa developed a habit of mentally checking out during tedious class activities. She'd daydream, then get into trouble for not knowing the answers. As her problems deepened in school, she began to withdraw and became morose at home. She started skipping homework, telling her parents it was done, and began to shun former close friends, who began seeing her as a troublemaker.

Her parents brought her to our clinic for a neuropsychological evaluation. Sure enough, her IQ was very high, but we couldn't find any problems substantial enough to formally diagnose. Although she didn't show enough emotional or behavioral symptoms to diagnose an anxiety disorder or depression, Lisa was clearly having trouble adjusting to school.

Lisa's school guidance counselor had provided several counseling sessions plus some advanced learning activities, which improved the situation for the rest of that school year. But when similar problems reemerged at age eleven, her school referred the family for private counseling. Several months of play therapy and family psychotherapy helped her family understand her frustration and boredom and helped Lisa learn to cope with her school situation. By the time she was ready for middle school, her family—by now fully aware of her need for challenge—enrolled her in an academically advanced program that emphasized science and technology. Lisa's case illustrates the value of several approaches, including family psychotherapy, behavioral therapy, and play therapy.

These behavioral approaches can really help put many children on the right track—children like Carl, who had struggled with early reading skills in first grade. Poor Carl had the bad luck to be part of a class of precocious readers. As a result, he tried to avoid reading whenever he could. Soon Carl showed signs of giving up, commenting sadly, "I just can't learn to read." He was also developing a habit of rushing through reading by arbitrarily guessing what a word was on the basis of initial letter sounds rather than applying his phonics analysis skills more carefully to the middle and ending portions of words.

Psychotherapy to the rescue! Carl did much better after a series of five sessions with a gentle, encouraging child psychologist, who also provided some helpful attitude coaching guidelines for his parents and teacher. For instance, the therapist helped parents and teachers give clearer positive feedback for Carl's effort in reading, even when he was struggling with the words. Carl himself learned to accept some frustration while still trying hard.

Play Therapy

It may sound like just fooling around, but play therapy is a common type of psychosocial intervention often used with preschool and elementary-age children. Children often find emotions confusing and difficult to express.

Through play, children can often more clearly reveal how they really feel and think. Because play is a child's natural form of communication, even the most talkative kids often express themselves more fully through their play.

Most good child psychotherapists are trained to use play to help children cope with uncomfortable emotions and find solutions to their problems. This may take the form of a variety of treatment methods, all of which make use of one or more of the natural benefits of play. During play therapy, your child will work with a play therapist who guides the play sessions to help the child resolve problems. Different play therapists may use different methods; some work more directly with a child's problems, while others use play to gain insight into the child's personality and perceptions.

Because it's important for your child to feel safe during play therapy, most therapists will keep confidential what your child specifically says and does in play therapy, but they can share general themes and progress with you. This lets your child feel she can fully express herself without worrying about your reactions. Good therapists also will meet with you from time to time to discuss your concerns. Play therapists also may conduct family therapy sessions in which family members may participate to work toward helping a child.

Cognitive Behavioral Therapy

This type of treatment combines two effective traditions in psychotherapy: cognitive therapy and behavior therapy. It's often the preferred treatment for many emotional and behavioral problems, because many studies have shown it really works. You'd be surprised how many children develop the habit of negative thinking that interferes with their everyday life. A child with this pattern might say to herself, "I'm terrible at math. I'm the worst kid in this class—heck, I'm the worst at math in the entire *grade*. I'll never get better at math because I'm just stupid. So there's no point in trying. I'm just a terrible math student, and there's nothing I can do about it."

Cognitive therapy can show your child how distorted thinking like this can make him feel anxious or depressed or angry, and how he can change his thoughts to more helpful ways of thinking.

Behavior therapy can teach your child how to calm down his mind and body so he can feel better, think more clearly, and make better decisions. This might include things like muscle relaxation or new breathing techniques. Behavior therapy can also teach your child how to react differently in troublesome situations.

A good cognitive behavioral therapist combines these two treatments, helping your child see how uncomfortable thoughts can affect everyday life, and showing your child how to substitute more positive thoughts and behavior.

Family Therapy

Nothing exists in a vacuum. Your family's behavior directly influences your child, just as your child influences all of the different ways family members interact with each other. As a result, treatment involving the whole family can sometimes be really helpful. If your child is already in individual therapy, the therapist may bring other family members into the treatment sessions. Alternatively, your doctor or school may recommend a family therapist to start working with the whole family. It may sound scary, but family therapy doesn't have to be grim, confrontational, or traumatic. Humor is one of the hallmarks of a healthy family, and it can actually be a goal in therapy!

In family-oriented therapy with your child, the focus of the therapist is on the whole set of your family relationships. This type of therapy is often brief and focused on finding solutions to specific problems. There are many different family therapy approaches; some concentrate on changing relationship patterns and emotional communication, whereas others offer more structured directions.

One of my therapy supervisors was fond of reminding us that "all therapy is family therapy." That's because the emotional connections and communication patterns in families are so important and so strong that no matter what the problem, if one member is in therapy, it's virtually certain that the entire family's interactions are part of the agenda. For example, many times I've had to bring mom and dad into treatment with a high schooler who has ADHD because of the tricky balance between a teenager's need for independence and the parents' realization that their child needed supervision to cope with ADHD.

Behavior Management and Behavior Modification

If you tell your child, "No dessert until you clean your plate," that's "behavior management." Behavior management includes most things that we say or do to a child, including when and how we give commands and praise, use rewards, and apply negative consequences. Behavior management methods are the most thoroughly researched and popular methods that mental health professionals use to change children's behavior.

However, certain methods are more effective with different behavior patterns or disorders. For instance, the quick timing, clarity, and consistency of rewards are essential for success in a behavior program for a child with ADHD. Combining these principles with negotiation and choices becomes more critical as the child with ADHD grows into adolescence.

Behavior *modification* refers to a group of behavior management methods that are more formal and specific. These might include using charts and token reward systems. These methods are more often used with problems such as disruptive behavior disorders rather than other issues, such as mood problems.

Try This Test!

Do things sometimes feel confrontational around your house? Parents are often surprised when I tell them that most things we say to our children are either commands or questions. (By the way, your child experiences every question you ask partly as a command: "Listen to what I'm saying, then give me an answer.")

Try this test! See if you can increase the number of things you say to your kids without asking a question or giving an order. Talk about something you feel like, things you observe, or news about something of mutual interest. Tell them something you like about them, or information you'd like to share.

If you do this enough, only *some* rather than *most* of what you say to your children will be a command or a question. It might make you a lot more effective as a parent, and your kids might not feel bossed around as much.

Social Skills Training

How a child relates to kids his own age is such an important part of a child's life that it deserves special attention. Kids with ADHD, autism, and nonverbal learning disorders often have trouble in this area. Fortunately, social skills training can be included in individual and family therapy sessions, particularly the basic kind of help needed by children with autistic spectrum disorders. On the other hand, social skills training sessions can be helpful when taught in groups of children so they can have hands-on practice with issues such as cooperative play and handling conflict.

There are many different kinds of social skills training. A child may work on a particular problem in the social area, such as making eye contact or appropriate conversation. Perhaps a child needs to be taught how to ask another child to let her join a game. Social skills training would also be used to help a child conquer disruptive problems such as being too aggressive with classmates.

Combined Approaches

In many cases, your doctor or school system may recommend a combination of different types of psychosocial treatment—behavior management, play therapy, family therapy, cognitive behavioral therapy, and so on. This can be helpful if more than one problem is going on—such as the teenager struggling with depression, an eating disorder, and alcohol abuse.

The combination approach is what we eventually recommended for Henry, a busy, cute four-year-old whose parents felt he never completely grew out of the "terrible twos." They were getting frustrated with the ever-increasing tantrums and confessed that they often found themselves ignoring their child as a way of coping with his problems. When his preschool teacher suggested an evaluation, his parents asked Henry's pediatrician for advice.

The pediatrician was familiar with our thorough methods and cautious approach to diagnosis, so she referred Henry for a neuropsychological evaluation, even though he didn't show evidence of the kinds of thinking and learning problems we typically handle. Testing revealed he was just above average in general IQ, and his language and early academic skills were solidly average. He was a bit impulsive at school, but not at home. In fact, he was able to pay attention in most activities—except when he got into a power struggle with an adult.

We didn't believe that Henry had ADHD or a serious emotional disorder. Instead, we thought he had a mild *tendency* toward "oppositional defiant disorder." Some professionals call this kind of kid a strong-willed child or a difficult child. However, in Henry's case, it wasn't just his will. Instead, the demands of the different situations and his parents' sometimes overbearing responses contributed to the problem. Henry improved with play therapy aimed at easing his anger about his parents' tendency to ignore him. We also referred Henry's parents for some behavioral management coaching, and I chatted with his preschool teacher to help coordinate everyone's efforts. Over two months of weekly meetings with a good child psychologist, Henry became happier and more consistently cooperative. Occasional follow-up meetings with the psychologist over the next several months helped make the improvements more lasting as Henry got ready to enter kindergarten in the fall.

Doctor, Why Can't You Tell Me Precisely What's Going On?

Figuring out what's going on inside your child just isn't an exact science. If you get different answers from different tests, don't despair. Keep working with your doctor to try to clarify the picture, or to at least narrow the list of possible explanations. Often, your doctor will choose a treatment based on a best estimate of the problem, rather than definite answers. You may find yourself hedging your bets by trying some things that could be appropriate for more than one possible diagnosis.

Keep in mind that as your child grows and changes, his problems may change, too. This means that some treatments will be outgrown and replaced with different approaches.

Your biggest pitfall is black/white thinking. Instead, it's all a matter of degree—or shades of gray, like the clouds, with enough silver linings to make it worth your efforts as a parent!

Can't vs. Won't

Do you ever wonder if your child really can't learn something, control his behavior, or manage his emotions? Or is he just making bad choices and not willing to work hard enough? Does George truly have a hard time concentrating on his homework, or is he just manipulating the situation to get out of doing it? Would Anna feel so anxious and overwhelmed about the idea of going to school if she would only "put her mind to it" that she has to go?

This is a common debate among parents, teachers, and mental health professionals. One side effect of this debate is that the more an adult sees the child's behavior as a lack of *capability* (such as attention and impulse control in ADHD, or mood in depression), the more likely the idea of medication will be considered. Psychotherapy is more likely to be suggested if there is hope that children can learn how to change their motivation or feelings.

I often find myself talking with parents about just how much *can't* vs. how much *won't* is involved in their children's behavior patterns. However, virtually *all* children's behavior or emotional problems involve some degree of *can't* and some degree of *won't*. In addition, the degrees shift in different situations. To tell the truth, most things that appear to be *can't* should be more accurately viewed as the child having a harder time doing something, rather than absolutely not being able to do it at all, as *can't* would imply. So I'd advise you to avoid black/white thinking in this matter. If you make too big a deal about what your child can't do, you may be making excuses and letting him off the hook for responsibilities that he really could learn to handle. If you don't face how hard it is for your child to do some kinds of life tasks, you may be setting everyone up for extra frustration.

Paying for Care

In these times of rising health care costs and shrinking health insurance coverage, you'll need to realistically figure cost of the evaluation into your family budget. For most families, paying for evaluation and treatment is a real concern. We like to think we'd do anything for our family, but for all too many of us paying for care can be a serious problem. What do you do if you make too much money to qualify for Medicaid coverage—but not enough to pay for all of the evaluations, treatments, and medications?

Few families can afford to do absolutely everything they'd like to do, or everything that professionals recommend, to help children with the kinds of problems covered in this book. And for that matter, few schools have enough resources to provide an ideal intervention program! Even when a child qualifies for special education, the school's legal requirement is to provide a program that provides educational benefit and a "free appropriate public education"—*not necessarily the ideal program.*

Fortunately, if you need help paying for care, there are a few options you can check out. You can look into free community-based services, consider taking on a second job, or share child care with other parents so you can spend a bit more time with the one who needs your attention at the moment. What better choice is there than to do something that really helps you help your kid grow up?

Medical Insurance

If you've got health insurance, you can work with your primary care physician, the insurance company, the evaluator's office, and your employer or union to get the evaluation paid for. Health insurance gatekeepers often object that these evaluations are the school's responsibility. While this may be true to some extent, most of the behavioral, emotional, and neurologically based issues that we discuss in this book go far beyond the area of "educational" problems. However, even with the best medical insurance policies, some of the cost is usually borne by the family.

Most families with medical insurance have to deal with another problem: the best evaluators in your area may be "out of network," which either raises your copay expense or means your policy won't cover the person at all. Think of it this way: the evaluation is a onetime expense, rather than something you're going to have to keep paying for as treatment continues. If possible, see if you can pay for this yourself to get the quality you want, rather than accepting the lower-quality "expert" your plan is willing to cover. Family finances are a personal and often delicate matter, but I strongly encourage you to think of good-quality evaluation and treatment as an important investment in your child's future.

Piecing Something Together

When it comes to getting an evaluation, remember that a partial or approximate map is better than no map at all—but an inaccurate or misleading map won't help anybody. You'll certainly want to get some essential tests done, but you may be able to drop some others. Ask your evaluator for help on this one.

Get the School to Pay

Sometimes your school district will pay for some or all of a private evaluation—but only if it's needed to determine if your child is eligible for an IEP. Remember, you don't have a right to demand from the school any testing that you want.

Shop Around

Shop around for price and quality by asking for suggestions from other parents and experts you trust. Look into what you can learn to do yourself, especially for intervention after you've gotten a good professional evaluation. For example, you could take a course on how to help children with reading disabilities, using training that is available for parents and tutors (such as the Orton-Gillingham method). Look into bartering treatment for your child with a service that you can provide (although there are ethical limitations for this when something as personal as psychotherapy is involved).

Medication Costs

Many of the medications used to treat some of the disorders I discuss in this book are expensive. However, if you don't have insurance or your plan doesn't include a prescription-drug benefit, you do have a few options.

Government Entitlement Programs

- **Medicaid:** This state-run public health program covers many types of treatments, mental health care, case management, and transportation to doctors. States are required to cover a core set of benefits, including hospital, outpatient, doctor services, and home health services. If they wish, states can also cover services by psychologists, social workers, and services provided in clinics. You'll need to check with your state Medicaid office to see precisely what is covered where you live and what the income limits are.

- **Supplemental security income (SSI):** This federal program provides cash benefits to low-income people who meet financial eligibility requirements and the government's definitions of disability.

Many physicians will offer their pharmaceutical samples free to patients who can't afford them. If your doctor doesn't offer, ask if any samples are available.

You may not realize that most drug companies offer free medications to patients who can't afford them. These special programs are typically called "patient assistance programs" or "indigent drug programs." They're designed as a last resort for needy patients who are unable to pay for their medications. The programs typically require a doctor's consent and proof of financial status, and proof that you have no health insurance or no prescription-drug benefit.

Patient Assistance Programs Web Sites

Although individual drug companies may have their own programs online, two Web sites are designed to provide information about many patient assistance programs that provide free prescription medications to eligible participants. Check out:

NeedyMeds (www.needymeds.com)
RxOutreach (www.rxassist.org)

In the Next Chapter . . .

Now that you have an idea of the experts and types of treatment you may need in your quest for help, it's time to think about exactly what kinds of tests your child might need. In the next chapter, I'll discuss the typical tests administered to children, what you can expect, and what the results may mean.

5

It's Test Time: What You
and Your Child Can Expect

MENTAL HEALTH CARE professionals and education specialists have lots of tools to help them diagnose children with behavioral, emotional, or learning problems. But before you can figure out the best treatment, you've got to really understand your child's strengths and weaknesses—and that's why a good-quality evaluation is so important. For many years I've used all kinds of psychological, neuropsychological, and educational tests, and I've found that many parents are confused about testing. At the very least, parents sometimes have unrealistic expectations.

Let me set the record straight: *Testing can help you understand your child's problems, including how serious they are. Tests can pinpoint strengths and weaknesses and help you understand if your child needs special education.*

Tests came in handy in figuring out what was going on with David, who'd had trouble with numbers and shapes from the beginning. His worried parents worked with him at home as his kindergarten teacher had suggested, but by first grade, his problems continued. Although his reading and spelling were strong, he had trouble decoding a clockface. Eventually he mastered telling time—with lots of review—but he didn't enjoy drawing at all, and he needed help each time a project required charts or pictures.

David made gradual progress in math with extra tutoring after school during second and third grade. His sensitive parochial school acknowledged his struggles with math tests, and he visited the school's learning center to review math lessons. He also started taking some math tests in the learning center, where the resource teacher helped him interpret diagrams and directions and gave him extra time for any parts that he needed. However, his parents were worried about his growing frustration and his slow pace, so in third grade they asked for an evaluation by the special education team in his public school district. Although they loved the parish school he attended with his brothers, David's parents were willing to switch him to the public school for more specialized instruction there if he needed it.

David's parents were relieved when the IEP team decided he could get learning disabilities services in math at the public school, along with occupational therapy to help with fine motor coordination. The school psychologist explained that there was a large gap between David's high-average IQ, his low-average arithmetic calculation skills, and his below-average math reasoning skills. But his parents were confused: How could they make sense of all these scores? What was causing the contradiction between his high-average IQ scores and his poor daily schoolwork?

When they brought David to our clinic for a neuropsychological evaluation to sort out their confusion, we updated the assessment of his academic skills with a different test battery than the one the IEP team had used. We also tested some additional important areas such as memory and tactile perception to clarify exactly what was going on with his learning disability pattern. We also wanted to pinpoint his basic mental processing strengths and weaknesses. Building on the school's testing, rather than just repeating everything, we successfully pieced together which of David's areas were average and which were below average—along with a clear picture of *how far below average*. We also offered the most likely explanations for the pattern, taking into account the benefits that he'd received from his extra instruction so far.

David's parents walked away from this additional evaluation with a much clearer understanding of what was going on with their son and what to do next, both because of the information from the additional tests and the careful explanation they'd received about what all the test results meant.

Testing Helped Amos

Alas, not all cases are so straightforward. Amos was one of our patients who'd been tested and tested and tested—in fact, his file in our neuropsychology clinic was about three inches thick! His parents had asked for his first evaluation during late kindergarten, because they weren't sure that testing by a special education team at school would give them as much detail as they wanted to know about his problems with attention and pre-reading skills. At that time, he appeared at risk for dyslexia, but it was too early to know for sure, because kindergarten students aren't really expected to be reading yet.

Brief retesting of key academic and language skills during second grade verified that Amos had developed enough delays in reading and spelling to confirm a dyslexia diagnosis, particularly since he'd received lots of good-quality extra help during first grade but was still behind in several important areas.

The specialized dyslexia tutoring center that Amos attended during second and third grades was careful about documenting his progress with tests of many different reading skills every six months. He also returned to the neuropsychology clinic twice for updates during late elementary school, where we eventually decided that he showed an additional pattern of borderline attention-deficit/hyperactivity disorder. His parents brought him three more times for weekly testing of his response to medication to improve his attention.

Amos's encouraging progress, along with some continuing signs of struggle, actually followed a quite consistent pattern in the assessments over the years. So why were his parents requesting testing yet again just before he entered sixth grade? It was quite simple: the way that we chose, timed, and explained the testing to Amos's parents and teachers helped them understand both his problems and his progress in important ways that contributed to planning for the next steps in his education. And that was reason enough to do it.

When Testing Makes Sense

A thorough assessment is vital in choosing the best treatment. It's also a critical element in convincing other people (such as school administrators) to take action to help your child. Testing can be used to supplement, refine, readjust, or even redefine the informal impressions and observations about your child. I remember one seven-year-old boy whose testing reassured his parents that he just had ADHD, not a learning disability. This knowledge helped them work with their son to get him more organized and better at managing his study time, right through college. He's now a successful optometrist!

By the way, some of you may be afraid that your child will be upset or feel bad about himself if he's taken in for testing. If you explain to the child in kid-friendly language that the testing is a kind of team discovery about how best to help him, and if the tester is supportive, your child will probably actually enjoy the testing. Amos, for example, feels interested, respected, and has fun with the psychometrist every time he comes in, even though he'd rather be at school with his friends now that he's in middle school.

No Test Is Perfect

Some parents think test results will give them all the answers—they won't! In fact, all tests have certain limitations. For instance, some experts question the accuracy of giving certain tests to children when the tests were originally designed for adults. You should remember that the results of psychological testing won't give you an "absolute" score or a foolproof diagnosis. We must combine these results with information from many different sources.

If several areas of your child's function need to be assessed, such as attention *and* intelligence *and* school skills, be prepared for some lengthy appointments! In particular, neuropsychological and psychoeducational assessment batteries can be long when used in their complete form.

What If the Experts Don't Agree?

Suppose you and your spouse think that your child might really benefit from an assessment of his or her problems. What happens if your child's pediatrician or teacher doesn't think your child needs to be tested? Sometimes, you'll need to respectfully move beyond your primary care physician and teachers and go ahead and get further testing on your own, even if experts you've consulted thus far believe your child will "grow out of" problem behaviors or moods. You're perfectly within your rights to set up an appointment with an outside psychologist or clinic and have your child independently evaluated. (Check chapter 4 to help decide what type of specialist you'd like to contact for testing.)

Preparing Your Child for Testing

Once you've set up an appointment for testing, you'll want to get your child ready for the assessment. Jenny might be shy about meeting a stranger who will ask a lot of questions. Sue may not like being separated from you. Dan could be nervous that you'll find out what's "really bad" about him. Pete might argue that there's nothing wrong with him and he's "not stupid."

Break the News

If you can, place a brief phone call to the evaluator in advance to see what you can learn about the upcoming testing. If you don't have an opportunity for this discussion, you can tell your child that he or she will be visiting a "talking doctor" or a "thinking and learning doctor." (Of course, you would use a different term, such as *teacher* or *helper*, if the expert has a master's degree rather than a doctoral-level degree.) Explain that the evaluator's job is to help parents and teachers understand how the child learns best.

You'll also want to prepare your child for some of the things that might happen during the appointment. I often tell children that I'll ask some questions, do puzzles or play word games, work on school stuff, or give them some things to remember. You'll be amazed to find out how many kids, preteen and below, worry that they'll get a shot or be hurt somehow during testing. Whether or not they ask, I'd suggest that you promise them that this won't happen (unless you think it might with the particular specialist you're seeing, such as a psychiatrist who might take a blood test).

Listen to Their Concerns

Listening to your child is actually much more important than any kind of organized speeches that you may give, particularly if you get resistance about the idea of going for testing in the first place. Try to really understand how your child feels, what the reluctance is about, or why your son or daughter might even feel relieved or curious about the test.

Be Honest!

You should be honest about what will happen, how long the testing sessions will take, and what you know or don't yet know about what goes on. Most testing of children older than early preschool takes place without the parent in the room, but some testing and/or interviewing may involve the parent and child together. If you've already met the evaluator, tell your child any positive impressions about the person—maybe the person seems nice, respects kids, is friendly—whatever you think is relevant, reassuring, and honestly likely to be true.

Making Mistakes

Explain that some of the items on the test may be easier and some may be harder, and that your child shouldn't worry if he feels that he's not getting all the answers right. Reassure him that the most important thing is for him to try his best; in fact, children beyond preschool age can probably understand if you explain the concept that the tester has to ask some things that he might not know or can't do completely, just to see how much he does know and can do.

Give a Pep Talk

If you suspect that your child might not cooperate fully or might have problems paying attention to the tests, try a pep talk. If you think it would help, it is legitimate to promise a modest reward (such as ice cream) right after the testing if the examiner reports that your child tried hard.

Where You'll Be

Tell your child if you'll be in the waiting room or out doing errands during testing. If there's any chance your child would be most comfortable with you being in the waiting room, make arrangements to stay right there. Children will do best if they know they can count on your support, participation, and presence, even in the background.

Medication

If your child is taking medication for problems with attention, behavior, or emotional issues, ask the evaluator in advance if medication should be stopped on testing day. There are pros and cons in each situation, so a case-by-case decision is important, especially if the medication is helping a lot or seems to cause side effects that could interfere with testing (such as sleepiness). For instance, if your child already takes medication for attention and self-control, but you're trying to find out whether a diagnosis of ADHD is appropriate, it may be best to have your child stop taking medication before the test. On the other hand, if your child takes medicine for something you're not testing for (such as depression)—and you're assessing a learning disability—then continuing the medication is probably a good idea.

And don't forget, since some medications take several days or even weeks to fully clear out of a child's system when discontinued, there might be no point in temporarily stopping the drug for testing day.

"I Won't Go!"

This variation on the familiar Peter Pan song may crop up, despite your best efforts to pave the way as I outlined above. These situations can lead parents to sigh, wring their hands, or even pull out their hair. While there's no single answer to this one, two old sayings come to mind that can help: First, there's more than one way to skin a cat—you should trust that seasoned professionals are used to this sort of thing, and they may have some tricks to coax cooperation once you drag the reluctant one to the doctor's office. Second, it's true that you can lead a horse to water, but you can't make him drink—but it's your job as a parent to get the horse to the water trough.

Types of Tests

Once you've decided to have an evaluator test your child, you may be surprised at the number of different tests that professional may choose. Over the years, I've found that parents are sometimes confused about what a "psychological test" really is. Actually, there are several different types of tests your evaluator may be considering for your child, including assessments of skills, abilities, feelings, and behavior patterns. I won't try to give you a complete catalog here, but I do want to illustrate some of the options. Keep in mind that there is some overlap among these different testing areas.

Psychological Tests

Broadly speaking, psychological tests observe and record a child's behavior, emotions, interests, or abilities. Personality tests are one type of psychological testing, covering issues such as emotions, behavior, personality, and how your child relates to other people. There are many variations on personality testing, such as questionnaires that assess different aspects of anxiety.

Neuropsychological Tests

These tests can measure specific skills, such as memory, concentration, problem solving, and learning. This type of testing may sound complex or intimidating, but really it just refers to tests that reveal how the brain and nervous system interact with thinking and behavior. A complete neuropsychological evaluation begins with the collection of information about a child's education and physical, social, and psychological development. Then tests are used to measure a wide range of areas, including focus and attention, motor skills, sensory acuity, working memory, learning, intelligence, language, arithmetic skills, problem solving, judgment, abstract thinking, mood, temperament, the ability to interpret and apply meaning to visual information, and other skills. A neuropsychological examination might be recommended if your child has experienced:

- changes in emotions or thinking that can't easily be identified
- a medical condition or injury that could affect the brain
- a sudden or unexpected change in thinking
- failure to improve with therapy or special education help
- complex learning and behavior patterns that other evaluations haven't clarified

Psychoeducational Tests

These tests generally include individually administered assessments of intelligence and academic skills, giving IQ scores and levels of performance in areas such as reading, math, and written language. Most of these tests have subsections that offer more detail in each area, such as both verbal skills and visual-spatial skills in IQ testing, or accuracy in both reading *words* and reading *comprehension.*

Standardized Educational Testing

This includes those tests you think of as "standardized tests" or "achievement tests"—the evaluation of academic skills such as reading, comprehension, and math—typically administered at school.

So what's the difference between a "psychoeducational" test and a "standardized educational" test? A psychoeducational test is usually used for an individual child for a particular purpose, whereas a standardized educational test is typically given to large groups of kids at regular intervals in school.

Most states require public schools to administer national standardized tests as a way of assessing competency. It's important to realize that these achievement tests are usually given to many children at once in groups, such as in the classroom or an ACT testing session. The most reliable, usually most detailed achievement tests are a different type, given in a one-to-one session between the tester and the child, as noted in the category of psychoeducational testing referred to above; this can be called individual testing or individually administered tests.

Other Tests

These assessments include those that therapists use to assess speech, motor skills, and sensory areas. Each of these evaluators will consider many different possibilities, but should begin by taking a good history and doing some observation. For basic hearing and vision tests, you'd typically visit different specialists than the ones we focus on in this book. The highest levels of expertise would be a pediatric audiologist for hearing and a pediatric ophthalmologist for vision.

Testing Goals

I usually start my first interview with a parent by asking the most important questions: "What do you want to find out from this evaluation? What are your main questions for us?" The answers to these questions help me decide if testing is needed and what type of testing would be most helpful.

Recently, I got the following response from one beleaguered parent: "I don't mean this to come across as mean or harsh, but my biggest question is, 'Where did this kid come from?'" This mom, Judith, was genuinely puzzled about why her son sassed adults, flew into temper tantrums, and was constantly kicking his little sister over the slightest provocation. "We keep trying to teach him our values, but he just doesn't seem to get it," his mother said. "He isn't like anyone else in our family!"

This mom was just trying to answer the question that perplexes many parents most: *How can I make sense of these problems?* That's where testing comes in, along with all the other information we've gathered from checklists and behavior diaries as discussed in chapter 2.

Common Tests

In each testing category, many, many different tests are available, but I'd like to familiarize you with just a few types and selected examples (although new versions are published all the time). It's important to understand that testing categories overlap, and that very different tests could be relevant within a category at different ages:

- **Intelligence or overall cognitive ability:** Wechsler Intelligence Scale for Children, 4th Edition, or WISC-IV
- **Academic achievement:** Woodcock-Johnson 3 Tests of Achievement
- **Speech and language:** Clinical Evaluation of Language Fundamentals, 4th Edition
- **Visual-spatial skills:** Test of Visual Motor Integration, 4th Edition, and Judgment of Line Orientation
- **Personality, emotional adjustment, and social function**: MMPI-A and Child Behavior Checklist
- **Other neuropsychological functions:**

  - Attention and impulse control (Continuous Performance Tasks)
  - Executive functioning (Wisconsin Card Sorting Test)
  - Memory (Wide Range Assessment of Memory and Learning, 2nd Edition)
  - Motor and sensory skills (Finger Tapping subtest from Halstead-Reitan Battery, and Grooved Pegboard from the Wisconsin Motor Steadiness Battery)
  - Phonological awareness (Comprehensive Test of Phonological Processing)
  - Processing speed (Coding from WISC-IV)

In Judith's case, we got a much clearer picture of her son's problems when we sat down to go over the test results and other information. I explained that her son's impulsivity—which was part of a bigger problem with ADHD—made it harder for him to stop and think before acting. "This is a clear example of what people mean when they say, 'His brain is wired differently,'" I told Judith. "He *understands* what you tell him and *knows* the rules, but it's harder for him to hold back an urge to do something else." In addition, as he got older, his behavior triggered negative responses from the people around him. I also pointed out that her son's values had been shaped by this combination of "built-in" ADHD characteristics and the consequences he'd experienced. When he impulsively slapped his sister, Judith reacted by yelling at him. When he talked back because he couldn't control his angry impulses, he was punished. When he jumped out of his seat at school to answer the teacher's question, he was punished. Time after time, he'd act impulsively, other people would respond with anger or punishment, and he began to believe he was bad, naughty, and a failure.

A Word About Statistics

When they start hearing words like *mean, percentile*, and the ever-confusing *standard deviation*, most parents' eyes start to glaze over. While you don't need to be a statistics major to decode test results, there are some basic terms experts use that you'll need to know. It's also helpful to understand statistics as they relate to the standardized achievement tests that are administered from time to time to all children in public schools, since interpretations of your child's scores are used by many schools to place your child in certain programs. The three concepts that I'd really like you to understand are *percentile, mean*, and *bell curve.*

Percentile

A percentile is the percentage of scores of typical children that are equal to or below your child's score. For example, if Steve took a standardized test and was ranked at the 65th percentile, this means that he scored better than 65 percent of other kids his age on the same test. I usually explain it to parents this way: "If we took a hundred random kids exactly Steve's age from across the whole country and lined them up with kid number one as the weakest to kid number one hundred as the strongest on this particular skill—say, vocabulary—Steve would be kid number sixty-five. That's in the upper half of the average range."

Knowing your child's percentile tells you how your child's score ranks among other scores. Many standardized educational tests given in school give both a "national" percentile (like my example for Steve) and a "local" percentile (which compares your child to typical children *in his school or district or region*; you need to find out which of the latter it is to understand it correctly). So a kid who earned a national percentile of 95 in reading would have scored higher than about 95 percent of the students in the nation in that skill—he would be kid number ninety-five out of one hundred in our lineup.

Keep in mind, when interpreting percentiles, there is quite a large "average range." Different test publishers and evaluators differ somewhat in exactly what they consider average, but a general rule of thumb would be to include the middle half—which includes the 25th to the 75th percentiles.

How to divide the top quarter of people is a matter of some debate, but as an example, most IQ tests label approximately the 75th through 90th percentiles "high average," the 90th through the 98th percentiles "superior," and above the 98th percentile "very superior." Often, this top 2 percent is considered in the gifted and talented range.

The most important area for you to understand is the bottom quarter of scores, because this is where you get the most information for your map of your child's difficulties. Most IQ tests label approximately the 10th through 25th percentiles "low average," the 2nd through 10th percentiles "borderline" (referring to borderline cognitive disability, borderline mental deficiency, or borderline mental retardation), and below the 2nd percentile as "mild," "moderate," or "severe" cognitive disability, mental deficiency, or mental retardation.

On the other hand, many of the skills that we measure with tests become significant problems for children in school and in everyday life when they get near or below the 25th percentile, so the terms that different evaluators use for the below-average scores can depend on the skill being measured. I typically consider reading, math, and written language scores from the 10th through 25th percentiles "below average," and scores lower than the 10th percentile "well below average," particularly where your child's school has challenging standards or students who tend to achieve above the average range. Many experts refer to scores for specific mental-processing functions such as receptive language, spatial skills, or attention as "borderline impaired" between the 15th and 25th percentiles, "mildly impaired" between the 2nd and 15th percentiles, and "moderately to severely impaired" below the 2nd percentile.

Mean

Mean is another word for "average," and it provides a way of comparing one score with the pattern in the overall group. If Sally scores a 67, it's not possible to determine if this is a good score unless we know the mean. If the mean is 200, then 67 isn't so good, but if the mean is 40, then 67 may be quite good.

The Bell Curve

You may recognize this term from your own school career or from things you've read in the popular press. It's not hard to understand—basically, it just refers to a graph of how often something occurs. For example, if you lined up a number of people, with the tallest at one end and the shortest at the other, only a few would be at the very shortest and very tallest points. Most of the people would be clustered near the middle—the average height. This is represented by a bell curve—a curved line that is fatter in the middle than at the extremes, and which resembles a bell.

One of the basic observations in most educational and psychological testing is that children's scores also fall along a bell curve. Therefore, in any typical group of children, most of their scores would fall closer to the middle; only a few would score the highest or the lowest.

Assessing Special Needs

Although psychological tests have traditionally been used by clinical psychologists to help figure out why some children behave in certain ways, special educators also use testing as a regular part of assessing children to see if they have special needs. As you learned in chapter 3, these tests can suggest why some kids have trouble learning to read or developing arithmetic reasoning skills and can be used to help determine the best learning environment for the child. They also can help teachers more effectively serve children with learning disabilities. Educators have turned to these types of tests to comply with recent laws for students with disabilities or handicaps.

Your child's ability to learn can be affected by many factors. Maybe your daughter can't read because she wasn't taught phonics or other closely related language skills directly enough. Or maybe she's been sick a lot and missing school or has emotional problems that interfere with learning. Perhaps she can't sit still and listen to instruction, or maybe she has a subtle brain dysfunction that prevents her from acquiring information via traditional methods. To separate the many overlapping factors and provide the most accurate diagnosis possible, you'll want to have your evaluator use the best diagnostic tests available.

As I discussed in chapter 3, in a complete assessment for an Individualized Education Program, the team of special education experts gathers and analyzes information about your child's development physically, socially, scholastically, and psychologically. You may be asked for your observations, because you're typically the person who knows the most about things such as when your child learned to talk, how well she holds a pencil and uses her hands, and so on. In addition, the experts will observe your child pronounce words, figure out arithmetic problems, copy pictures, or perform other tasks.

Because public schools are bound by federal and state laws that specify who qualifies for special education, as you learned in chapter 3, some children with mild or borderline presentations of disorders "fall through the cracks," even if the teachers and administrators would truly like to provide services. Beyond that kind of scenario, which is frustrating for everybody, there's usually a range of kids who qualify for services if the rules are interpreted flexibly—but not if the rules are interpreted more strictly. The interpretation often depends on how financially strapped the school district is. (The less money there is, the more pressure on the administration to interpret rules strictly.) In other cases, tight budgets may mean that the school is reluctant to qualify children with mild problems for special help, because special educators don't have time to serve all the students who might benefit.

While these are reality-based issues, special education law specifically states that school budget problems can't be an excuse for not providing services that the school evaluation team judges that a child needs.

In conducting assessments in the medical center, I always welcome information from school evaluations. I sometimes suggest that parents first ask for testing at school, and I always request information from past school evaluations, even if I sometimes interpret the school results differently from the way the school did. The main problem with getting a school evaluation done first is that it sometimes takes longer, particularly if the school district staff are overworked. There's also the risk of triggering an adversarial relationship between parents and school staff.

If you're trying to get an independent evaluation in addition to the testing at school, I'd strongly encourage you to have both sets of professionals share results with each other, even if they've come to different conclusions. This may be confusing for you at first, but only by carefully considering all the information and opinions can either you or the professionals try sorting out the reasons for the different impressions.

If Results Don't Fit . . .

The situation gets stickier when the scores from the special education evaluation at school don't fit your child's overall clinical picture, or they contradict testing results from an independent evaluation at a clinic. When this happens at our clinic, we need to do some careful sorting to figure out the true picture. If this has happened to you, you may have found that a careful independent evaluator tends to trust his or her own test results over results from another source. However, sometimes the school's results are more accurate—for example, if a child has been resistant or reluctant during testing in the unfamiliar clinic situation.

Even if the results from two testing situations don't match at first, they can still be helpful—just as in Allen's case. Allen's pediatrician referred him for a neuropsychological evaluation at age eleven because of a frustrating disparity in test results.

Allen had been diagnosed with a reading disability three years before in a sound psychological evaluation by a respected developmental clinic, but the school district's evaluation six months ago didn't show the necessary pattern for him to qualify for special education services. There were three reasons why this happened.

First, government laws defining learning disabilities have traditionally required a discrepancy between IQ scores and academic skills, but Allen didn't fit this pattern. His overall IQ was slightly below average (19th percentile), which wasn't different enough from his 10th percentile basic reading skills in the previous clinic testing. The IQ score was also close to his 21st percentile reading skills in the school evaluation, certainly not indicating a required discrepancy. His math and written language scores were at similar levels. Although most researchers now agree that a discrepancy between IQ and academic skills isn't necessary for a learning disability diagnosis, most state laws haven't quite caught up with this new thinking.

Second, Allen also had ADHD and an expressive-language disorder that added to his problems and affected the findings in the school evaluation. Specifically, his IQ score was lowered by his language problems, so it wasn't fair to use a traditional IQ test as the most valid indicator of his learning potential. School procedures require that different IQ tests that don't rely so much on verbal skills be substituted, but this step had been missed in Allen's situation.

Third, and most important, while he attended a parochial school through third grade, Allen received extra reading help outside of school for several years, which improved his reading and written language skills a bit—but not into the normal range. In the neuropsychological evaluation, we concluded that Allen's academic problems deserved a diagnosis of what we called a *mild, partially treated reading disability or dyslexia*, which would probably have been at a moderate rather than mild level if it hadn't been for the extra help he'd received. Many parents in this situation end up regretting getting extra help outside of school, because the benefits can mean that the child no longer formally qualifies for special education services! Nevertheless, I firmly believe that the extra help is almost always worth it in these cases, because anything that improves the child's abilities is good, even if it complicates qualifying for services later.

Allen didn't end up receiving special education services through his public school district. Instead, his family kept him at his parochial school, where the staff helped tremendously by increasing its flexible accommodations in the curriculum to account for his learning disability. His family also expanded his outside tutoring. Although his parents could have gone back to the public school and pressured them for more tests, they decided that it would be best to make changes in his current school situation and add extra help outside of school. It also helped that they now understood how his schoolwork had gotten off track.

What Do All the Test Results Mean?

After testing, you should be given a description of your child's strengths and weaknesses, often accompanied by a diagnosis. In our clinic, this is the time when I carefully explain what test results mean, how parents should interpret and weigh those results, and when some findings can be "hedged" or even ignored.

This was important to Colleen, whose fifth-grade son, Michael, was doing well in special education. This program involved both speech/language therapy and extra help from the learning disabilities teacher. When Michael's neurologist referred him to our clinic to clarify whether his anxious responses to stress might be triggering his migraines, Colleen told me she was also curious about his school skills. He got 100s on his spelling tests and seemed to do okay in reading, but he was really struggling in math.

As we reviewed the information that Colleen had brought with her to our meeting, I noticed some interesting discrepancies. Michael's IQ score in kindergarten was at the first percentile, which is in the mild range of mental retardation. On his standardized test at the end of first grade, he scored at a not-so-strong 27th percentile in reading, comfortably average 64th percentile in vocabulary, but concerningly low 11th percentile in math. What did all these numbers mean? What testing did we need to do to answer Colleen's questions?

I explained to his parents that although Michael's updated overall intelligence score in our testing was in the borderline mentally retarded range, with verbal and spatial problems at about the second and third percentile, his overall pattern seemed more like a severe learning disability with an unusual pattern of strengths and weaknesses. It's not that rare for children with several different learning disabilities to earn scores near or even within the mentally retarded range when given IQ testing; more detailed assessment is definitely needed in these situations to find out exactly what's going on.

In fact, Michael's reading and language arts skills were happily in the lower part of the average range on our updated testing, although his math skills were well below average. This was unusual, because most students with learning disabilities have weaknesses in basic reading and writing skills as the main problem. Even more unusual, our testing showed that Michael had a mixed receptive and expressive language disorder, but he could speak and explain much better than he could understand. Most kids with language deficits have the opposite problem, struggling more with speaking than with understanding. We felt that Michael's unusual pattern in the language area strongly implied that he'd been helped by treating his speaking skills in speech/language therapy over the past few years, but he clearly had processing problems that hadn't responded much to treatment.

This pattern raised the possibility that he might have what is sometimes called an auditory processing deficit—a complex problem that occurs in a part of the brain responsible for recognizing and interpreting sounds. When this happens, the child may not recognize slight differences between word sounds, even if the sounds themselves are loud and clear.

Finally, we explained that Michael didn't have weaknesses just in the language and verbal areas, but also in the spatial area—he had trouble putting block designs together and figuring out complex pictures. His combination of spatial and receptive language problems suggested to me that he had a basic difficulty with abstract conceptual reasoning—that is, "getting the big picture"—as he approached late elementary age. This meant that he might begin to have more and more problems in reading comprehension and written expression in coming years, as these tasks became more complex and demanding.

On the basis of these tests, we told his mother that Michael didn't seem to be mentally retarded at all, although he certainly had learning problems. We explained we would refer him to an audiologist for further detailed hearing tests, and we'd also want to consider computer-based training for his hearing system, as well as special help in the classroom so he could understand what everyone else was saying. Michael was in a good school program, but he clearly needed help in many areas, so his parents and I discussed how to take this information back to the school to make his program even more intensive. We also started planning how he could get extra instruction during summers, so he wouldn't slip back too much in his skills during that time.

As Michael's tests showed, intelligence is an important concept, and the intelligence basics that IQ tests measure can fairly well predict how well the child will perform in school. On the other hand, summary scores of general intelligence (sometimes using similar terms, such as *general cognitive ability*) can often represent a mixture of apples and oranges. These summary IQ scores usually include verbal skills along with nonverbal and/or spatial skills, working or short-term memory, processing speed, abstract/conceptual reasoning, and quantitative skills. The bigger the difference among the different factors of intelligence in a particular child's profile, the more the summary score may reveal an artificial or misleading statistical average that glosses over important underlying patterns of strength and weakness.

As you can see, appropriate and thoughtful testing can provide a thorough understanding of your child's strengths and weaknesses—and that's why a good-quality evaluation is so important.

6

Learning Difficulties: Thinking, Academics, Language, Speech, and Motor Skills

KARLA AND STEVE had known for several years that their son Jim was struggling with reading, but they were nevertheless startled when his third-grade teacher wanted the school psychologist to evaluate him.

"The shrink?" his father shouted. "He's not that bad off! And he's certainly not crazy!" Steve in particular was offended that the teacher didn't understand that Jim's slow progress in reading was simply because he was a busy child who just didn't care for books. Jim's parents became unduly suspicious of the school's motives, so they consulted me for an independent evaluation. When I reviewed Jim's report cards from the last several years, I saw clearly that each teacher had noticed signs of learning struggles, but it was hard for Jim's parents to face these observations. As we talked, Karla became teary. "I had such high hopes for him!" she confessed. "All we want is for him to go to a good college, and now I'm afraid he won't make it!" When I suggested that we assess if Jim might have a reading disability, she found the idea hard to handle.

You're Not Alone

Karla and Steve's reaction wasn't unusual or surprising. We all have dreams for our children and want them to succeed. The idea that your child could have a significant learning problem may seem like a crushing blow at first—but a learning difficulty like this doesn't mean that failure is on the horizon. What's more, it's not that uncommon! If you suspect your child has a learning disability, he's not alone. Nearly 4 million other school-age children and teens have learning disabilities, too.

It's also important to remember that not all learning *problems* are necessarily learning *disabilities*. Just because your child has trouble learning new math skills or studying for a test doesn't mean he should be diagnosed with a learning disability—the problem has to be bigger and longer-lasting than that for a diagnosis.

Many years ago, I had a colleague whose preschool son had trouble making himself understood, which perplexed his father, a renowned medical school professor. It turned out that his son didn't have a learning disability—just a learning problem. His son improved quickly with small-group speech and language therapy at a clinic during kindergarten. As he's grown older, he's never been a strong writer, but he's also never needed special education. Now he's a star engineering student in his junior year at a state university.

Keep in mind that some of the areas that we list here under the category of "learning difficulties" could be considered more basic brain-processing issues, such as problems involved in speaking, drawing, or printing. These movement problems may not translate to bigger problems in mental or "cognitive" areas involving more complex thinking skills.

Many children are slow to develop certain skills, or they have a normal range of strengths and weaknesses. Just because your child doesn't score near the top in reading and writing skills doesn't mean there's a diagnosable problem—it could well be that your child's school has high standards and that most students there achieve a notch above average, or that the teaching methods in your school's curriculum haven't "caught on" yet for your child. Children show natural differences in their rate of development, so sometimes what seems to be a learning disability may be a mild or temporary delay in acquiring certain skills.

In addition, there are often different ways to learn the same material, and some children find other ways around learning hurdles. Thus, they can't really be said to have a disability. John was a client of mine who learned best by doing and practicing. Rob learned better by listening in class; Andy preferred to read class material.

Sometimes, what seems to be a learning disability may just be a temporary developmental lag, a reaction to a lifestyle change, or a detour in priorities—but soon the child will catch up to or even surpass other kids in the class.

A Bumpy Road

That's what happened to thirteen-year-old Kate. She'd been a bright, inquisitive child who had consistently scored above the 90th percentile on the standardized achievement tests throughout her school career. She'd started reading on her own in kindergarten, and by second grade she was devouring Harry Potter books. You can imagine her parents' consternation when in eighth grade, she seemed to have developed a problem with reading comprehension. As she moved through middle school, the required reading list became much more challenging, and Kate brought home her first D on a literature test. Could it be that she'd had some type of learning disability all along that had never been diagnosed? This was an understandable question that needed to be answered to decide how to help Kate overcome this slip.

Actually, you'd be surprised how many parents face this issue. Although most learning disabilities can be identified during early to middle elementary school, some kinds of learning disabilities aren't really identified until later. Sometimes a significant problem doesn't appear until adolescence, when the work and expectations become far more challenging. Remember that the brain and your child's learning skills continue to develop throughout her school career, and that at times a particular cognitive task may simply be too challenging for your child *at that moment*.

This turned out *not* to be the case in Kate's situation. "While it's possible that Kate *might* have a learning disorder," her English teacher told her worried parents, "I really don't think that's the problem." The teacher explained that Kate, who had always been quiet and studious, had suddenly become social and busy with friends, often chatting and giggling in class, which interfered with her concentration on many days. The teacher, who had twenty years of experience in middle and high schools, wisely realized that this surge of socializing was an important developmental stage for Kate. He explained to her parents that her social skills development was every bit as important as her intellectual advancement at this time.

In addition to ongoing developmental issues, he also pointed out that many students have never really been *taught* how to study or develop good strategies for understanding what they read, especially with complex text. Bright students may have been able to get by without doing much work—just "soaking things in" when they were younger. As they face more challenging assignments in middle school or high school, Kate's teacher explained, they may tend to approach the material as if they were reading a light novel for enjoyment, skimming the pages quickly. "Then they slam the book shut," the teacher said, "and they think they've studied." He recommended that over the summer, her parents help Kate tune up her reading comprehension strategies, as well as brush up on more effective ways to study. He also suggested her parents watch her performance closely in the fall to see whether the problem had improved. If she was still struggling, she could be tested for a learning disability then.

But as the teacher predicted, Kate continued to mature throughout the summer, and by the fall her problems in comprehension had largely disappeared. Aided by some coaching on reading and test-taking strategies with a tutor over the summer, she was now successfully tackling far more challenging literature assignments, getting A's again on tests of Dante's *Inferno* and Shakespeare's *Macbeth*.

Of course, not all situations will have this easy ending. Some teens who begin to struggle will ultimately outgrow their problems, but others do have a genuine undiagnosed learning difficulty. Teachers can often aid in guessing what the likely problems might be. It was entirely appropriate in Kate's case to provide a bit of extra help and then watch to see if she was simply struggling with a developmental stage.

So What IS a Learning Disability?

Broadly speaking, a learning disability (LD) is a problem that gets in the way of how kids receive, process, or express information. This affects the ability to learn—most often in reading, writing, or math, but also sometimes in speaking and listening. The way our brains process information is extremely complex. For example, to understand speech, you have to recognize the sounds in the words, combine the sounds together, interpret the meaning, and figure out the significance of the statements. These activities take place in many separate but connected parts of the brain.

A child with a learning disability has a problem with the way the brain handles some kinds of information, which hinders the normal learning process, affecting the ability to receive, process, analyze, store, organize, or communicate information. Usually a child with this problem won't learn as quickly in one or more key school areas as another child.

In this book, I use the term *learning disorders* in a broad sense, which includes both specific academic *learning disabilities* and some other problems in the development of mental or complex motor skills. To have a learning disorder, your child must show basic symptoms in at least one of four important broad areas that I'll cover later in this chapter:

- "information processing" abilities that are closely related to reading, writing, or math
- language or speech skills
- coordination problems
- intelligence or overall thinking and reasoning abilities

Don't worry about the fact that different experts may use different terms for this broad umbrella category of skill problems. For instance, the diagnostic code book that psychiatrists use (*Diagnostic and Statistical Manual, Fourth Edition–Text Revision*, or *DSM-IV-TR*) labels these categories *developmental disorders*, which is also quite reasonable.

Sometimes overlooked as "hidden handicaps," learning disabilities are often not easily recognized, accepted, or considered serious once they are detected. The impact of the disability, which often runs in families, ranges

from relatively mild to severe. Learning disabilities can be lifelong conditions that, in some cases, affect school, daily routines, friendships, and
family life. On the other hand, many learning disabilities are preventable
if treated early, or they can be at least partly correctable later.

Potential or Performance?

Most definitions of learning disabilities in the past have required a substantial difference between how well a child actually does in school versus
how well he *could* do, considering what his intelligence is. Each state has
determined just how big the gap must be for a child to qualify for LD services in the public schools.

But these definitions are changing, bolstered by research and federal
law. First, experts recognize that IQ or aptitude tests reveal a lot more
about what your child's thinking skills are like *right now* than what your
child's mental potential was at birth or when she started school. It's just
not true that an IQ score is a solid, stable benchmark of how well a child
should be able to learn; in fact, IQ levels can actually drop as a result of
learning problems. This means that a discrepancy between an IQ score
and achievement isn't as meaningful as we once thought it was.

Second, a lot of research supports the idea that reading disability—
the most common kind of learning disability—should be diagnosed only if
your child shows a significant academic delay *after* receiving treatment.
This is a dramatic change in the way that learning disabilities can be defined. The 2004 revision of IDEA allows local school districts to override
the part of the old definition that required a severe discrepancy between
aptitude and achievement, so major changes are on the way for how some
students are evaluated for LD in the public schools.

I think it's still important to have a clear idea of a child's basic intelligence. But it's even more important to understand your child's specific
mental processing skills that are most relevant to the learning problems
outlined below in deciding if your child has a particular learning disability.

What LDs Are NOT . . .

It's important to understand that learning disabilities are *not* the same as mental retardation, autism, deafness, blindness, or behavioral disorders. Although two or more out of every ten children with learning disabilities also have attention-deficit/hyperactivity disorder, *ADHD is not a learning disability in itself*. (We'll discuss ADHD more fully in the next chapter.)

Clues That Might Signal a Learning Disability

Your child is a poor speller. Is that a learning disability? Another child doesn't read well out loud, but does okay on tests. Does she have LD? What about the kid who just can't seem to get the hang of math—is he just slow? Math phobic?

Obviously, learning disabilities affect a broad range of skills and abilities, and there isn't just one symptom you can look for. In fact, at one time or another, most children *should* struggle with some parts of what they're learning in school, or it means they aren't being challenged enough. What you should be concerned with is a child who has a *consistent, significant* problem with a particular set of basic skills in reading, writing, or arithmetic.

You may first have noticed a problem when your child began to have trouble speaking, reading, writing, understanding numbers, or paying attention in class. Most kids with LDs are diagnosed in grade school, after a parent or a teacher notices the child struggling to complete work he should be able to do easily. Sometimes, however, children develop sophisticated ways of covering up their problems, so learning disabilities aren't recognized until the teen years as schoolwork gets more complex.

Preschool

Your preschool child might be at risk for developing a learning disability if he's had problems learning the alphabet, rhyming words, connecting sounds and letters, counting, or learning numbers. Perhaps he learned to speak late, doesn't use many words or phrases, or can't find the right word. Maybe she can't rapidly name words in a specific category or has trouble being understood when speaking to a stranger. Or there might be a problem in using scissors, crayons, or paint, remembering names of colors, or learning to write the letters in his name.

Kindergarten Through Mid–Elementary School

At this age, you might suspect a problem if your child is slow to learn the connections between letters and sounds, can't blend sounds to make words, makes consistent reading and spelling errors, has problems remembering sequences and telling time, is slow to learn number skills, or has difficulty planning. Perhaps there are problems in following directions, comprehending, drawing, or copying shapes. There also might be a problem if he has trouble holding a pencil or doing math problems.

Late Elementary School Through Adolescence

By now, you may notice your child is slow to learn complex word parts such as prefixes and suffixes, or to use strategies for reading comprehension, or avoids reading. He may have trouble with word problems in math or may misspell the same word differently in a single piece of writing. Your child may have trouble remembering or understanding what she's read. He may work slowly and have trouble generalizing concepts, misreading directions. Symptoms might include problems deciding what information presented in class is important, modulating his voice, organizing, or meeting deadlines.

What You Should Expect from Your School

Learning disabilities tend to be diagnosed in the elementary grades because this is when the school focuses on the basic skills in reading, writing, math, listening, speaking, and reasoning. If the teacher notices that your child isn't learning in some areas as expected, the school may ask to evaluate your child to try to figure out what's causing the problem. But even if the teacher hasn't said anything and you're the one who's worried, don't hesitate to share your concerns with a teacher, principal, or school counselor. Bring your child's recent tests, report cards from earlier grades, and any comments other teachers may have made. Write down your concerns using the guidelines in chapter 2, with examples to back up what you've noticed. If the school is also worried, you can ask the school to diagnose the problem, as we outlined in chapter 3. (And don't forget that it's important to rule out basic vision or hearing problems.)

Remember—the school is obligated to find out if your child may have a disability and may need special education services, whether she attends a public or private school. However, the school isn't legally required to provide a medical or psychological diagnosis, perform unnecessary testing, or conduct testing just because it's requested by outside professionals such as her tutor.

LD Assessment

As we discussed in chapter 3, laws require that learning disabilities as defined legally in the public schools be identified by the IEP team. After an assessment, the team will meet with you to discuss the results and decide if your child is eligible for special education services. Even if your child isn't eligible for these services, test results can be used to plan an educational program in the regular curriculum at school, and to help your child understand her learning struggles and find ways to be successful.

If the school's tests don't seem to indicate a problem but you're still convinced there might be one, you can have your child tested outside of school by a psychologist or learning specialist who can use specific tests to help clarify the problems. These tests could help pinpoint your child's learning strengths and weaknesses, in addition to revealing any particular learning disability that may not have fit the legal definition. You may even have started with an independent evaluation rather than an evaluation conducted by the specialists at school. However, while public schools must consider reports you obtained privately, they have the right to directly assess your child before making any decisions.

Most of the parents of children I see are quite concerned when their child has been diagnosed with a learning disability. I tell them to think of it like this: A careful diagnosis is actually the first step in addressing the problem.

There's a lot you can do to help your child, once you know what's going on. Many parents are relieved to finally understand that their child's learning problems aren't just a sign that Junior is "slow"—it's just that he may have a specific glitch in acquiring knowledge, along with some important strengths in other areas.

Once an expert has pinpointed your child's particular weak and strong areas, there are strategies you and the school can use to help your child cope with the problem, such as intensive training in phonics skills for a child who can't read words well. Other strategies can help your child use her strengths to compensate for the weakness, such as listening to books on tape instead of reading them.

Remember, it's *never* too late to get help, no matter how old your child is when he's diagnosed. For example, Megan's parents weren't surprised when her first formal evaluation in high school identified a learning disability in reading comprehension, because she'd always struggled in elementary and middle school. Her small, flexible rural school had worked with her, giving her easier books to read and allowing her to be tested orally. But the expectations at her urban high school were daunting. You can take heart from the fact that most children with learning disabilities, like Megan, learn to adapt to their learning differences, and they can often learn strategies that help them accomplish goals and dreams.

My message to you as you seek a good initial evaluation is this: Don't be scared to the point that you whitewash or minimize your child's problems. It's important to understand your child's problems as clearly as you can. In the end, an understanding and acceptance of your child's diagnosis may help her develop a gentler self-perspective. For instance, she may decide that she has "learning differences" and just needs some extra help from the learning resource center. This may include the attractive opportunity for some individual attention from some nice "extra" teachers. There are good books, videotapes, and Web sites to help both you and your child with her self-esteem.

If the School Finds a Need for Special Education

As you may recall from chapter 3, if your school's evaluation results show that your child has a learning disability or other special education needs, you and the school will develop an IEP. Remember that, among other things, the IEP describes your child's current level and identifies specific services your child will need.

Intensive instruction to improve weak skills is the most important service for a student with learning disabilities. Your child's school district is required to have special education teachers trained to help students overcome learning problems. Students with learning disabilities can work with these experts to learn special study skills, note-taking strategies, or organizational techniques that can help them compensate for their learning disability. If your child has a mild or limited learning disability, he may only need help for the subjects that give him the most trouble.

To boost the effectiveness of supports or changes in the classroom, many students with LD use "assistive technology," ranging from tape recorders to computer voice-recognition systems that allow students to "write" by talking to the computer. Accommodations may also include taped textbooks available through Recording for the Blind and Dyslexic, extra time to take tests, tutoring, use of a note-taker during class, or use of a scribe during tests. Your child might also need a "reader" during test taking if he has trouble reading test questions. Other accommodations might include tape-recorded class lectures or testing in a quiet place.

Types of Academic Learning Disabilities

Now it's time to discuss specific types of learning disabilities. Let's start with the seven types listed in federal and state laws governing special education services for learning disabilities:

SEVEN LEARNING DISABILITY CATEGORIES
UNDER FEDERAL LAW

Special education law uses the following seven academic skill categories to determine if a child has a learning disability in the public schools.

- **oral expression:** saying what you mean accurately
- **listening comprehension:** understanding what you hear
- **written expression:** writing what you mean accurately
- **basic reading skills:** reading words accurately and efficiently, whether or not you understand them
- **reading comprehension:** understanding what you read
- **math calculation:** addition, subtraction, multiplication, and division—computing with the numbers
- **math reasoning:** the more complicated parts of math, such as word problems and algebra

These are the definitions that your public school district must use. Most experts outside the school think in these terms, too. Problems that are limited to one subject, such as spelling or French, are too narrow to be considered learning disabilities.

On the other hand, most students who do have learning disabilities struggle in more than one kind of overlapping area, since many aspects of speaking, listening, reading, writing, and arithmetic build on the same brain capabilities. For example, you need to be able to understand language to be able to speak, so a problem in understanding language usually interferes with the ability to speak, which can in turn hinder learning to read and write. As you can see, a single problem in the brain's operation can go on to disrupt many types of activities.

For these reasons, I'll focus on two of the most important underlying learning disability patterns: *developmental dyslexia (reading disability)* and *nonverbal learning disability*. Then I'll describe other main types of learning disorders that aren't typically classified as learning disabilities themselves, although some of them sometimes fit into other special education categories. Near the end of the chapter, we'll return to the seven types of learning disabilities in the law and show how they relate to the underlying patterns and other learning disorders.

Dyslexia—Reading Disability

Dyslexia is the most common and well-known of all the learning disabilities. It involves problems with accurate or fluent reading word recognition, and it's usually accompanied by problems with spelling and phonics decoding abilities.

Although reading or decoding the words is the main problem for youngsters with dyslexia, other difficulties are often linked to this main problem, including reading comprehension, written expression, and solving math word problems. Some (but not all) children with dyslexia also have trouble memorizing math facts, reverse letters when reading or writing, or have trouble retrieving words. Kids with dyslexia learn some academic skills at a level lower than others of their same age and IQ level, but they may do other things quite well. They may be talented in the arts, great with computers, or whizzes in geometry. You should encourage these gifts.

Caution!

I need to warn you: *dyslexia* can be defined in a variety of ways, depending on who's talking—a scientist, a teacher, a doctor, or the media. These definitions are often inconsistent and incomplete, and many parents seeking help for their children with learning problems are understandably confused about what *dyslexia* really means. I often tell parents and teachers that *dyslexia* is one of the most well-misunderstood terms in education, psychology, and medicine!

Although the legal, medical, and scientific references to dyslexia aren't always consistent with each other, major researchers and organizations such as the National Institutes of Health and the International Dyslexia Association have during the past decade been working on clarifying exactly what *dyslexia* means. At present, it usually refers to the same thing as *reading disability*. Some broader terms, such as *developmental reading disorder*, include both the concept of dyslexia and/or problems with reading comprehension despite adequate reading decoding skills. In the box below, I've given you the exact definition as adopted by the International Dyslexia Association. It means essentially what I've already explained in previous paragraphs.

International Dyslexia Association (IDA) Definition

D yslexia is a specific learning disability that is neurological in origin, characterized by difficulties with accurate and/or fluent word recognition and by poor spelling and decoding abilities. These difficulties typically result from a deficit in the phonological component of language that is often unexpected in relation to other cognitive abilities and the provision of effective classroom instruction. Secondary consequences may include problems in reading comprehension and reduced reading experience that can impede growth of vocabulary and background knowledge.

Adopted by the IDA Board of Directors, November 12, 2002. This definition is also used by the National Institute of Child Health and Human Development (NICHHD).

The bottom line: When talking with your child's teachers or other professionals about dyslexia—find out exactly what they mean by the terms they're using. If the other person's definition doesn't fit the up-to-date version in the box above, talk to each other so you can figure out exactly what each of you *is* talking about.

Core Deficits

Virtually all researchers agree that children with dyslexia have trouble distinguishing, separating, and working with the sounds in spoken words. (Note that this is different from the federal learning disability of "listening comprehension," which involves understanding the meaning of what's said, not how each sound relates.) For example, Jim might not be able to identify the word *dog* by hearing someone exaggerate the individual letter sounds: *duh-aw-g*—or Sally might have trouble playing rhyming games. These types of problems fall into the areas called phonemic awareness, phonological awareness, and phonological processing. While researchers use these three terms in slightly different ways, what's important for you to understand as a parent is that this is the layer of language that makes up the foundation of phonics, which in turn has to do with the link between sound segments and the printed word.

Children who are weak in phonological processing end up having trouble learning how to decode words when they read. Since phonological processing skills can usually be tested in kindergarten, we're getting better at predicting which students are at risk for dyslexia. Testing is an important part of any evaluation for dyslexia, whether a child is just learning how to read or has already developed significant delays in reading word recognition skills.

Diagnosis

There isn't one accepted dyslexia test. If you suspect this problem, you'll want to assess your child's ability to read words accurately and quickly in comparison to other children the same age. Other helpful tests include assessments of spelling and reading comprehension, phonological processing, IQ, and perhaps some other information-processing skills. As you learned in chapter 3, these test results can determine eligibility for special education services and will be used to make educational recommendations for treatment.

The most useful time to see if a child is *at risk* for dyslexia is kindergarten or first grade. On the other hand, it's usually most reliable to confirm an actual diagnosis of dyslexia in second grade or later. At any age, the testing can help determine whether your child is reading at the expected level and takes into account family background and overall school performance.

This testing can be conducted by school or private specialists, either a single person or a team—but whoever is conducting the test should have a background in psychology, reading, language, and education. The tester must understand how children learn to read and must also understand appropriate reading interventions so as to make the best recommendations.

Causes

Research suggests that there are probably both a genetic/brain basis and environmental factors. The exact causes of dyslexia aren't clear, but brain scan studies have found differences in how the brain of a dyslexic person develops and functions compared to those of people who are not dyslexic.

Treatment

Treatment should focus on the specific learning problems, modifying teaching methods in the classroom to meet your child's needs. Typically, a child with dyslexia should be taught the basic sounds associated with letters of the alphabet (phonemic awareness), and how to put these together and take them apart. It's important for you to understand that phonemic awareness training is more basic than traditional phonics training. Both are needed.

For example, Mike spent most of his first two months of tutoring playing word games, such as counting the number of sounds in the word *tell*. This was phonemic awareness. Then he moved on to beginning phonics exercises, practicing how to relate both the printed letters *c* and *k* to the beginning sound in *cat* and the ending sound in his name. After that, his tutor started reading Dr. Seuss books with him, emphasizing all the wonderful rhymes. Sometimes the tutor would emphasize the phonological processing by having Mike just listen, other times they would work directly on phonics by having Mike read himself. Other methods, such as "repeated reading" (having children read the same material several times), are effective for improving reading speed.

The earlier the problem is uncovered, the better. If your child gets appropriate phonological training in kindergarten and first grade, she'll have many fewer problems in learning to read at grade level than do children who aren't identified until third or fourth grade. On the other hand, it's never too late for children with dyslexia to improve their reading skills. It just takes longer to make headway in key phonological and phonics training if it's started past early elementary age.

There are many brand-named teaching methods that emphasize phonological and/or phonics skills. Don't get hung up on one particular brand name (such as the well-known Orton-Gillingham or the Wilson methods).

But instruction isn't the only way to treat dyslexia. Virtually all kids with dyslexia need both intensive instruction in reading decoding skills *and* coping strategies and modifications to help them succeed in school. The school will probably suggest academic modifications to help your child succeed. For example, as part of the IEP that we illustrated in chapter 3, Jason's teacher gave him extra time to complete in-class writing assignments. She also modified his homework requirements: when the rest of the class had to write a three-page paper, she assigned Jason a one-page essay on a similar topic. She made him photocopies of a strong class-mate's class lecture notes while he listened closely and jotted down key points only during class, and she gave him taped tests. Jason's family signed him up to borrow books on tape from an organization called Recording for the Blind and Dyslexic. He composed most of his assign-ments and tests on a computer, always using the spelling checker as much as he was capable.

I remember one patient I saw for a mild tendency toward dyslexia, first in second grade and then again as a high school sophomore. Between the two evaluations—when she was in middle school—she'd had two years of intensive tutoring from a dyslexia specialist. By high school, my patient was thriving in a tough private school as a result of a combination of in-terventions: her own dogged persistence, tutoring, and accommodations that the school allowed—she was given some tests orally and used both audiotapes and computer-scanning technology to "read" the difficult college-level texts her courses demanded.

Mental Health Support Can Help

Having learning problems at school can make a child feel emotion-ally vulnerable, too. Even in the most supportive school environ-ments, children can be acutely aware of who needs "special" help, and a label may make your child feel he's just dumb. Mental health specialists can help your child cope with these frustrations, anxieties, and funks.

How You Can Help

You can expect that your child with dyslexia may need a little or a lot of one-on-one help to progress, so be prepared to spend extra time reading and working together. Try to remain supportive, and don't be too critical as your child works hard to overcome her disability. Depending on your child's particular pattern, there will be many specific things you can do to reinforce the extra instruction your child is getting from the professionals.

Nonverbal Learning Disabilities

Perhaps your child has had problems drawing or catching a ball. Maybe he daydreams in class and struggles to understand math concepts. Perhaps he doesn't seem to be able to look at an angry face on the school playground and understand that his friend is irritated. Maybe there are also academic problems in reading comprehension or mechanics of written language, although he's a great speller. If so, your child might have a nonverbal learning disability (NLD), or what some experts call a nonverbal processing deficit or a right-hemisphere processing deficit.

Did you know that most communication is nonverbal? Unfortunately, too many schools tend to ignore a child's nonverbal problems, so these issues can go unrecognized. The discovery of this pattern of problems really got going in the 1970s when researchers began to notice children who had much weaker performance IQ (putting block patterns or puzzles together) than verbal IQ (defining vocabulary words or explaining answers to commonsense questions).

Core Deficits

NLD usually causes a pattern of strengths and weaknesses, rather than a couple of basic symptoms. Children with NLD almost always have trouble processing complex visual material. This is because NLD affects how the brain interprets complex visual patterns, designs, shapes, angles, distance, and direction—what we call visual-spatial processing or visual perception. Kids with NLD usually have trouble making sense of visual details, such as numbers on a blackboard. An elementary-school child with

NLD may confuse the plus sign with the division sign, for example, and some even need to work hard to remind themselves not to make this slip as they get older. Abstract concepts, such as fractions, are often difficult to master for adolescents with NLD.

Other problems that occur with NLD may include difficulties with visual-motor coordination—these kids can be clumsy, struggling to kick a ball, shoot a basket, or cut things out with scissors. They may also have trouble with perception of touch or emotions, attention, abstract reasoning, and problem solving. Many kids with NLD also have trouble with nonverbal language and nonverbal communication. They struggle to understand another's tone of voice, facial expressions, and gestures. Instead of being able to sense another person's social cues ("he's frowning and turning away—that means he's upset"), children with this problem rely on memories of past experiences or the other person's words. In fact, most kids with NLD have trouble adapting to new situations or reading nonverbal signals or cues. They may not understand by looking at another person's face what that person is feeling, which can affect social situations profoundly.

Because many children with NLD have only some of these basic symptoms, I consider NLD to be a set of related or overlapping disabilities, rather than a single condition. That's one of the reasons it's not yet recognized as a defined diagnosis in codebooks such as *DSM-IV-TR*. For example, many kids with real problems in processing visual information don't have any trouble with social and emotional communication. One patient of mine with NLD couldn't interpret a simple graph or read a map, but she was the best writer in her class! She was a whiz at explaining her thoughts clearly and efficiently in words. She had great social skills, but she kept getting into minor car accidents because she didn't develop the automatic-attention habit of scanning the road that most of us develop naturally. She ended up deciding to live in a big city with good public transportation so she wouldn't have to own a car, after graduating from college with honors in history and library science!

At the same time, most children with NLD have relatively strong basic language-processing skills such as vocabulary knowledge and grammar, rote verbal memory, reading word recognition, and spelling. On the other hand, there appears to be an increased risk for social relationship problems and depression. My patient who couldn't draw or drive has great social skills, but this didn't protect her from periods of discouragement and depression before we clarified her pattern of strengths and weaknesses during middle school and got her some good therapy. She still goes through low periods at times now as an adult.

Diagnosis

Testing for NLD must cover all the potential areas of strength and weakness mentioned in the previous section. We usually start with standard IQ and achievement tests, followed by tests of other information-processing areas such as fine motor skills, touch, attention, conceptual reasoning, and memory.

All too often, children with NLD are never diagnosed because their early verbal skills are a source of pride to parents and teachers. Verbally precocious kids with NLD can even be considered gifted in their early school careers and are often able to read at an early age. As they move on to late elementary and then middle school, however, nonverbal and conceptual reasoning problems become more obvious. Despite the early verbal ability, they begin to have trouble organizing written work. They start handing in assignments late (if at all). Their skills at memorization may not be enough to meet the demands of high school. By the time teachers and parents notice that the child isn't doing well, the child may already have begun to give up.

A child with unrecognized NLD is especially prone to developing depression and anxiety problems, especially if he's told he's just "not working up to ability" or "not working hard enough." You'll want to be sure your child also has a sensitive emotional-status evaluation in addition to testing.

Causes

The brain is divided into right and left hemispheres that work together, but that also handle different jobs. For example, if someone tells you, "Oh, you're so smart!" with an angry face, your right hemisphere helps you understand that he really means the opposite. It's the right hemisphere that understands anything unusual or contradictory between verbal and nonverbal messages. The brain problems in NLD are usually attributed to skills that are associated with this right cerebral hemisphere.

Indeed, NLD is sometimes called right hemisphere processing deficit or developmental right hemisphere syndrome.

If there has been an interruption in the development of your child's central nervous system, mental functions associated with the right hemisphere or with efficient processing of brain signals are likely to be affected. Any injury, tumor, or seizure in the right hemisphere also can cause problems with NLD.

Treatment

Intervention should involve a combination of extra instruction and compensation (such as keyboard training to sidestep bad handwriting)— and the earlier the better. But because NLD is different from a *language-based* learning disability, the treatment is different from what would be done to treat reading and language disorders. Academic subjects that many kids with NLD need help with include math, some aspects of written language, reading comprehension, and complex visual tasks such as understanding and creating maps, charts, and graphs.

A comprehensive IEP should outline what help might be given in speech and language therapy to improve social communication, as well as what kind of occupational therapy should be provided to address visual perception and fine motor skills. On the other hand, since NLD as an underlying pattern is not itself one of the thirteen categories of special education or the seven specific types under the category of learning disability in federal law, you and the school should look closely for any way to qualify your child under one of these existing categories. Pay particular attention to problems with math computation, math reasoning, reading comprehension, and written expression.

During class, your child's teacher should be careful to speak clearly and outline expectations without ambiguity. You should try to avoid having your child copy text either from the board or a text—but simplifying test taking will help. (For example, your child shouldn't be penalized for putting the right answer in the wrong space.) Whenever possible, timed tests should be eliminated.

How You Can Help

Give your child graph paper to help line up her math problems, and let her use a computer to complete written assignments. You'll have to help your child with any projects that require arranging materials (such as producing a poster), using scissors, or folding. In addition, your child's schedule should be as clear, straightforward, and predictable as possible. If there's going to be a test or a trip, prepare your child ahead of time—don't spring anything on him. At the same time, all directions, expectations, and requests need to be clear and specific. Don't expect your child to read between the lines or somehow "pick up" what you want her to do from your tone of voice.

Don't use sarcasm or idioms when speaking to your child, and try to avoid harsh criticism or blame—the more supportive and positive you can be, the better. If you must give complex directions, write them down. Your child may benefit from coaching on organizational and study skills and interpersonal communication.

Developmental Speech and Language Disorders

Children with problems in this category have trouble producing speech sounds, understanding what others say, or using spoken language to communicate. Speech and language problems are often the earliest indicators of a learning disability. The disorders in this group include:

- developmental articulation disorder
- developmental receptive language disorder
- developmental expressive language disorder

Core Deficits and Other Signs

If you're like most parents whose child has a problem with speech skills or language processing, you probably noticed some difficulties in early childhood. Perhaps your daughter didn't learn to speak when the others in the neighborhood were asking for "Mama" or "Dada." You may have noticed your son's sentences were shorter than his brother's, or his vocabulary seemed more limited. When you asked him a question, maybe he didn't seem to answer you appropriately—or did it drive you crazy when you sent him to the kitchen for milk and he came back with soda? Do you find yourself pronouncing your words carefully or correcting your child's grammar more often than for other children her age? Perhaps you've noticed that your child can handle simple commands, such as "Put this book away," but when you move on to more complex requests, you may notice things break down: "Can you go get your backpack out of the kitchen, and then bring me your test paper after you put your assignment book on your desk?"

Although all kids sometimes mispronounce words, pronunciation can be a problem for children with language processing disorders long after you'd expect these problems to have disappeared. For example, your child might still be saying "am-na-mal" instead of "animal." Word sequencing is also a problem, so that a child may not be able to tell the difference between "hitting a block" and "blocking a hit."

Diagnosis

Thorough assessment in this area includes the child's history provided by parents and teachers, standardized tests, direct observation of a child's play and interaction with caregivers, and a detailed analysis of everyday speech samples. It may take several testing sessions and evaluations to get enough information to make an accurate diagnosis. Speech pathologists or neuropsychologists are the best experts to assess these problems.

Developmental Articulation and Other Speech Disorders

A child with a developmental articulation disorder may have trouble controlling how fast he speaks, or he may lag behind his friends in learning how to make speech sounds. My friend's daughter gets speech therapy at school because she still pronounces the *s* sound like *th* at age nine, which should have disappeared by age eight.

Phonological disorder and *speech dysfluency* are two technical terms for different types of these speech problems, in which a child substitutes sounds, stutters, or doesn't use age-appropriate speech sounds. Although these disorders are actually fairly common, affecting at least one out of every ten children under age eight, most outgrow the problem or are successfully treated with speech therapy. Related pronunciation problems are called speech apraxia or oral-motor apraxia; with this condition, a child can't organize the movements necessary to produce a speech sequence.

Developmental Receptive and Expressive Language Disorders

These problems affect the way a child hears or expresses language. Because using and understanding speech are strongly related, most children with receptive language disorders also have expressive language problems.

If your child has trouble making sense of what others say, he may be diagnosed with a developmental *receptive* language disorder. This is what's going on with a toddler who doesn't respond to his name even though he can hear, or the teen who can't seem to follow complex directions even though she's paying attention and wants to cooperate. It's not poor hearing that causes the difficulties with speech input—it's just that the child can't make sense of certain sounds, words, or sentences.

Children with developmental *expressive* language disorders have trouble expressing themselves while speaking, call objects by the wrong names, speak only in short phrases, or can't answer simple questions. For example, a three-year-old child who can't speak in more than two-word phrases may have an expressive language disorder.

A combination of receptive and expressive language disorders affect a child's understanding or production of language in one or more common patterns. Some kids with these problems don't completely understand what others are saying to them, even though they may appear to understand some parts. Others have trouble organizing their speech into conventional grammar. Some don't understand word meanings.

Other children develop adequate skills in the above areas, but they don't receive or produce language well enough to be able to communicate or interact with others. These kids have a variation of a language processing problem called a *semantic/pragmatic language disorder*.

Treatment

If your child is diagnosed with a significant speech or language problem, he would probably benefit from speech therapy (or what is sometimes called speech/language therapy). Most professionals agree that if a speech or language disorder is suspected, treatment should begin as soon as possible—even in very early childhood, before your child *begins* to speak. For instance, if your doctor notices that your child has missed an important developmental milestone (such as not using single words by age two or not using phrases by age three), a speech or language disorder may be suspected.

How You Can Help

Follow suggestions from your child's speech pathologist. Reinforcement at home can be an important support to the time your child spends in therapy each week, particularly in younger children.

Coordination Disorders

Developmental coordination disorder is a broad term that applies to movements using large muscles, such as waving or jumping (gross motor), and smaller muscle movements of the hands, such as writing or drawing (fine motor). I'll focus on the fine motor area here, because it interferes much more clearly with thinking and learning skills than do gross motor problems.

Core Deficits and Other Signs

You should suspect a fine motor disability if you notice that your child drops or spills things a lot or seems clumsy or awkward during play, especially with activities that require delicate hand movements. Check to see if your child has trouble handling small puzzle pieces and toys, using scissors, or holding pencils and crayons too loosely or too tightly. Do your child's drawings look messier than the work of other children the same age? Does she need help with buttons, zippers, and laces, although other children the same age can dress themselves? At school, does her teacher complain that her handwriting is sloppy, or that her written work is too short and often unfinished? Does she write slowly, with great effort, or turn in papers that are torn and crumpled, with lots of erasures? Perhaps he says he just doesn't like writing and drawing, or maybe you've noticed he makes careless mistakes in math because his work is illegible or incorrectly aligned. As your child gets older, he may have trouble learning to type.

Fine motor disabilities can affect other areas unrelated to writing or copying. In science, children with this problem may have trouble dissecting. They may spill food at lunch, trip over the ball in gym, splatter paint on their clothes in art class, or knock their books off their desk in study hall. As you can imagine, this could quickly lead to a negative self-image and teasing from their classmates. Children with fine motor difficulties sometimes have trouble with articulation, which only compounds their communication problems.

Diagnosis

If you suspect a fine motor disability, a school psychologist or neuropsychologist might help with initial screening to see if further evaluation is needed. Your child might be asked to draw, copy designs, or place pegs in a board as fast as possible. To be thorough and to provide specific treatment recommendations, you should also get an evaluation by a pediatric occupational therapist. A neurologist should examine any child with fine motor problems that might be related to a brain injury or brain disease in case any medical treatment would be recommended, such as medication for epilepsy or for a severe tremor.

Cause

A fine motor disability is caused by a problem in the areas of the brain that control the planning and execution of hand-muscle movements. A fine motor problem doesn't directly affect intellectual ability, but it can certainly affect school performance when it interferes with the ability to write. These kids find it hard to concentrate on *what* they're writing, because they're so busy telling their hands *how* to write. As a result, their good ideas may not get down on paper. To write, your child may need to concentrate so fiercely on making each letter that she doesn't have any energy left to develop what to say!

Treatment

While there's no medical cure for fine motor disabilities, your child's skills will usually improve with time, extra practice, and occupational therapy. Typing or dictating assignments can be helpful. See if the teacher will allow your child to dictate reports or write shorter reports and then discuss the work with the teacher. Perhaps other students or the teacher could provide copies of notes and tape-record school assignments.

How You Can Help

I think it's often a good idea for parents to boost children's confidence and interest in school in the face of penmanship problems by offering to perform some writing or typing for them, and by encouraging them to develop ideas out loud. Take some time to discuss the day's events. In fact, you should encourage your child to talk, since this can also develop many of the skills needed in writing: the ability to organize thoughts and present them clearly, and developing an ear for language.

Many children with fine motor problems have no difficulty with gross motor skills, easily jumping, running, or dancing. In fact, they may become accomplished athletes in areas not requiring fine motor skills, such as in the long jump or track.

Below-Average Intelligence

Below-average intelligence isn't usually labeled with a formal diagnosis, unless the level is quite low and there are problems with important self-care skills, in which case the child may have mental retardation. So why do we discuss this pattern along with the learning disorders?

There are two main reasons: First, below-average intelligence (whether at low-average to borderline level, or actual mental retardation) involves problems in abilities or thinking skills, just as the other learning disorders do. Second, many professionals believe that children with delays in *most* or *all* of the main mental-processing skills needed for learning deserve extra help every bit as much as those with a learning disorder in only one or a few areas. Therefore, we should design this extra help for them with a broad range of needs in mind. In the past, this pattern of low intelligence has sometimes been called dull normal or slow learner, which are both pejorative and unfairly imply that we should just lower our expectations for these students.

Sometimes, below-average intelligence is really a combination of several of the other learning disorders in one child. However, the only types of low IQ that are official "disorders" in *DSM-IV-TR* and that are official categories in special education law are the different levels of mental retardation.

Still, kids with "in between" IQ who aren't mentally retarded and don't fit the diagnosis for another type of learning disorder have needs, even if they don't have a formal diagnosis.

That's what happened for seven-year-old Sally, who had received special education help during preschool and kindergarten, including early-childhood special education classroom placement, speech/language therapy, and occupational and physical therapy. When her IQ tested in the low-average range at school after her first kindergarten year, her parents and teachers hoped that an extra year in kindergarten would help her catch up. Unfortunately, once she finally moved into first grade, she continued to struggle with early academic skills and seemed socially immature.

Sally's pediatrician referred her to me for a neuropsychological evaluation to help clarify her developmental delays, balance and coordination problems, and continuing learning struggles. At that time, we found her overall intelligence in the borderline range (73), including below-average performance in all key areas of the IQ test. Her lower scores on this second test only a year after the first was probably due to differences in the requirements for success on the tests at different ages, as well as gradually increasing gaps in Sally's general thinking skills over time. I didn't think she was actually losing skills, but she was certainly developing abilities at a slower rate than her peers.

After our evaluation, Sally's school looked over the information closely and developed a new IEP for her, with about half of her school day in the regular classroom for social studies, science, music, physical education, and art, as well as recess and lunch periods. The rest of her time was spent working at a slower pace in reading, math, and written language in a classroom for students with borderline to mild mental retardation. She began to flourish in this more appropriate placement, and she was significantly less frustrated.

Diagnosis

A child has mental retardation if the IQ score is below 70 to 75; there are significant limitations in two or more adaptive skill areas; and the child has had the condition since childhood. The first step in getting an appropriate diagnosis is to have a psychologist give standardized IQ tests. If there is also a developmental language disorder, alternative IQ testing (often called nonverbal IQ testing) is necessary.

However, IQ tests only measure some aspects of a child's overall function. Mental ability isn't enough by itself to define any degree of mental retardation, because being able to learn some key academic skills at a higher level, or to adapt and live everyday life, can counterbalance the score on a test. Tests don't just indicate what capacity the brain has; tests combine "brainpower" with experience, including cultural upbringing, schooling, motivation, and effort in learning activities. Some of this is included in the popularized term *emotional intelligence*.

Therefore, the next step is to have a psychologist or special education expert assess your child's *adaptive skills* in all aspects of life, using a standardized interview with parents and teacher. Adaptive skills involve the abilities a child needs to live, work, play, and socialize, including communication, self-care, home living, social skills, leisure, health and safety, and self-direction. A child with limited intelligence but who doesn't have limits in at least two of these adaptive skill areas shouldn't be diagnosed with mental retardation.

Once you know how well your child is functioning in all these areas, the IEP team at school or an independent evaluator can recommend how much support your child will need. Some kids might need only occasional extra help with schoolwork or in finding a job; others might require more intensive support over a limited period, such as to help make a transition from school to work.

Can IQ Scores Change?

It's important to realize that IQ scores do sometimes change over time, particularly if your child has been tested before age six—but it can also change at older ages. It's also important to understand that any of the more specific learning disorders I discussed earlier in this chapter can interfere with both the development of intelligence *and* the accurate measurement of intelligence, particularly learning disorders that affect language or fine motor skills.

A few children show IQ changes as they get older even without a brain disease or injury. For example, William walked and spoke at a normal age, but his delays in combining words led to speech therapy and placement in a special education preschool classroom at age three. An evaluation at school during first grade revealed low-average overall intelligence, with weaknesses in reading, expressive vocabulary, verbal problem solving, visual processing, visual-motor skills, fine motor skills, and sensory motor integration. William's school gave him a reading intervention program, speech/language therapy, and occupational therapy in a broad effort to improve his functioning over the years.

Despite the extra help, a brief follow-up assessment at school in eighth grade showed poor reading and written language skills. Shocked, William's parents moved him to a private program based in a nearby psychiatric hospital, even though he didn't have major behavior or emotional problems. Although William liked the new school, it turns out that they'd made a wrong turn—because they didn't have a good map. Within a few weeks, staff at the new school told William's parents they suspected mild mental retardation and sent him to us for a neuropsychological evaluation. In his first really thorough assessment since elementary school, we found that William's verbal skills, reading, and written language had slipped below the first percentile, and his visual-spatial problem-solving skills and math were below the second percentile. In the adaptive areas, he showed communication at the first percentile, social skills at the fifth percentile, and daily living skills at the tenth percentile. All this had transpired even though he had no signs of brain disease or damage!

William's parents transferred him from the inappropriate psychiatric school back to the public high school for his freshman year, where he finally began to flourish in a strong program for students with borderline to mild mental retardation, bolstered by speech/language therapy.

William's situation illustrates how a child's IQ scores can gradually decline between early childhood and adolescence. This often seems to be related to the following scenario: In the earlier years some children can get by with relative strengths in concrete or rote learning, but later, problems start cropping up as both the IQ tests and the school curriculum demand more abstract reasoning. All too often, resource-strapped school systems assume that a child's IQ will remain stable after mid–elementary school, sometimes skipping the important periodic IQ reassessment when the required IEP reevaluations are held every few years. If a child's map of developmental skills isn't updated often enough or thoroughly enough, you can be in for disappointment if your expectations have become too optimistic.

Causes

Most kids who are eventually diagnosed with mental retardation show some developmental delays in some important areas in early childhood, even if caution dictates that a formal diagnosis be deferred. This was the case in both Sally's and William's situations, and their parents were startled to find that they were at borderline to mild levels of mental retardation when appropriately assessed later. They had no idea how this could have happened. Although low IQ and mental retardation can be caused by any number of conditions that impair development of the brain, these two kids had no such problems. Although we've discovered several hundred rare causes of mental retardation, about a third of the time the cause remains unknown—as with Sally and William.

The three most common known causes of mental retardation are Down syndrome, fetal alcohol syndrome, and fragile X syndrome. Mental retardation can also be linked to abnormal genes inherited from either parent, or to gene mutations that weren't part of the parents' makeup.

Prognosis

The long-term effects of mental retardation vary considerably. About 87 percent of children who are mentally retarded test in the "mild" range and may not be easily diagnosed until they go to school. Because children with low-average or borderline IQ may have trouble communicating, interacting with others, and developing good independent judgment, parents may worry about how well they can take care of themselves and stay safe when they grow up. Not all skills are necessarily impaired, however, and many of these youngsters learn to function independently in many areas. However, education programs providing skilled assistance and ongoing support are necessary.

While the term *mental retardation* still exists as a clinical diagnosis, contemporary usage is moving toward other terms, such as *developmental disabilities* or *cognitive disabilities*, which some believe do not carry the same negative connotations or misuse. In the past, those who were mildly or moderately retarded were traditionally divided by IQ scores into *educable* or *trainable*. Today, the more commonly used terms for the whole range of below-average intelligence include *low average* (80 to 89), *borderline* (70 to 79), *mild* (55 to 69), *moderate* (40 to 54), or *severe to profound* (below 40). It's important to remember that children with low IQ and mild mental retardation aren't all the same—they have widely differing levels of function.

Virtually all children with low IQ struggle in school. However, many with mild retardation are capable of learning basic academic subjects, then later are able to live and work relatively independently. Children who are moderately retarded can usually learn some basic functional academics and vocational skills, sometimes achieving coached employment goals and living with limited assistance.

Treatment

One of the most important issues you'll need to face is how much time your child can spend in the regular classroom, and how much time she should be pulled out to work in a special education resource room. This will be determined in part by any behavior problems, in addition to her current mental and adaptive skill levels. It also may depend on how flexible your school's regular curriculum is, and how big the gap is between your child's mental abilities and academic skills compared to her peers in the classroom.

I believe a balanced mix of regular and special placement is often best, even though the "inclusion" model of doing as much regular classroom placement as possible is popular in schools these days. Sometimes there can be too *much* inclusion, particularly when children with mental limitations are spending lots of time in classroom instruction that is way over their heads.

I also believe that in general it's a good idea for a child to spend a good portion of time in school grouped with peers who are modestly but not overwhelmingly above his own level. Of course, this isn't statistically possible for all children, since some mix of higher- and lower-functioning kids is necessary in any classroom.

Your child's curriculum should combine basic academic skills (including continuing work on his areas of strength, such as reading decoding or spelling) and academic accommodations. Speech/language, occupational, and physical therapies are more likely to make an impact in the early years, from birth through preschool, then sometimes through kindergarten or possibly as far as middle elementary school.

You and the teachers should also try to strengthen conceptual skills if your child is in the low-average to mildly retarded range, although it may be hard to make much progress. For example, in reading comprehension, the teacher should "walk through" the main idea, details, and implications with your child, relating material in the reading passage to familiar or personal information as much as possible. In math reasoning problems, the teacher should ask your child to start at the end of the problem, ask himself what he needs to know to obtain the answer, and work backward gathering and sorting the necessary information. It would often be necessary to use multiple-choice questioning in this process.

In areas such as social studies and science, the teacher should illustrate concrete examples step-by-step, using words as well as pictures or diagrams, relating the new material to the student's previous knowledge and experience, and asking routine sets of key questions (for instance, what, when, why; what's first, second, and so on). In middle school and especially high school, your child will benefit from life-skills training, supervised extracurricular and recreational involvements, prevocational training, careful vocational counseling, work-study, and internships.

In adulthood, your child may want to take advantage of specialized technical training in slower-paced or basic-skills programs (such as paraprofessional), on-the-job coaching, regular supervision from you or a counselor about financial matters, enrollment in activities such as Special Olympics, and perhaps supervised living in a group home.

Reviewing the Learning Disability Types

Now that we've summarized the most common broad kinds of learning disorders, let's return to wrap up the specific categories of *learning disabilities*. The box below shows how varying combinations of the core deficits that we've outlined in this chapter relate to or produce the LD categories in the public school laws.

Patterns Underlying the Federal Learning Disability Categories

Here's how the seven federal learning disabilities categories (in bold type) typically relate to the explanations of the broad learning disorder patterns that make up the bulk of this chapter:

- **oral expression** problems overlap mostly with expressive language disorder
- **listening comprehension** problems are due to receptive language disorder
- **written expression** can be impaired by some combination of dyslexia, expressive language disorder, and sometimes fine motor coordination problems
- **basic reading skills** are the most common form of learning disability and are essentially the same thing as dyslexia
- **reading comprehension** can be impaired by some combination of dyslexia, receptive language disorder, and/or expressive language disorder
- **math calculation** difficulty is most often related to nonverbal learning disability and can also be impacted by dyslexia or language disorders
- **math reasoning** problems are most often due to some aspect of language disorder and/or nonverbal learning disability

---

Note that problems in academic skills in narrower areas (such as penmanship, spelling, or foreign languages) or in academic subjects such as science or social studies aren't legally considered "learning disabilities." Most children with mental retardation have problems in many or all of the specific learning disabilities as outlined in the law, which is part of the reason that additional LD diagnoses aren't actually applied in those cases. On the other hand, the new options for defining learning disabilities in the updated IDEA may offer more help to kids with reduced intelligence in what has historically been called the "gray area" between learning disabilities and mental retardation. In the past, these children had fallen through the cracks with the old discrepancy-based definition for LD.

Learning Disorders: The Bottom Line . . .

A wise psychologist friend of mine used to tell her patients with mental health problems, "It isn't cancer. It's not going to kill you." As a parent, it's important to remind yourself of this when grappling with the hard work of identifying and helping with your child's learning problems. The statistics on children's success in overcoming learning disorders vary widely, depending on the number and severity of problems, as well as the quality and timing of treatment.

Optimistically, some current researchers estimate that almost all reading disability cases could be prevented if they were identified and treated during kindergarten and early elementary school. On the other hand, long-term studies have suggested that most children with reading disabilities in mid–elementary school still have reading problems in higher grades. Even successfully treated children with reading disabilities usually still read more slowly and spell poorly as adults than students who didn't have reading disabilities.

What does all this mean? Most children with learning disorders make important progress, although they still feel frustrated in certain learning tasks. All find ways of getting around their problems to some extent. But once they graduate, most find satisfying careers because they're able to explore careers that have little to do with the demands they faced in school.

A few end up becoming fantastic special education teachers themselves, because they know what their students are coping with!

My friend Gloria is a perfect example. Her dyslexia was identified by second grade, and her resourceful parents had already enrolled her in the learning resource room at her parochial school, supplemented by an ongoing schedule of extra tutoring over the next several years using phonics-intensive methods. While her reading accuracy never was normal, by middle school she'd learned how to guess many of the words she couldn't decode. Listening to books on tape and using a voice-activated computer program that typed for her helped, and she was allowed to expand orally on her written test answers at school. These accommodations and compensations helped highlight her other thinking and learning skills.

When she graduated from middle school, she earned the school's award for the student who'd made the most academic effort and progress. By that time, she'd developed a gift for singing, so she attended a high school with a strong vocal music program. The last time I heard from her, she was on her way to one of the state university campuses with a strong learning support program, where she plans to become a music teacher.

Remaining Questions

I'll end each of the chapters 6 through 10 with reflections on important controversies, key questions, or areas that need more scientific research. Sometimes in these chapter-ending comments, I'll venture my own opinions about subjects that we don't yet have enough research-based answers on, because we as parents and frontline professionals need to decide how to proceed.

Here's one of the most important puzzles in evaluating learning difficulties: Why are there so many different tests for the problems that were discussed in this chapter, and why do different experts have so many competing ideas on how to classify these learning problems? Why will another professional use a fancy term such as *dysgraphia* to label something that I'd call a fine-motor coordination problem, an offshoot of dyslexia, or the effects of expressive language difficulties in written expression? Of course, some professionals just like fancy terms, but I think the main rea-

LD Online Web Site

www.ldonline.org

This Web site has lots of information on many aspects of learning disabilities, as well as related areas including ADHD. It also offers a monthly newsletter.

son for these different terms is the conflicting research into the different problems we've reviewed in this chapter. Unfortunately, sometimes it turns out that the less research, the fancier the term! For example, there's been a lot of information in the past twenty-five years about reading skills and reading problems—but far less research into the important nonverbal processing problems.

I'd suggest that you ignore the more unusual, fancy terms unless they've been backed up by scientific research *and* there's enough agreement about what the terms mean. Make sure to get current, solid information about the diagnoses that you're looking into, and keep updating this information as you help your child progress. You should also try to narrow your focus to a few key core deficits, rather than thinking about a long laundry list of issues. Keep in mind that most of these learning problems can improve with treatment.

And while I wouldn't discourage you from experimenting with new, cutting-edge interventions (as long as you're sure they are safe and have at least some value), make sure to put most of your energy into more valid methods that we know will work.

7

Attention-Deficit/ Hyperactivity Disorder and Other Disruptive Behavior Patterns

BETH'S TEACHER called Beth's mother after the second week of school complaining that her daughter showed signs of attention-deficit/hyperactivity disorder (ADHD). None of Beth's other teachers had ever mentioned this, and her mom was quite confused. Could Beth really have ADHD? She didn't seem hyperactive at home.

Beth's parents were already well aware that she had a learning disability in basic reading skills, and she had an appropriate IEP at school for that problem. They also knew that she often got nervous when reading a difficult book. Beth cared a lot about what her friends thought, so she was embarrassed about her problems with reading. She'd finally accepted special ed classes for extra help, and her parents and teachers had done a good job of helping her understand her learning disability. The extra time she spent on homework didn't threaten her self-esteem. But she got restless when she was asked to read material in the regular classroom that was above her own reading level. She also fidgeted and worried during silent reading, because she knew she was going to be the last one to finish, and her teacher would be moving on to other activities while she was scrambling to complete the last pages of her book. You can imagine how she felt about the prospect of being called on to read aloud in class!

Beth's parents had always thought these behavior patterns were just reactions to her reading disability, but her teacher thought there might be another cause, and they suspected at least a mild component of inattention.

Attention-Deficit/ Hyperactivity Disorder (ADHD)

You can hear ADHD being discussed everywhere these days, on the radio and TV, in books and magazine articles. The moment a child seems restless or bouncy, some parents and teachers immediately think, *Hyperactive!* But certainly not every busy, curious child has ADHD. So how do you tell the difference between an active, challenging, or naughty-but-not-mean child versus one with a diagnosable disruptive behavior disorder such as ADHD?

To a great extent, it's a matter of degree—in other words, how frequent and how impairing are the problems? Are there other plausible causes of the behavior, such as an abusive or chaotic environment? ADHD is a behavior pattern with core deficits in two major areas—impulse control and focusing on tasks. It's one of the most common psychological conditions affecting children—between 3 to 8 percent of school-age children are estimated to have ADHD (or about one out of every twenty kids). Most often, ADHD is diagnosed between the ages of four and ten and appears about three times as often in boys.

Children with the most common form of ADHD are repeatedly inattentive, impulsive, and hyperactive. They'll blurt out answers, interrupt, and won't wait their turn. Because of problems with following rules and explosive energy, children with ADHD often get into trouble with parents, teachers, and other kids. By adolescence, the hyperactivity often subsides into more subtle signs of fidgeting and restlessness, but problems with attention, concentration, and impulsivity usually continue into adulthood.

Although ADHD is a common childhood behavior problem, it can be hard to diagnose and even harder to understand. We once thought ADHD was a condition in childhood featuring gross-motor overactivity and the inability to pay attention, but lots of more recent research suggests that ADHD is both more complicated and probably centered on a child's lack of *behavioral inhibition.* In other words, the behavior you see is more likely because "he doesn't stop and think" rather than "he can't sit still." In fact, ADHD may *not* include physical restlessness or hyperactive behavior at all ages, and children don't typically outgrow the condition completely even if they stop appearing "hyper."

Teens who have ADHD often end up with other problems, such as depression, anxiety, or poor school performance. They may also be at greater risk for smoking and using drugs, especially if ADHD isn't treated. On the other hand, most adults who had ADHD as children lead successful lives. That's what happened to a twenty-four-year-old former patient of my colleague, whose parents had complained that he always "rose to the minimum expectation" in school. He'd never earned more than a few college credits despite clear ability, worked a few odd jobs, wandered into debt and hard feelings with his family, and lost his girlfriend due to irresponsibility and lying. He finally turned his life around when he joined the Marine Corps—the structure and discipline of the military matched his ADHD "needs" perfectly, and he developed pride and self-esteem that had eluded him for years. Now he's back on track to get his associate's degree as a veterinarian's technician.

Does My Child Have ADHD?

Many parents agonize over whether to have their child assessed for ADHD, because the picture isn't necessarily simple or straightforward. That's what happened in Jonathan's situation. When he wasn't speaking much more than two words by his second birthday, his parents asked the pediatrician if Jonathan should be tested for a speech delay. The doctor dismissed their concerns, explaining that boys were often slower than girls to talk. He offered to refer Jonathan to the speech and hearing center at the Children's Hospital, but they decided to wait and watch. By Jonathan's third birthday, his fourteen-month-old sister had a better vocabulary than he did, and she was able to connect more words together in phrases. They realized it was time for an evaluation.

The hospital speech pathologist reported Jonathan's language comprehension and vocabulary were average, but noted that all of his expressive language skills were mildly to moderately delayed when carefully compared to other kids his age. Jonathan started speech/language therapy and a special education preschool program in his local public school.

Right away, the teachers noticed something else: he seemed to have trouble settling down for story time or nap time. And despite his sweet disposition, friendly manner, and popularity with the other students, Jonathan started getting into trouble for grabbing and hitting. Even at this young age, he was aware that this behavior wasn't acceptable, so he was usually dreadfully sorry afterward. Throughout kindergarten and first grade, his teachers worked patiently with good behavior-management strategies, but Jonathan continued to struggle with self-control.

By the time he came to me for a neuropsychological evaluation at age seven, Jonathan was doing well with his language skills, so school staff happily predicted that he might no longer need therapy by the end of second grade. He was a bit behind in reading and writing, but an evaluation at school at the end of first grade didn't find enough delay to qualify him for learning disabilities placement. However, his inattention and lack of impulse control were becoming more of a problem. His parents wondered if the legal guidelines for qualification that the school was required to use might be missing a more subtle learning disability. Even more important, they raised the chicken-and-egg question about whether attention problems might be causing the mild learning delays, or was it the other way around?

In this situation, since the school had recently completed a range of academic and IQ tests, we had the luxury of zeroing in on some specific neuropsychological areas, including attention, impulse control, executive mental functions, and memory. Considering his previous language delays followed by encouraging progress, we concluded that he was at mild risk for developing learning disabilities as time went on. However, we saw clearly that he had a mild case of ADHD. We felt that his slight signs of learning disabilities were probably caused by the mild leftover effects of his language problems, plus his problems in paying attention to instructions and practicing his academic skills. We hoped that his academic skills would improve if the other two issues were treated.

While his parents were disappointed with the ADHD diagnosis, they were relieved to better understand this complex picture. His parents first worked on their behavior management strategies at home by attending the parent training group in our clinic. They also started consulting regularly with the teacher and school psychologist to figure out how they could best work with school staff to reinforce his homework strategies. They also enrolled Jonathan for extra reading help available at school for children with mild learning problems. Finally, after a few months, they returned to their pediatrician to try various doses of a couple of different medications for ADHD until they found the most effective option. With all this support, Jonathan is now doing much better with his attention, organization, and self-control, and we think he should be able to overcome his learning disability risks.

As you can see in Jonathan's example, ADHD is often a tricky condition to identify. It can coexist with a number of other problems, including learning issues, mood problems, or specific impulse control disorders (such as eating disorders or alcohol abuse). Some children may have symptoms of depression in reaction to their problems with ADHD, whereas others may have a depression independent of ADHD. Nearly half of all children with ADHD also have a condition known as oppositional defiant disorder (ODD) characterized by stubbornness, outbursts of temper, and defiance, which I'll discuss later in the chapter.

Core Deficits and Other Symptoms

Of course, all children sometimes have trouble paying attention, following directions, or being quiet. But for children with ADHD, these behaviors occur more frequently and are more disruptive.

We use the name ADHD to refer to a disorder that actually has three subtypes with overlapping characteristics. The first, called the *predominantly inattentive type,* is marked by problems with paying attention, staying organized, and remembering things. A child with this problem has trouble sticking with tasks, following instructions, finishing work, and keeping track of books or homework. Most researchers believe that this type of ADHD is actually different from the other types and may really belong in the category of learning disorders rather than the disruptive behavior disorders.

The second category is called the *hyperactivity/impulsive type.* Kids with this problem fidget, feel restless, have trouble taking turns, and interrupt. This cluster of problems is closely related to the concept of behavior inhibition that we cited above, which is one of the most prominent theories about the underlying problem in ADHD.

The third type is the most common and combines the features of the first two. In fact, almost all children with the second type are preschool age, and their patterns tend to evolve into the combined type during elementary school.

Your child's doctor will probably diagnose ADHD using the criteria in the *Diagnostic and Statistical Manual of Mental Disorders, Fourth Edition (DSM-IV-TR)*, which requires that the child must display symptoms for at least six months, and that the problems appeared before age seven. In addition, the ADHD behavior must negatively affect at least two areas of a child's life, such as school, home, or friendships.

As we discussed above, a problem in paying attention is one basic symptom of ADHD. Of course, all of us daydream now and then. But inattention in ADHD involves constant failure to pay close attention to details or making careless mistakes in schoolwork or other activities, as well as trouble maintaining attention in tasks or play. Kids with this problem don't seem to listen when spoken to directly, and they don't follow through on instructions. They often fail to finish schoolwork, chores, or duties. Perhaps your child often has trouble organizing tasks and activities or often avoids, dislikes, or is reluctant to do anything that requires sustained mental effort, such as studying for a big test. Or maybe he loses toys, school assignments, pencils, books, or tools. Easy distractibility and forgetfulness are other examples of inattention.

If your child also is impulsive or hyperactive, the doctor might suspect the combined type of ADHD. In this case, your child probably often fidgets with his hands or feet or squirms in his seat or often gets up when remaining seated is expected, such as in class or church. Other signs of hyperactivity include often running around inappropriately (in teenagers, this might just be restlessness), problems playing quietly, or talking too much. Key symptoms of impulsivity include often blurting out answers, having trouble taking turns, or interrupting.

Other related issues can include trouble understanding the passage of time. In addition, children and teens with ADHD often have trouble getting started, lose focus, and don't finish projects. There may be problems with short- and long-term planning abilities. Your child may seem disorganized because he can't plan or complete even the most basic tasks, such as cleaning his room or setting the table. Teens with ADHD often take risks, become argumentative, and may have poor judgment.

At the same time, children with ADHD may also display puzzling behavior, such as the ability to focus intensively on a task of their own choosing over time. You can have ADHD and still have strong intellectual, verbal, and problem-solving skills, or extraordinary creativity. Because children with ADHD can sometimes perform well, especially when they are interested, subsequent failure to perform at the same level is often perceived as a lack of self-discipline or effort. In fact, research on ADHD provides more than passing support to the saying that "the only consistent thing is the inconsistency."

Causes

ADHD is assumed to be a problem with brain function. Research has identified differences in brain scans between children and adults with and without ADHD involving the frontal lobes and basal ganglia. We think an area within the frontal lobes is an important part of the brain's "command center," and the basal ganglia seem to help translate those commands into action. Some research suggests that not only may some brain areas be smaller or less active than normal in ADHD, but that the brain may actually use these areas differently. Some brain scans have shown an abnormal increase of activity in the front lobe and certain nearby areas that control voluntary action, which could mean that children with ADHD may need to work harder to control their impulses than those without ADHD. When patients with ADHD take medications such as Ritalin, their brain scans become more normal.

Certain imbalances in brain chemicals play a role in the development of ADHD, and many effective medications seem to work by boosting the availability of these chemicals in the brain. But the picture is not simple, and a wide variety of brain chemicals are also probably involved.

Genetics research has also clearly established that ADHD characteristics are often inherited. Other medical problems such as thyroid malfunction or medication reactions can occasionally cause ADHD symptoms.

Finally, a few children with ADHD have experienced brain damage of some sort, such as birth complications or traumatic brain injury; one of the most common results of any significant brain injury in childhood is some degree of ADHD.

Diagnosis

Perhaps your child's behavior patterns lead you to suspect ADHD. Or maybe your child's teacher thinks there may be an ADHD problem. ADHD can be tricky to diagnose and even harder to understand, and there aren't any reliable medical or individual psychological tests for ADHD at the moment. Many of the symptoms of ADHD are common to other psychiatric and medical conditions, and all of the symptoms occur at times in "perfectly normal" children, so you shouldn't try to diagnose your own child with any degree of certainty. Instead, you should seek a comprehensive evaluation from a qualified professional, or from a team with experience in ADHD. Keep in mind that the team may include professionals who don't work in the same place, but who work together for a brief time to help you figure out your child's behavior patterns. This team may include a pediatrician, a clinical psychologist or school psychologist, your child's teacher, and perhaps a medical pediatric specialist in neurology or psychiatry.

The American Academy of Pediatrics recommends a careful outline of procedures for an ADHD evaluation if your child shows signs of school problems, underachievement, problems with family members and peers, or other behavioral issues. The assessment should include information about symptoms and how they affect the child's life, obtained from parents or caregivers and school professionals. At our clinic, we diagnose ADHD with a combination of

- a comprehensive clinical interview to assess the child's symptoms
- individual and family history
- information about behavior from parents and teachers
- a limited set of testing and observation in the clinic to evaluate the symptoms along with any coexisting conditions.

We also want to know about any medications, social adjustment, and general day-to-day function.

Testing is usually more useful for ruling out other possible problems than confirming ADHD, since we know that patterns we see in the clinic may be quite different from what you see at home and school. Typically, I administer tests to children to evaluate inattention, distractibility, behavioral inhibition, memory, and executive functions such as planning, organization, and problem solving. As mentioned above, evaluation should include looking for coexisting conditions such as learning and language problems, aggression, disruptive behavior, depression, or anxiety. If the picture is complicated or unclear, testing shouldn't be a brief, cursory exam, but an in-depth survey that takes several hours. Ideally, the interview should rely on several people, including at least one parent.

Of course, we always want to rule out certain psychiatric or medical conditions that could also cause problems with attention. At our clinic, we prefer to make a careful, cautious diagnosis after we've gathered all necessary medical, psychological, and behavioral information, rather than do a quick screening approach.

Is ADHD overdiagnosed these days? In some situations, the answer is probably yes. One father brought his son to our clinic for a second opinion on his son's ADHD diagnosis after he was astounded to learn at a Cub Scout campfire that five out of the seven boys in his son's den were on medication for ADHD! On the other hand, many diagnoses of ADHD may actually be missed in situations where medical services and thorough evaluation aren't available, or when parents avoid getting a needed evaluation because they're afraid someone will negatively label their child—or, worse yet, dare to suggest medication!

About one out of twenty children in the United States has ADHD, although we're continuing to debate if this rate is accurate. In other countries, symptoms are interpreted with different levels of sensitivity, making comparisons difficult. When reasonably similar comparison methods have been used with some of these disorders (especially ADHD), roughly similar prevalence rates have been found. I'd urge you to refocus your questions about whether too many children are diagnosed with ADHD on *your own child's situation.* Do you think the professionals suggesting your child has ADHD usually so identify more than one out of twenty children? If not, I wouldn't worry about overdiagnosis.

Treatment

There is no cure for ADHD, so we try to manage symptoms and reduce other problems associated with ADHD. You and all other adults working closely with your child need thorough information about ADHD. Behavior management and medication are the only two treatment approaches that have demonstrated real power to change the core symptoms of ADHD. No matter how much we professionals with expertise in teaching behavior management methods believe in our treatment, we need to acknowledge that reliable research demonstrates at least slightly more powerful benefit from medication for ADHD than from other therapies.

Behavior Management

Both you and the teachers need to consistently apply good behavior management strategies, which I have briefly described in chapter 4. Hundreds of good studies have identified which behavior management approaches are most effective for children with ADHD at home, at school, and in social situations. These methods have been summarized in several good books that you should read if you have a child with this diagnosis (see especially Dr. Barkley's *Taking Charge of ADHD* in appendix A). I'll give you a few examples of these methods here, but there are many others that you should learn and practice if you have a child with ADHD.

- *Break down complex tasks:* First, you should help your child break complex tasks into smaller steps. Give commands one or two at a time; longer commands should be repeated, rehearsed, or written down.

- *Attentional cuing:* It's also a good idea to provide "attentional cuing": "Look at this now!" or "This is important to pay attention to." It may be a challenge, but you should try to avoid getting frustrated with the need to direct your child's attention.

- *Reward systems:* Shaping behavior using chips or charts is a powerful tool, because this makes positive reinforcement more explicit, consistent, and quickly available after positive behaviors occur.

In addition, many kids with ADHD and other disruptive behavior problems need social skills training groups to work on ways to stop acting so impulsively around their friends, using "stop and think" and "problem-solving" routines. These kids also need more basic instruction in exactly how to interact with their friends.

Medication

Trials of one or more medications are appropriate and worthwhile. For most children with ADHD, medication isn't used to control behavior, but to ease the symptoms. But remember, there are often other aspects of a child's problem that medication won't affect.

Traditionally, ADHD has been treated with regular doses of stimulants such as Ritalin or Concerta (methylphenidate), Dexedrine or Dex-troStat (dextroamphetamine), or Adderall (amphetamine). With any of these medications, it's vital to adjust the dosage for each child's particular symptoms. This can be a trial-and-error effort—if one stimulant medication doesn't work, your doctor may want to try another.

Stimulants appear to help children with ADHD by altering the levels of transmitters in the brain by which different nerve cells communicate. Between 70 to 90 percent of children with ADHD respond positively to these medications, with anywhere from a little to a lot of improvement in attention span, impulsivity, and behavior. Some children also become better able to tolerate frustration, become more compliant, and even develop more legible handwriting. Relationships with parents, peers, and teachers may also improve. Older teens with ADHD sometimes report the medications bring more control and organization to their lives.

The newest drug used to treat ADHD is Strattera (atomoxetine), a nonstimulant medication approved for teens and children over age six. It boosts the level of norepinephrine, a chemical messenger believed to be

Cylert Alert

Cylert (pemoline) is a stimulant medication that had been used for thirty years to treat ADHD. It was discontinued by the manufacturer in the spring of 2005 because of declining sales. This drop in sales occurred in the wake of a few reported cases of serious liver damage in patients taking Cylert.

important in regulating impulse control, organization, and attention. The exact way that Strattera works in ADHD is not known, but the drug has been prescribed for more than 2 million patients since 2002.

Other medications (such as antidepressants like Elavil, Prozac, Tofranil, or Norpramin) can be helpful for children with depression, phobic, panic, anxiety, and/or obsessive-compulsive disorders in addition to ADHD. Clonidine, a drug normally used to treat high blood pressure, may also ease some symptoms of ADHD.

A doctor should prescribe medication for ADHD only after medical, psychological, behavioral, and (if needed) educational assessments. Although the drugs clearly reduce the symptoms of ADHD, no studies have continued long enough to convincingly determine if they have a lasting effect on academic performance or social behavior.

All medications can cause side effects, and for that reason, I believe the potential side effects should be observed closely and carefully weighed against the benefits for each individual child with ADHD. While taking stimulants, for example, some children may have stomachaches or less appetite and temporarily grow more slowly. Others may have trouble falling asleep or become irritable. There is a concern that stimulants may worsen the symptoms of Tourette's syndrome, although recent research suggests this may not be true. If your child's height, weight, and overall development are carefully monitored, the benefits of medication for most children outweigh the potential side effects. Side effects that do occur can often be handled by reducing the dosage.

I typically tell parents that as a nonphysician, I can't be the final authority on medication matters for their child, and they need to discuss medications with the prescribing physician. When medications are approved by the FDA, I generally trust that the regulatory process has established an adequate level of safety. Taken as a whole, the large number of good studies examining the long-term side effects of the stimulants haven't documented reliable, significant concerns. To make good use of science to improve our kids' lives, the occasional not-so-good studies that have suggested otherwise need to be examined carefully, and with extreme caution.

When an individual child experiences a short-term side effect of a stimulant medication, parents and the physician must balance the benefits of the medication against the side effects. For instance, how much improvement should George show to make it worth how much trouble he has going to sleep at night? Is there something else we can do to help George go to sleep, such as changes in bedtime routine, relaxation therapy, or warm milk? If the problems with side effects are too severe, the child shouldn't keep taking that medication. Other doses, other medications, or (if drug options have been exhausted) behavior management alone can be considered. And remember, just as ADHD is sometimes overdiagnosed, medication is sometimes overprescribed. Just as ADHD is sometimes underdiagnosed, medication is sometimes underprescribed.

Psychotherapy

It's also important to keep in mind that many children with ADHD develop some of the other problems we discuss in this book. The daily frustrations that are a part of having ADHD can make children feel abnormal or mentally slow. In some cases, the cycle of frustration and anger has persisted for so long that it may take a long time to alleviate. For these reasons, I sometimes also recommend individual, family, or group counseling, to help a child build more hope, sometimes including work to clarify how the disability might be linked to his or her history of below-average performance. Counseling may also help reduce mood swings, stabilize relationships, and ease discouragement. As we discussed in chapter 4, several behavioral therapy approaches are available, and different therapists tend to prefer one approach or another. You might want to reread that chapter, since understanding the various types of interventions makes it easier for you to choose the best therapist for your own situation.

Investigate Support Groups

Because ADHD affects all aspects of a child's home and school life, I highly recommend that you consider joining a support group to learn how other parents in your shoes help their children cope with frustration, organize their lives, and develop problem-solving skills. You may find it useful to join a local or national support group such as CHADD (Children and Adults with Attention Deficit Disorder; see appendix B for contact information.)

Other Disruptive Behavior Problems

Of course, ADHD is not the only "acting out" behavior disorder, although it's the most commonly recognized one. Perhaps your child has exhibited problems with defiance, rule-breaking, or aggression. If so—and if the pattern has persisted for at least six months—you may need to consider the possibility of either an oppositional defiant disorder (ODD) or a conduct disorder (CD).

Many children with either of these conditions also have ADHD. It's also important to realize that many children can have tendencies toward ODD or CD without severe or persistent enough problems to get a full diagnosis—but these kids need help, too.

Children and Adults with Attention Deficit Disorder (CHADD) Web Site

www.chadd.org

CHADD is one of the largest and most effective advocacy organizations for developmental disorders. This site is similar to the sites, programs, and publications of other major advocacy groups that are directed by a combination of parents and professionals (such as the Learning Disabilities Association) in that they tend to blend recommendations that have strong research support with others that should be seen as more speculative. (See appendix B for contact information.)

Oppositional Defiant Disorder

A child with an oppositional defiant disorder (ODD) shows repeated serious problems with negative behavior, such as temper outbursts, arguing, or deliberately doing things to annoy others. ODD occurs in between 2 and 15 percent of school-age children, depending on exactly how the symptoms are defined. In younger children, ODD is more common in boys than girls, but as they grow older, the rate evens out. Children who have oppositional behavior also often have ADHD or some of the other problems I discuss in this book.

Eleven-year-old Mitchell showed this frustrating, draining combination of patterns. During the past two years, he became increasingly disorganized, had trouble with schoolwork, and began showing more and more signs of oppositional behavior—fighting with his brother, his parents, and his friends. Academic testing at school found low-average basic reading and mildly below-average math calculation skills, but not to the extent that could account for his failing grades in several subjects. On recent report cards, many teachers noted he didn't turn in assignments on time. His parents arranged for extra tutoring, summer school, and reduced workloads in hopes of improving his academic performance—and then made an appointment to visit our clinic.

In the evaluation interview, Mitchell's parents and I carefully reviewed his behavior patterns over the years. He'd been mildly inattentive and disorganized since beginning school. Both parents and teachers had repeatedly noticed that he seemed to be able to focus on tasks he liked, but he didn't bother to work when he wasn't interested. He'd been arguing constantly at home over the past several years, had started to throw things at his brothers and parents, and threatened to hurt people. He deliberately annoyed family members—he'd grab his brother's toys and run away, interrupt his parents, and look his parents straight in the eye as he defied them. Interestingly, these oppositional behaviors weren't noticeable at school, although he could be passive-aggressive in his slow, partial completion of classwork. Mitchell had been counseled for his outbursts in fourth grade, but his busy parents weren't able to get him to regular sessions.

Mitchell's mother's responses to a behavior checklist showed that her son had a higher level of oppositional and aggressive behavior than 97 percent of boys in his age group. He also had higher levels of attention problems and anxious, depressed symptoms than 93 percent of boys his age. However, his father's responses to the questionnaire suggested his son was within normal limits. Responses on questionnaires completed by Mitchell's teachers showed variable results. Two teachers noted no compliance problems in a variety of school settings, whereas three indicated mild compliance problems in classroom activities such as individual deskwork, small-group work, and lectures.

During testing, Mitchell appeared sleepy and irritable. His emotional expression was flat throughout much of the day, especially during conversation. He often got stuck on an item or mumbled to himself about whether previous answers were correct. He seemed to be anxious during testing, getting flushed, swinging his legs, and tapping his pencil. He rarely made eye contact with the examiner, never initiated conversation, and ignored others in the room. His responses to questions were short, and he was hesitant to reveal personal information. For example, he said his relationships with his brothers and friends were "all right," and that his relationship with his parents was "fine." How different this was from his mother's stories about family interactions!

Mitchell displayed a pattern of significantly more oppositional defiant symptoms in some situations than others, with worsening problems as time passed. His oppositional behaviors were clearly intertwined with other attention, anxiety, and mood symptoms.

Coexisting Conditions

As Mitchell's example shows, it's fairly uncommon in our clinic to evaluate children who *only* have oppositional defiant disorder; usually, the child has another disorder as well—often ADHD or learning disabilities. Other specialists in our community see a lot more children with ODD as their main or only problem. On the other hand, research suggests that a child with ADHD has a 30 to 40 percent risk of also having ODD, and many behavioral problems associated with ADHD may in fact be symptoms of ODD. Other conditions that may appear in a child with ODD include mood problems (such as depression or bipolar disorder) and anxiety disorders. It's important to diagnose these coexisting issues, because it may be difficult to improve the symptoms of ODD without also treating the other problems.

Core Problems

ODD is characterized by various forms of aggressiveness and resistance, but it's not the same as the impulsiveness of ADHD. Often, children with ODD annoy others or challenge authority on purpose, making their symptoms much more difficult to live with. The social skills problems in ODD may include thoughtless actions, such as jumping into situations insensitively, but more importantly they include being bossy, mean, or manipulative with peers.

For example, a child who has only ADHD may impulsively push another child out of a tree or knock a child down, but he'd probably be sorry afterward. A child with more ODD tendencies than ADHD might push the child out of the tree and then deny it or even brag about it to his friends later. Children with combined ADHD and ODD often get in big-time trouble because their impulsiveness and hyperactivity can set off fights, way too much rough play, and temper tantrums. Without treatment, ODD doesn't usually improve with age; instead, these children can develop signs of mood disorders or anxiety as they get older. On the other hand, some of the psychological factors in ODD may respond with really good, intensive psychotherapy.

You should consider ODD if your child shows a pattern of negative, hostile, defiant behavior lasting at least six months that causes significant problems at home, at school, or with friends. ODD should also be considered if your child often loses his temper, argues with adults, actively defies or refuses to comply with requests or rules, and deliberately annoys people. He may blame others for mistakes or misbehavior, get easily annoyed, and seem angry, resentful, spiteful, or vindictive.

Of course, most children may occasionally annoy someone, lose their temper, or feel angry or resentful. The key difference is that a child with ODD *often* displays these symptoms. What's "often"? That's hard to say, but research suggests you should be concerned if you notice that your child is angry and resentful or deliberately annoys people at least four times a week; or is touchy, easily annoyed by others, loses his temper, argues with adults, or actively defies or refuses to comply with your requests or rules at least twice per week.

The ODD behavior pattern in early to middle childhood may evolve into the more severe problem of conduct disorder by teenage years, or sometimes even younger, as discussed below.

Causes

There are probably many different causes for ODD. Some parents report that their child with ODD was more rigid and demanding than their other youngsters at an early age, which could suggest that a "built in" difficult temperament might predispose a child to ODD. Biological, genetic, and environmental factors may play a role. Some experts believe ODD may be linked to how a child was disciplined. Family interaction patterns often need to be examined to fully understand and work on changing the opposition.

Treatment

Many research studies have found that kids with ODD only sometimes respond well to treatment, so cautious expectations are in order. Although there have been no major research breakthroughs in finding constructive ways to handle this condition, there have been some small improvements, especially with interventions based on improved parenting.

Children with oppositional and defiant behavior along with attention problems typically benefit from some form of structured behavior-management program at home and school. Learning the techniques outlined below, and also working with your child in therapy, is most effective.

- Use clear, specific commands.
- Reinforce positive behaviors: "I know you were frustrated when Bill beat you in tennis, and you did a great job of handling your emotions. You even shook hands with him and smiled. Good going!"

- Use consistent negative consequences delivered in a neutral way in response to inappropriate behaviors.
- Use more positive incentives than reprimands.

Conduct Disorder

ODD sometimes worsens into the far more serious condition of conduct disorder, characterized by excessive, sustained aggression against people or animals, antisocial behavior, property destruction, lying, theft, or other serious rule-breaking. It may affect at least 6 percent of boys and 2 percent of girls under age eighteen, but it's important to distinguish between children who act like this because of strong group pressure (for instance, as members of a rough gang) versus those who are less socially connected.

Coexisting Conditions

Many children with a conduct disorder may have other problems such as anxiety, mood disorders, post-traumatic stress disorder, substance abuse, learning problems, ADHD, or thought disorders.

Core Problems

In addition to the basic symptoms found in ODD, children with conduct disorder typically lack remorse for their actions or refuse to accept responsibility for them, and they often lack empathy toward others. These central issues are probably behind the observation that cruelty to animals, deliberate or repeated fire setting, and vandalism are among common ways that kids with CD can violate the rights of others in dramatic ways. They may have trouble learning how to solve problems, establish peer relationships, and control their anger. Because of these troubling issues, children with CD are likely to attract attention from teachers and parents, to be referred for services, and to receive some treatment at an early age for their misbehavior.

That's what happened to Ethan, who was sixteen when he was referred to us for a neuropsychological evaluation of his thinking skills in reference to his anger-control problems, his long history of ODD, and his more recent substance abuse. In particular, his worried parents wondered if his problems had gotten worse as a result of a concussion he'd suffered the previous year and his past history of daily marijuana use. They also suspected he might have had undiagnosed ADHD since early childhood.

Ethan's medical history also included three episodes of unsteady gait, confusion, bloodshot eyes, disorientation, and facial tics after taking excessive doses of Robitussin. He was treated in the ER with activated charcoal and placed on heart monitors each time, but there were no significant complications and the symptoms passed quickly.

As we learned his complex story, we became most concerned about Ethan's years of behavior problems since early childhood. He'd always been shy, with poor social skills. By age two he'd developed ODD and prolonged temper tantrums. At first, these fits of temper and defiance only occurred at home with his parents, but during kindergarten he began acting up at school and in the community. He showed some obsessive symptoms when younger, such as wanting his parents to say the same thing when he went to bed at night or touching certain things on the way to the car, but these gradually declined and then disappeared as he got older. By middle school, Ethan was withdrawn in class, didn't want to do schoolwork, and got into control struggles with many teachers. As a teenager he began to steal money and charge cards from home, once taking his mother's car without permission.

Our IQ testing verified Ethan's parents' impression that he had superior overall IQ, including strengths in both verbal and visual-spatial areas. Detailed neuropsychological testing suggested that he fit the usual picture of complete long-term recovery after his concussion. I felt that his accompanying symptoms of depression and anxiety could account for his fluctuating inattention in the testing, and there was little compelling evidence for either a diagnosis of ADHD or any residual effects of his overdoses of cough medicine or previous marijuana use. Unfortunately, Ethan was clearly in big trouble in many areas of his life and had a conduct disorder.

Ethan's parents had learned over the years that he responded best to strict limits, such as not being allowed to get his driver's license right away. After the neuropsychological evaluation at our clinic, he completed a treatment program for children with conduct disorder at a local hospital where he appeared to have made progress. Still, we all worry that he might slip back into his old ways, as do a significant portion of adolescents with conduct disorders, even after successful treatment.

Causes

Many factors can contribute to the development of a conduct disorder, including genetic vulnerability, history of ADHD or ODD, long-term chaotic family situation, chronic school failure, child abuse, psychological trauma, dangerous "models" for behavior, or brain injury.

Treatment

Treatment of children with conduct disorder can be complex and frustrating, especially because of the child's uncooperative attitude, anger, and distrust of adults. Without treatment, many children with conduct disorder are unable to adapt to the demands of adulthood and continue to have severe problems with relationships and responsibility. They often break laws or behave in an antisocial manner. Because these more aggressive behavior patterns in children and adolescents are hard to change after they've become ingrained, the earlier the problem is identified and treated, the better. Family psychotherapy and behavior therapy may help the child learn how to express and manage anger.

School programs that target bullying are getting more popular these days. These programs can sometimes help with this frequent symptom of CD, even when other aspects of CD often continue. These programs typically include coaching teachers to be more aware of the problem, how to handle bullying, and how to intervene in specific cases. Some of the most effective programs for CD are those that deal with a variety of potential problems at home and at school. A program that combines classroom social skills, a playground behavior program, parent training, and regular communication between parents and teachers has been shown to reduce short-term aggression and boost some classroom skills.

Certain medications (including mood stabilizers, antipsychotics, or stimulants) are sometimes used to treat severe CD, cases complicated by a coexisting diagnosis, or CD that hasn't responded to other treatments. Unfortunately, there hasn't been a lot of research in children. Some studies have suggested that medications are only partly helpful in improving symptoms in these situations and must be combined with other types of treatment, such as psychotherapy, to be most effective.

More on Bullying and "the Difficult Child"

Bullying is a serious problem—both because of how often it happens and because of the psychological damage it can have on victims. Many bullies have ODD or CD. Even if your child bullies repeatedly without also having a full disruptive-behavior diagnosis, it's a big problem—whether it involves siblings or kids outside the family. I'd advise you to take your child to a mental health professional as soon as possible to find out whether treatment is needed. You could be taking the first step toward nipping ODD or CD in the bud, before the bullying becomes more ingrained and harder to treat.

I believe there's a big overlap between what some professionals call "the difficult child" and the oppositional behavior patterns that make up ODD. In fact, I think they should usually be seen as different degrees of the same basic behavioral problems. Experts who write about how to parent "the difficult child" often directly state or strongly imply that the child's behavior became difficult because of some traits that were "built in" to the child's temperament from the beginning, rather than caused by things such as less-than-perfect parenting approaches. While this is probably true to some degree in many cases, it can also be a dangerous cop-out—because it points the finger only toward the child.

In parenting, one sure thing is that no one's perfect. And genes, physical makeup, school environment, peers, and, yes, parenting—*all matter*. You shouldn't have a problem in shouldering part of the responsibility here, because this can help you get ready to roll up your sleeves to do the hard work of changing what you do as a parent.

The Importance of Taking Action

A word of caution—the patterns outlined in this chapter tend to continue rather than disappear if you try to "wait it out." This is one reason why a good evaluation is important. Be prepared for some ongoing work on these issues with a mental health professional that you trust. Other family members are often affected by these patterns, so get some skilled coaching in behavior management strategies, and find ways of giving everybody in the family a break from these challenging problems. The sooner you start, the more chance you have of reducing or avoiding some of the emotional complications discussed in chapters 9 and 10, for both your child and other family members.

Remaining Questions

I'd like to emphasize three issues you should be thinking about if you suspect your child may have ADHD. First, one of my colleagues (who's an international expert in the field) reminds us repeatedly that it's easy to make a diagnosis of ADHD, but it's much harder to make a good *differential diagnosis*. This means that it's often hard to tell whether a behavior pattern that looks similar to ADHD may be caused by something else. What *kind* of "something else"? Here's where it gets tricky, because you need to have your eyes open, but avoid both guilt and blaming: Is there enough structure in this home or this classroom for this particular child's needs? Could this kid have minor tendencies toward ADHD, combined with stress in his life, that make it appear to be a full-blown case of ADHD? Am I looking for an easy way out by seeking a diagnosis of ADHD that implies a brain-related cause, rather than something like ODD that may require some hard work on family relationships? Do we know enough about what's going on in your child's "inside life," such as feelings of anxiety or frustration or sadness, to rule these out as the main causes of the symptoms? These are important questions to consider in making a good differential diagnosis.

Second, some of the children with ADHD diagnoses in the United States probably wouldn't get this diagnosis in many other parts of the

A Parent's Letter to the Doctor

When I explain things to parents, I like to anticipate what their questions might be, so I'm guessing there's one you might have right now. It would go like this:

Dear Doctor:
Come on! Isn't there such a thing as "lazy bum syndrome"?

Dear Parent:
Absolutely. Usually we call it something like "inadequate motivation." Believe it or not, things like this actually have official labels in the diagnostic codebooks, although medical insurance companies usually don't pay for therapy for this!

Dear Doctor:
So how can I tell if my child has this "inadequate motivation" thing, or if it's really a little ADHD, or a little ODD, or a little LD, or . . . ?

Dear Parent:
That may be why you're reading this book, and why I hope you'll think of taking your child for an evaluation. You may find that it's a little of several things, perhaps even including a little "lazy bum."

Dear Doctor:
If we do have some lazy bum going on, could it be because I've "spoiled" my child and not asked for enough "nose to the grindstone"?

Dear Parent:
Could be. But every kid is different. In fact, there may be ways that you could help by actually giving your child *more* or *different* from what we usually mean by "spoiling." Dig in with the evaluator to figure out the behavior sequences. You can probably change your own approach to situations in a way that would make a big difference for your child, if you do your homework.

world—especially in many European countries, where mental health and primary medical care professionals take a more conservative approach to ADHD criteria. It would be inappropriate to say that any particular society's approach to this problem is "right."

I'd encourage you to feel confident in getting behavioral treatment if you're convinced after careful evaluation that your child has *some degree* of ADHD, reserving medication unless you're also convinced that your child is more likely to have ADHD than nineteen out of twenty other kids the same age *and* the symptoms are causing significant problems in his life.

Finally, the inattentive type of ADHD may have been diagnosed more often since its definition was clarified and revised in 1994, but this hasn't made the concept any less slippery. Eventually researchers may agree that only a small number of children can truly be diagnosed with the inattentive type, and that these children really show a form of learning problem rather than a disruptive behavior disorder. Furthermore, many professionals (including me) believe that lots of children are misdiagnosed with this inattentive type, when they really have more important underlying anxiety and mood problems usually treatable with good psychotherapy. Therefore, if someone suggests your child has the inattentive type of ADHD, think hard and ask careful questions before agreeing with the diagnosis.

8

Autistic Spectrum Disorders

JESSICA first came to see me at age ten, after her parents had spent years consulting other professionals, searching for the reasons why she seemed so different from her siblings and friends. Over the years, her parents had spent long hours working with specialists at school, and anxiously anticipating how she'd react to medications. Many different ideas had been discussed, but none of the previous suggestions about Jessica's basic problems seemed to really capture the whole picture, and her parents weren't sure how to proceed. "What exactly *is* her problem?" her bewildered parents asked me.

Ever since she'd been a toddler, Jessica had seemed distant. While other kids her age would happily stack blocks together or share a playhouse, Jessica preferred to sit alone and draw, moving away from other kids when they approached. In kindergarten, her pediatrician suggested a diagnosis of ADHD, and Jessica seemed to improve a bit with the medication he'd prescribed for her in early elementary school. Beginning in second grade, Jessica got help from the special education staff in learning how to be less rigid when it was time to move from task to task in the classroom. She had a lot of trouble making friends, preferring to sit alone instead of joining in with the others playing tag or swinging, and in class she kept falling behind in her work because she would get "stuck" on a certain idea.

Jessica's school had diagnosed her with an emotional/behavioral disability in order to give her special education help, but this unfortunately placed her with other students who had temper tantrums or were aggressive or agitated. She didn't throw things at her classmates, kick her teachers, or slam books onto her desk; she didn't attack her friends or scream in frustration.

I carefully reviewed Jessica's interactions with classmates and family members, and I observed her play interview interactions. The neuropsychological tests revealed that she scored as "high-average" in both intelligence and academic skills, and her parents told me about her almost obsessive interest in odd history topics over the previous few years. Combining all available information, we came up with a revised diagnosis of Asperger's syndrome—a condition on the mild end of the autistic disorders spectrum.

After a long discussion about this concept in our follow-up interview, Jessica's mom and dad started regaining their sense of direction. When her mom called me two weeks later to set up further "coaching" sessions for themselves, I could hear both relief and a touch of excitement in her voice at the prospect of taking some new approaches to her daughter's problems. The next time we met, her father was far less grim, and his usual demand for a clear-cut, simple solution had been replaced with a certain softness and forgiving flexibility.

Once we realized Jessica was coping with a problem on the autism spectrum, she made strides with training in groups and in family psychotherapy over the years. She learned helpful ways to interact with other students in social skills training groups in school, moving into outpatient clinic training groups in middle school. She got better and better at interacting with people through early high school, in response to sensitive coaching from her special education staff about what to do and what to avoid in trying to connect with peers. "Jessica," her coach would prompt during a role-playing session, "try this: If you want to play with Emily at recess, you could say, 'Hi, Emily. Do you want to play?'"

Participation in Girl Scouts and some carefully selected activities such as orchestra and stage crew boosted her self-esteem. Her grades improved when her parents began to closely monitor her homework and scheduled her study time carefully. Because trials of several medications yielded mixed results, her family stopped medication during middle school.

We arranged for Jessica to receive careful counseling about college planning, and her school submitted a formal application for an accommodation of extra time when taking the ACT. She's now attending a carefully selected small private college, with the benefit of support from the student disabilities office. She recently decided herself to consult again with her psychiatrist, hoping to find a new medication strategy for this stage of her life.

Types of Autism Spectrum Problems

Jessica was fortunate in that her experience with Asperger's syndrome was fairly mild, and her parents were able to get special help for her in time to make a real difference. The autistic spectrum disorders (ASD) (also called pervasive developmental disorders) are a group of related problems including not only Asperger's, but also autistic disorder (what many people call autism), pervasive developmental disorder–not otherwise specified (PDD-NOS), and a rare childhood condition called Rett disorder, which I'll discuss in chapter 11.

As you may already have realized, many of these diagnostic terms for problems on the autistic spectrum overlap. Still, they have a number of things in common. Each condition appears early in a child's life, and each affects three primary areas: social interaction, the ability to communicate ideas and feelings, and flexibility in adapting.

From time to time, it's not unusual for a child to behave oddly or seem shy. What differentiates children with an autism spectrum disorder is the *consistency* and *severity* of the unusual behavior that affects every part of their lives.

In this chapter, we'll discuss three separate types of autistic spectrum disorders, but keep in mind that many professionals believe these three main types overlap to such a degree that they should be considered as different levels of severity along the same disorder spectrum. The three main types include:

- *Autism or autistic disorder:* This condition seriously affects verbal and nonverbal communication as well as the ability to relate to others and includes various restricted, repetitive, or stereotyped behavior patterns.

- *Asperger's syndrome:* This milder condition features social deficits and certain types of unusual behavior patterns, without significant impairment in overall intelligence or basic language skills. Many experts think Asperger's syndrome overlaps with "high-functioning autism" (autism with minimal deficits in language, IQ, and/or adaptive skills) or nonverbal learning disabilities (which I discussed in chapter 6).

- *Pervasive Developmental Disorder–Not Otherwise Specified:* This category includes children with significant enough autistic symptoms to receive a diagnosis, but who don't fit completely into either of the other two categories just listed.

A Growing Problem?

If you think your child might have an autistic spectrum disorder and you start doing some reading in this area, you'll soon discover quite a bit of controversy on just about every aspect of these puzzling conditions. Historically, experts suggested that one out of every five hundred children had some type of autistic spectrum disorder, including autism itself, which was thought to occur only in one out of every two thousand to five thousand children. More recent reviews have suggested that one in a thousand children may have autism itself. The current estimated chance of having some type of autistic spectrum disorder is one in 150 to 200 children. The Centers for Disease Control estimates that autism could affect one out of every 166 children—meaning 24,000 of the 4 million children born every year could be diagnosed with an autism spectrum disorder.

Sketchy available data on other specific subtypes of autism have suggested that Asperger's syndrome may occur less often than autism (2.5 per 10,000), but changes in the way scientists are thinking about the milder autistic spectrum disorders may signal a higher prevalence rate for Asperger's. Rett syndrome is clearly much more rare, occurring less often than once in every ten thousand births. In fact, at my clinic, I've never evaluated a child with Rett syndrome—nor have most of my colleagues.

In any case, experts do agree that there has been a dramatic increase in reported cases of autistic spectrum disorders in the past decade, especially in certain states such as California. Most serious, research-oriented experts believe that there aren't actually that many more cases of autism spectrum disorder now than before—it's just that we're more likely to identify it. This is because more people are aware of autism, there has been more research into the disorder, and because more services (such as intensive behavior modification) are now available only for a child with a formal diagnosis in this spectrum. In addition, professionals working in this area are clearly loosening the definition of autism to include milder forms. In my opinion, we're seeing more kids with autistic spectrum disorders mostly by redefining it to include milder cases. There is little sound evidence at this time that either genetics or environmental exposure to toxins is causing a big increase in the actual number of cases.

Core Deficits

If you're wondering whether your child might have autism, you've probably been noticing some unusual behavior since infancy or early childhood. You might be concerned that your child doesn't try to get your attention when he sees something that interests him. Perhaps you're wondering if it's normal the way your child shrinks from being touched or stands with her arms at her sides when she's being hugged. Maybe you've noticed your young child seldom looks you in the eye or spends a lot of time lining up toy dinosaurs alone in his bedroom. Autistic disorders have unique patterns of symptoms and areas of relative strength, and they typically have lifelong effects on how children learn to interact with others, take care of themselves, and participate in the community.

Not everybody with autism has exactly the same symptoms—it varies depending on where along the autistic spectrum one falls. To make things even more complex, many children with autism also have symptoms of depression, anxiety, attention-deficit/hyperactivity disorder (ADHD), or bipolar disorder. Because autism often occurs together with mental retardation or language disorders, educational planning must address all of these needs.

To be diagnosed with an autistic spectrum disorder, your child must have trouble communicating and getting along with other kids or making friends. You'll also notice eccentric, odd, or unusual stereotyped behavior, interests, and activities. For example, your child may be hypersensitive, so that sounds seem louder, lights brighter, taste sharper, and smells stronger. Although many kids with autism have below-average IQ and adaptive skills, some are of average or high intelligence.

Of course, not all children with social relationship problems or odd behaviors have ASD. Indeed, the stereotyped behavior patterns and social attachment problems that are seen in many kids subjected to difficult early environments can be mistaken for autism, when the cause is actually quite different. This is why careful evaluation, observation, and history-taking is vital in these situations.

Social Relationships

Most experts agree that the core problem in autistic spectrum disorders is the inability to relate to others socially. Put briefly, these kids just don't "get it" when it comes to the social give-and-take that most of us find effortless. From the beginning, children with autism aren't very interested in others and often prefer to be alone. Even as toddlers, they may not care whether their parents are paying attention to the same things that interest them. As these kids get older, they often have trouble with nonverbal communication skills—facial expressions, body posture, or eye contact. Your child may have trouble making friends, since this requires sharing interests and emotions with others. Children with autism may also not be very empathetic and may have trouble understanding someone else's feelings. You might notice that your child invades others' personal spaces. If a friend gets angry or is hurt, your child may seem unaware of what's going on.

This was Sharon's problem. As a preschooler, she had absolutely no interest in other kids. Instead, she'd happily sit beside them, playing with a truck by the hour. When other children came near, she'd get upset and refuse to involve others in what she was doing. Her parents were sad that she didn't have friends, but they told each other that at least she seemed content by herself. She'd softly repeat to herself phrases from her favorite movies, but otherwise she was silent, despite involvement in special-education-classroom and speech/language therapy.

Communication

Problems with both spoken language and nonverbal communication are real issues for kids with autism, which makes it hard for them to respond to others. Many of these children have significant language delays; some learn to speak later than average, while others never learn to speak at all. Some children with autism use language in odd ways, repeating words or sentences (called echolalia) or using only single words to communicate. Language problems may make behavioral problems worse. Eventually, frustrated by their inability to use language, kids with autism may start screaming.

Odd Behaviors

Many kids with autism just seem to have a lot of odd, eccentric, or stereotyped behaviors, which can be among the most challenging symptoms you can face. They may be oversensitive to certain sounds or have narrow, obsessive interests in mechanical items or rigid daily routines. They may get upset when a chair is out of place or their backpack is moved a fraction of an inch. Peculiar physical movements can include hand flapping, finger snapping, rocking, or head banging. These patterns are inappropriate, repetitive, and sometimes aggressive or even dangerous. Some children with autism may try to hurt themselves, gouging their skin or biting their fingers. They may show little or no sensitivity to pain. Any sort of change—such as ending play when it's time to go home—may trigger tantrums. These behaviors can be triggered by a variety of situations: the demands of a classroom, your commands or expectations, limitations in communication, social problems, or confusion about consequences.

Adolescence

The teenage years are a time of stress and confusion for most kids, no matter what kind of problems they're struggling with. Although some autistic behaviors can improve during the teenage years, others may get worse. Increased autistic or aggressive behavior may be one way some teens express their newfound tension and confusion. Adolescence is also a time when children become more socially sensitive. At a time when most teenagers are concerned with popularity, grades, and dates, teens with milder autism spectrum characteristics may realize that they are different from their peers. They may wonder why they aren't dating or why no one is expecting them to have a career. For some, the sadness that comes with this realization motivates them to try to learn new behaviors and acquire better social skills.

When I first saw Greg at the age of eight, he'd already been diagnosed with autism, mental retardation, and mixed receptive and expressive language disorder. He came to see me at the clinic when he became so aggressive that his in-home intensive therapy program was put on hold. His parents were frantic as they watched him deteriorate, refusing to work with his therapists and throwing tantrums several times a day.

Greg had developed classic symptoms of autism in early childhood. He was mute, he had significant social problems, and he would incessantly line up objects and tap his forehead with his palms. As you can imagine, his mother and father were confused and worried about these early problems, but they began to relax as the behaviors gradually improved during his toddler and preschool years. However, by the time Greg entered junior kindergarten, he still wasn't interested in playing with other kids his age.

When I saw him, he was involved in therapy at home that emphasized "floor time" with his parents, who would join in his activities and follow his lead. Floor time was supposed to improve his ability to relate to others— but he wasn't reacting well. He'd jump up from the floor and race around the room or lash out at adults. When his mother asked him to come to the dinner table, he'd grab the nearest book and fling it across the room. His parents wondered if Greg had some type of brain disease or psychiatric illness. As he neared puberty, his moods would swing wildly from happiness to bleak depression.

Greg had been on several medications at different times for the last several years, including Strattera, Risperdal, Adderall, and Paxil, with mixed results. His parents were relatively pleased with his school program, which combined special and regular classes, and he was much calmer at school than at home. Although he had no close friends, he would speak to students at school and sometimes even play a game of tag or shoot some baskets with others. On the other hand, he'd put people off when he'd try to obsessively discuss his three main interests: Harry Potter, *The Cat in the Hat,* and vampires.

Noting how well he responded to the structure of his school program, I wasn't surprised that Greg never threw things or tried to hit adults during our testing sessions, although he was obviously still anxious. His parents had been worried that he might get out of control, but he never did. Each of the three mornings when he arrived at our center, he'd get disturbed when it was time to go to the testing room and start to cry. Once seated in the testing room, he'd cry, "Mommy, come back!" or "Mommy, Daddy, help!" Eventually, he was able to stay seated and play with a toy for a few minutes. He seemed to understand that if he was able to get work done, he could take a break to visit his mother. Each time he'd finish one test, he'd ask to see his mother, but after a short break with his parents, he had trouble separating from them. Once back in the testing room, however, he was able to settle down relatively quickly and completed three tasks with few disruptions. After a short snack break, he appeared to be more comfortable with the testing situation and became helpful and eager to please. Clearly, he was responding to the firm but supportive structure in our testing approach, which helped to ease his anxiety and the aggression associated with it. As testing progressed, he warmed up to the point that he would make piles of all the cards and ask to help the examiner put away the materials, echoing the examiner's earlier praise: "There you go!" he'd say cheerfully as he handed over a stack of cards. "Thank you, good job," he'd say.

Greg surprised his parents and school staff with a clear demonstration of nonverbal intelligence at the 10th percentile, higher than in any prior testing, although his verbal and language skills were still at the first to second percentiles. Even though this meant that his previous diagnosis with mental retardation was not fully accurate, we reconfirmed the rest of his condition—autism with language impairment.

I recommended that Greg continue in his special education program-ming with a strong emphasis on social and speech/language development. We also set up consultation sessions with his parents for behavior manage-ment strategies, suggested more structure for the in-home therapy ses-sions, and recommended his physician consider whether some of his behavior problems might be related to medication side effects.

Greg's parents struggled with their grief over their son's serious prob-lems that would probably limit his function throughout his life—but now they also realized they could learn ways to break the recent cycle of vio-lence that had so upset them. They now understood his problems in a way that gave them renewed hope.

What Causes Autism?

As you can see, autism can cause some distressing symptoms that can be a real challenge to cope with. It's clear that autistic spectrum disorders re-flect a problem in the developing brain. Although researchers can't claim yet to know exactly what causes it, there's growing evidence that it's linked to subtle abnormal changes in brain structure or differences in brain chemicals. In most cases, the onset of these problems is probably influ-enced by genetics and is much less likely to be triggered by the environ-ment or various toxins.

Brain studies have suggested that many different brain structures may play a role in the development of autism, including the cerebellum, cere-bral cortex, limbic system, corpus callosum, basal ganglia, and brain stem. It's possible that sudden, rapid head growth in an infant may be an early warning signal (although there are also other causes for spurts in head growth). If we're lucky, someday this kind of research might lead to early diagnosis and even effective biological prevention approaches for autism.

Heredity

Research suggests that autism is probably related to a combination of abnormal genes that affect brain development rather than a single "autism gene," beginning before birth or in the infant's first months. Indeed, families who have one child with autism have a higher risk of having a second, and an identical twin of a child on the autistic spectrum is quite likely to share the disorder.

Vaccines and Autism

In the past few years, a growing number of parents and some professionals have suggested a possible link between autism and the use of thimerosal, a mercury-based preservative once included in several vaccines, such as the measles-mumps-rubella (MMR) vaccine. Although mercury is no longer used in childhood vaccines in the United States, some parents still worry about an autism-vaccination link. However, a growing collection of well-designed, large-scale studies have failed to show a link between thimerosal and autism.

Diet/Allergies

Other parents suspect their child's autism might be caused by digestive system abnormalities, although more and more scientific evidence hasn't found any proof. As more good research is completed and published, parents will hopefully have less to worry about in this area.

Diagnosis

While many parents may not want to label their child as having an autism spectrum disorder, the earlier the diagnosis is made, the earlier treatment can begin. This is important, since evidence over the last fifteen years indicates that intensive early intervention and the best possible educational settings for at least two years during preschool and kindergarten time can improve the outlook for most young children with ASD.

Unfortunately, not every child is diagnosed this early. Cathy was referred to us for a neuropsychological evaluation during fifth grade because her psychologist was trying to figure out if she had ADHD, anxiety disorder, a combination of the two—or perhaps something else. Her behavior patterns over the years were contradictory and often confusing, and her parents were frustrated in their efforts to help her. No one had ever been able to figure out exactly what the problem was.

"Cathy is a Jekyll and Hyde personality," her mother told me. "Sometimes she's so sweet, nice, and caring," her father added, "but at other times she's vicious and manipulative." Occasionally greedy and untruthful, she seemed to delight in pinching and slapping her little brother. She even turned her anger against her peers and didn't seem to have any idea about the consequences of her actions toward others. One day, when her only friend didn't cooperate after Cathy told her where to stand during a game of Frisbee, Cathy grabbed her around the throat in a choke hold. When her friend burst into tears, Cathy was shocked, released her friend, and fled.

Alarmingly, she showed no remorse after punching, kicking, or choking other children. However, she was only occasionally aggressive, because she usually preferred to play alone, and because most of her classmates were afraid of her reactions and put off by her unusual manner. Fortunately for her parents, who were horrified when they got calls from school after such incidents, most of the aggression occurred at home or during play dates her parents arranged. She tended to be stubborn and didn't back down until she got what she wanted. One day, her parents told me, when it was time to go to school, she absolutely refused to put down her action figures until she'd finished the story she was enacting.

Yet others saw a very different Cathy. "How polite and well-mannered she is!" neighbors said when Cathy's family walked around the block and visited with their friends briefly as a group. Sunday school was also a bright spot, where Cathy actually liked her teacher's strict focus on lessons and routine. This was the same little girl who wasn't able to play a simple board game without wanting to strangle the child she was playing with.

"It's true we're not very consistent in disciplining Cathy," her parents confessed. They'd get so frustrated they'd lose their temper, threaten punishments, and sometimes resort to spanking. To their dismay, time-outs seemed to have no effect on her whatsoever. The only person who made significant headway with her was her second-grade teacher, who emphasized Cathy's positive behaviors, gave her responsibilities, and set up a daily pattern of "happy grams" to send home.

Although people described her as an introverted child who was quite content to play by herself, drifting alone in her own little world, her parents didn't think she was seriously sad or depressed. She could be quiet, appeared worried at times, and had trouble disengaging from her favorite solitary play activity, but she didn't express direct worries or have specific fears. By the time I saw her, she was beginning to be interested in making friends with other kids, but she was so controlling that few were willing to put up with her. "Come here!" she'd order. "We're going to play basketball now!" she'd tell another.

When I talked to Cathy during a play interview, I found that she was mildly inattentive, slightly overactive, and very impulsive. Testing showed excellent academic skills, which was no surprise, since she'd been placed in an advanced reading group during first grade and enrolled in gifted and talented programming at school twice a week in second grade. Her parents were concerned that her writing had become sloppy in recent years, despite a history of well-developed fine motor skills and previous pride in writing neatly, but testing of fine motor coordination, drawing skill, and penmanship were all average.

When reviewing the testing together, I told Cathy's parents that she was quite intelligent, but her specific skills ranged from below average to above average. Identifying her inconsistent attention and poor social communication skills in contrast with her superior IQ helped her parents understand why her performance frequently slipped.

We diagnosed Cathy with Asperger's syndrome and recommended a multifaceted treatment program, including parent training, social skills training, psychotherapy, and possible medication and special education.

What I Look for During an Evaluation

When I evaluate a child, the first things I look for are key behavioral characteristics that are related to the core deficits of individual problems. Some of the typical behaviors of children with an autism spectrum disorder may be apparent as early as the first year of life. In Cathy's case, those core-deficit "red flags" included her problems in social situations and unusual behavior during temper tantrums.

Your own observations and concerns about your child's development are of great importance. If you're at all worried about your child's behavior and you're wondering about autism, pay closest attention to her social responsiveness. Perhaps you've noticed that your son obsessively lines up action figures, repeats what others say to him, or throws tantrums when you ask him to move from one activity to something else that he usually enjoys. Maybe you've noticed how your daughter ignores the other children in the class, and you remember that she never really seemed to have a friend. Reviewing family videotapes, photos, and baby albums can help you remember when you first started noticing each of these problem behaviors. Looking at baby calendars and old diaries may help you remember when your child reached certain developmental milestones—took her first step, started playing with blocks, first smiled or clapped.

If you suspect an autistic spectrum disorder, make sure to mention your concerns during a developmental screening at the next "well child" checkup with your family doctor. If your child's pediatrician doesn't routinely check your child's development skills, ask for this type of screening if you have concerns. There are a number of basic screening tests for autism that your pediatrician can use—so ask if you're concerned.

SCREENING TESTS FOR AUTISM

Several screening instruments have been developed to quickly gather information about a child's social and communicative development, including:

- the Checklist of Autism in Toddlers (CHAT)
- the Modified Checklist for Autism in Toddlers (M-CHAT)
- the Screening Tool for Autism in Two-Year-Olds (STAT)
- the Social Communication Questionnaire (SCQ) for children four years of age and older

Some screening tests rely solely on a parent's responses to a questionnaire, and some rely on a combination of observations by parents and the screening professional. But no matter what, the experts are looking at several key items—such as social interaction or interest—that seem to set kids with autism apart from other kids before the age of two or three years. In particular, the pediatrician will be interested to see if your young child lacks "social referencing," such as whether your child looks at you when he discovers something new and interesting or tries to show you the discovery.

Of course, your child's pediatrician or other primary care physician can't come up with an individual diagnosis from a single screening test, but he or she can identify which children may need to be referred for more specific testing. Keep in mind, however, that these screening methods aren't often precise enough or sensitive enough to identify young children with mild ASD, such as those with high-functioning autism or Asperger's syndrome. That's why in recent years experts have come up with new tests to screen for Asperger's syndrome and high-functioning autism that concentrate on social and behavioral problems in children who don't have significant language delay. The Autism Spectrum Screening Questionnaire (ASSQ), the Australian Scale for Asperger Syndrome, and the Childhood Asperger Syndrome Test (CAST) are examples of screening tools that are sometimes used in this effort.

If Your Doctor Suspects ASD

If your child's doctor sees any of the key indicators of ASD, you may be referred for a consultation with one of the specialists mentioned in chapter 4, or for a comprehensive evaluation by a multidisciplinary team. To merit a diagnosis of ASD, significant problems must appear in social relationships, communication, and stereotyped behaviors. At this point, the doctor's diagnosis must be both comprehensive and careful, in order to accurately rule in or rule out an ASD or other developmental problem, and to estimate the seriousness of the ASD.

Because ASDs are complex and may involve other brain or genetic problems, the most comprehensive evaluations sometimes include brain and genetic assessment, along with in-depth intelligence and language testing. The evaluator may recommend a test to diagnose autism, such as the Autism Diagnosis Interview–Revised (ADI-R), which includes a structured interview about the child's communication, social interaction, and repetitive behaviors. Other tests involve observations of your child in different situations with and without your presence, such as the Autism Diagnostic Observation Schedule (ADOS).

Your doctor also may order tests of your child's hearing or for possible lead exposure or metabolic problems. Although some hearing loss can occur in children with ASD, many children with ASD may at first be incorrectly thought to have such a loss.

Understanding the Results

After the diagnostic team has thoroughly evaluated your child and come up with a formal diagnosis, they'll meet with you to explain the results. This can be a really difficult time. Although you may have been aware that something wasn't quite right with your child, to hear those words—*Your child has an autistic spectrum disorder*—might feel like a devastating blow. I know this is a rough time to focus on asking questions, but while evaluation team members are all together is the best chance you'll have to ask questions and get recommendations on what to do next. You'll want to leave this meeting with the names of professionals who will help determine treatment.

QUESTIONS TO ASK

1. How severe is my child's condition?
2. What can I expect from my child?
3. What's the prognosis for the future?
4. What's the next step?
5. Can you give me the names of experts with whom I can discuss treatment?
6. Are there local support groups that can help?

Treatment

Once your child has been diagnosed with an autism spectrum disorder, you'll face the next question: *Now what?* It's not unusual for parents to quail at this awesome responsibility. But take heart: there are things you can do to help your child, and the sooner you start, the better. It's important to remember that regardless of where your child falls on the autistic spectrum, treatment to improve function is available, even though claims for cures may be overblown. The basic social problems in autism can't typically be treated with medicine (although some people with autism may take medicine to lessen aggressive behavior or attention problems). Instead, children with autism are taught skills to help them do the things that are hard for them and coaxed (or even pressured) into greater participation with the rest of us. The best results are usually seen with children who start treatment in the preschool years.

As you begin to look at treatment options and at the types of aid available, you may find it useful to keep a notebook including a record of the doctors' reports and evaluations, so that eligibility for special programs will be documented. Learn everything you can about special programs for your child, because the more you know, the more effectively you can advocate. Although there's no single "best" treatment package for every child with ASD, most professionals agree that a highly structured, specialized program works best—and the sooner the better. However, this doesn't mean you have to rush out and sign up with the first treatment center you find. Before you make decisions about your child's treatment, you'll want to do your homework. Learn as much as you can, look at all the options, and make your decision based on your child's needs. You may want to visit public schools in your area to see the types of programs they offer to special needs children.

Any effective treatment program for a child with autism will build on the child's interests, offer a predictable schedule, teach tasks in a series of simple steps, actively engage the child's attention in highly structured activities, and reinforce positive behavior. Your involvement is a major factor in treatment success. You'll work with teachers and therapists to identify the behaviors that need to be changed and what skills need to be taught. Recognizing that parents are their child's earliest teachers, more programs are beginning to train parents to continue the therapy at home.

Questions About Potential Treatments

The Autism Society of America offers the following guidelines about potential treatments:

- Will the treatment harm my child? (Are there painful treatments used?)
- Has the treatment been scientifically validated?
- Does the program call for any special testing?
- How will the treatment be integrated into my child's current program?

The National Institute of Mental Health adds a few other questions:

- How successful has the program been for other children?
- How many children have gone on to placement in a regular school and how have they performed?
- Do staff members have training and experience working with children and adolescents with autism?
- How are activities planned and organized?
- Are there predictable daily schedules and routines?
- How much individual attention will the child receive?
- How is progress measured? Will the child's behavior be closely observed and recorded?
- Will the child be given tasks and rewards that are personally motivating?
- Is the environment designed to minimize distractions?
- Will the program prepare me to continue the therapy at home?
- What is the cost, time commitment, and location of the program?

Information in this box is reprinted courtesy of the National Institute of Mental Health.

Special Education Programs

Special education programs tailored to your child's individual needs are often the most effective available form of treatment, especially if they involve intensive behavior modification. These programs teach the child to communicate (sometimes by pointing or using pictures or sign language) and to interact with others. Basic living skills, such as how to cross a street safely or ask for directions, are also emphasized. A good treatment program might also include speech therapy, physical therapy, and/or occupational therapy.

Behavior Modification

Many of the interventions used to treat children with autism are based on the theory of applied behavior analysis (ABA), which simply means that behavior rewarded is more likely to be repeated than behavior ignored. Although ABA is a theory, many people also use the term to describe a specific treatment approach, and it's become widely accepted as an effective treatment. The goal of this type of behavioral management is simple: reinforce desirable behaviors and reduce undesirable ones. In fact, thirty years of research has demonstrated the usefulness of these behavioral methods in reducing inappropriate behavior and improving communication, learning, and social behavior in children with ASD.

The basic research, done by Ivar Lovaas and his colleagues at UCLA, recommends an intensive, one-on-one child-teacher interaction for forty hours a week. ABA often involves a structured interaction referred to as "discrete trial training"—an intensive approach with a professional who breaks tasks down into short, simple tasks (or "trials"). This approach is designed to teach basic daily living skills, such as dressing and eating, to more involved skills such as interacting with friends. When a task has successfully been completed, a reward is offered, reinforcing the behavior or task. Here's a sample of a discrete trial training exercise:

- a request to perform a specific action
- a response from the child
- a reaction from the therapist

In many parts of the United States, intensive in-home behavior modification programs using applied behavior analysis and discrete trial programs are available for up to thirty or forty hours a week. These programs are particularly effective in teaching the basic skills children need, such as paying attention to adults, maintaining eye contact, and following directions.

Typically, I recommend that children with a formal diagnosis of autism receive intensive behavior modification up to forty hours a week during the preschool years, often along with other methods such as speech/language therapy and "floor time," in which parents get down on the floor to play with their child. Floor time is a lot like play therapy; if the child wants to twirl a ball, the parent follows the child's lead, trying to get the child to interact rather than demanding that the child follow the parent's lead in an activity.

PECS

The inability to communicate is one of the main problems in autism; while some children with autism do speak, others never learn to talk. If this is a problem with your child, the child's doctor may recommend a communication program such as Picture Exchange Communication System (PECS) as a way of communicating with children who don't speak. With PECS, your child hands you a picture of something he wants, which you immediately honor. This way, it's easy for a child with autism to communicate with anyone. Verbal prompts aren't used, and eventually the pictures can be put together to form simple sentences. As PECS training proceeds, words are introduced and your child is taught to comment and to answer direct questions. Many preschoolers using PECS also begin developing speech.

Education

As soon as your child's disability has been identified, instruction should begin. Effective programs will teach early communication and social interaction skills. In children younger than age three, appropriate interventions may take place in a "birth-to-three" or "early childhood intervention" center and may also involve work in the home or a child care center. These treatments target specific problems in learning, language, imitation, attention, motivation, compliance, and interaction using behavioral methods, communication, occupational and physical therapy, along with social play interventions.

Children older than age three can usually enroll in individualized special education programs in their public school districts. High-functioning autistic children may be enrolled in mainstream classrooms and child care facilities, which can help them adapt their behavior to the behavior of normal children. However, if your child is overstimulated in a regular classroom, he may do better in a smaller, more structured environment. All through your child's school years, you'll want to be an active participant in the education program. Collaboration between parents and educators is essential in evaluating your child's progress.

Your Child's Rights

The education of children with autistic disorders was accepted as a public responsibility under the Education for All Handicapped Children Act of 1975 and has been reinforced with updates in the federal laws during the past three decades. Despite the federal mandate, however, the goals, methods, and resources available to treat kids with autism vary a lot from state to state and school system to school system.

Every child eligible for special programs must be given special education and services by the state. As you may recall from chapter 3, the Individuals with Disabilities Education Act (IDEA) is a federal program that assures a free and appropriate public education for children with diagnosed educational problems. Autistic spectrum disorders are included in this category.

Usually, children with autism are placed in public schools and the school district pays for services, which can include a speech therapist, occupational therapist, school psychologist, social worker, school nurse, and classroom aide. By law, the public schools must prepare and carry out a set of instruction goals for every child in a special education program known as an Individualized Education Program (IEP), which is basically an agreement between the school and the family about what the child's goals are and how they'll be met.

Medications

If other methods don't ease some of your child's problems with ASD, medications can sometimes be used to treat certain symptoms. This is particularly important if your child's symptoms are severe. If he is aggressive, injures himself, or has frequent tantrums, I encourage you to consult a psychiatrist—even as early as preschool age. Medication may improve your child's behavior and make it easier for him to benefit from the other types of treatments I've already discussed.

The medications typically used in ASD were developed to treat similar symptoms in other disorders. However, many available medications are prescribed "off-label," which means they haven't officially been approved for use in children, but the doctor prescribes the medications because they are appropriate for your child. Your doctor may try a variety of medications, depending on your child's problems. This is because no drug has been found to directly fix the basic social problems in ASD, but some drugs can help ease associated problems such as inattention or anxiety.

Stimulant medications such as methylphenidate (Ritalin), used effectively in children with ADHD, have also been prescribed for children with autism. These medications may control impulsivity and hyperactivity in some children, especially those with higher-functioning ASD.

Studies of the newer atypical antipsychotics are being conducted on children with autism, including risperidone (Risperdal) and olanzapine (Zyprexa). These are used more often than traditional antipsychotics such as haloperidol (Haldol), largely because they are not sedating.

The modern antidepressants called selective serotonin reuptake inhibitors, such as fluoxetine (Prozac) or sertraline (Zoloft), are sometimes prescribed for symptoms of anxiety, depression, or obsessive-compulsive disorder that may appear in children with ASD. Seizures occur in a significant minority of kids with ASD (most often in those who have low IQ or no expressive speech); they can be treated with an anticonvulsant such as carbamazepine (Tegretol) or valproic acid (Depakote). Although medication may reduce the number of seizures, it can't always eliminate them.

In the long run, further research needs to be done to ensure the usefulness and safety of drugs used to treat children and adolescents. Because a child with ASD may not respond in the same way to medications as typically developing children, it's important for you to work with a doctor who has experience with autism.

Alternative Treatments

In an effort to do everything possible to help their children, many parents seek out alternative treatments. But while an unproven treatment may seem to help a child, it's hard to tell whether it really helped unless it's been studied in a careful, consistent, scientific way.

Sensory Integration

Because they can't regulate their senses very well, children with autism often either under- or overreact to sounds, taste, touch, or bright lights. Sensory integration therapy, usually offered by occupational, physical, or speech therapists, focuses on desensitizing the child and helping to reorganize sensory information. For example, if a child resists being touched because the slightest pressure feels like a slap, therapy might include having the child handle lots of different materials with different textures. In an effort to reduce oversensitivity to sound, the child might need to listen to different sound frequencies coordinated to the level of impairment.

It's important to understand that these sensory treatments may reduce some autistic behaviors, but there isn't enough research to recommend them as a primary intervention for the full range of core autistic problems—especially social and communication difficulties.

Diets

Dietary interventions are based on the idea that food allergies or an insufficiency of a specific vitamin or mineral may cause some symptoms of autism. In the last few years some parents and experts have discussed the use of secretin to treat autism. Secretin is a substance approved as a single dose by the U.S. Food and Drug Administration to aid in diagnosis of a gastrointestinal problem. Anecdotal reports have suggested it may improve autism symptoms, including sleep patterns, eye contact, language skills, and alertness. However, several clinical trials in the last few years have found no significant improvements in symptoms of patients who received secretin.

Support Groups

Having a child with autism can be challenging to the entire family. At the same time, support and training for parents and siblings is an important component of treatment. In fact, learning more about autism and how to manage symptoms can reduce household stress and improve the child's function.

As soon as your child is diagnosed, it's a good idea to talk to your doctor and check out support groups available in your town. Family, friends, public agencies, and national or community organizations are all potential resources. Contact with other families who have an autistic child, and who can share the concerns and daily challenges, can be incredibly helpful. Local and national groups can help connect families and provide much-needed sources of information. (See appendix B for contact information.)

Prognosis

Despite the day-to-day problems, many people with autism make significant gains through appropriate early treatment and end up leading fulfilling, happy lives on their own or with help from friends and family. Most children with autism like school, and some can attend regular classes with everyone else. They have individual tastes and enjoy different activities. Some go on to vocational school or college, get married, and have successful careers.

Good quality long-term research into which treatments work the best is still going on. Despite growing strong evidence for important short-term benefits during childhood and adolescent years, you should be careful about relying on specific long-term benefits from any particular treatments.

Remaining Questions

Scientists have plenty of theories about the causes and symptoms of autistic spectrum disorders. Some of these ideas have been rejected—such as the idea that detached parents can make children autistic. At this point, almost all serious researchers and clinicians acknowledge that the basic psychological problem has something to do with a child's capacity to connect with other people—but no one is sure exactly how that develops. Is this inability to connect due to trouble with the capacity to think from another person's perspective? Is it a basic lack of integrated senses, including touch, balance, hearing, and seeing? Is there an imbalance in the child's capacity to deal with the "big picture" versus small details? While scientists continue investigating these important ideas—and the equally important genetic and brain-based causes—I believe that parents and professionals should focus their efforts on evaluating and treating the *social* problems these kids have, along with other attention and behavior control problems. The exact nature of the social problems in the autistic spectrum will become clearer over time. Until then, we can identify and improve the social function of a child with autism—we *can* make a difference!

9

Anxiety and Traumatic Disorders

NYONE WHO REMEMBERS what it was like to survive middle school knows just how anxiety-provoking childhood can be. But in addition to this "normal" anxiety and stress, children can suffer from anxiety disorders, just like adults. This was the case with Julie, age eight, who came to see me because of a long-standing history of anxiety symptoms. Almost every day at the beginning of school in the fall, she talked about not wanting to go to school, she worried about the teacher yelling at her, and she complained of stomachaches.

Looking back, these reactions weren't completely new. During kindergarten, Julie had seemed too concerned about how others would judge her ability to write and draw. She often had trouble completing schoolwork, and she wanted to rip up papers that weren't done perfectly. She was upset when she didn't finish things as fast as others. By first grade, she followed a rigid before-school routine and was fastidious about washing her hands with soap, although she didn't have other checking or cleaning rituals. She was afraid of storms and continued to obsessively worry about storms after they were over. She was fairly easygoing at school, but she was more rigid at home, getting upset when her parents asked her to do things that made her feel nervous.

Both her psychiatrist and I felt it was important for Julie and her parents to meet with a psychotherapist right away to deal with her school avoidance so it didn't become an ongoing pattern. Many children with school avoidance show other anxiety issues as well, and Julie's anxieties were treated in ongoing psychotherapy over the next several months.

Anxiety vs. Fear

Careful evaluation indicated that Julie had a real problem with anxiety, which we were able to treat successfully. But what's the difference between normal fears and a true anxiety disorder? Let's put it this way: *Fear* is a reaction to an actual danger, involving physical and mental tension that helps you spring into action to protect yourself from something that's happening. Once you know the danger has passed, the fear fades away.

The physical and mental tensions of *anxiety* seem a lot like fear. Anxiety can be a helpful warning of more subtle or complex risks or dangers. But with dysfunctional anxiety, there isn't always anything actually happening to trigger that intensity of feeling—or the emotional response can be out of proportion to the trigger. The feeling of anxiety is coming from the *anticipation* of future danger or something bad that *could* happen—there may be no danger happening now at all. For example, if you step off a curb and you jump back because a truck almost hits you—that's *fear*. If you see a parked truck in the distance and your heart starts to pound and waves of terror sweep over you because you once almost got hit by a truck, that's *dysfunctional anxiety*.

Stressful life events, such as starting school, moving, or losing a parent in death or divorce, are usually things that kids can live through. Sometimes, however, they can trigger the onset of an anxiety disorder. Other times, an anxiety disorder seems to appear out of nowhere—you don't have to experience a specific stress. If left untreated, however, children with anxiety disorders are at higher risk to perform poorly in school, to have less developed social skills, and to be more vulnerable to substance abuse.

As you'll see in this chapter, psychologists have tried to define the boundaries between ordinary fear and anxiety. I'll be discussing four of the important anxiety disorders:

- generalized anxiety disorder
- post-traumatic stress disorder
- specific phobias
- obsessive-compulsive disorder

How Common Are Anxiety Disorders?

Anxiety disorders are among the most common emotional and behavioral problems in childhood and adolescence. At least ten out of every one hundred children and adolescents ages nine to seventeen experience some kind of anxiety disorder (girls more often than boys). Moreover, about half of children and adolescents with anxiety disorders have a second diagnosis, such as depression or an additional anxiety disorder.

Colleen started psychotherapy when she kept getting angry every time one of her kindergarten girlfriends decided to play with someone else. She'd get worried that she'd lost the friend, and she'd get so angry she'd smack the little girl in frustration. During first grade, a school evaluation

It's a Matter of Timing and Degree

The problems in this chapter and the closely related mood issues in the next chapter can be temporary, mild, or related to particular situations or events in your child's life. Time-limited problems like this that represent reactions to stress, and that fade away without formal treatment, are called adjustment disorders. An otherwise resilient child can develop anxiety and mood problems if he finds himself in an ongoing tough situation, such as facing a bully in the classroom or dysfunction in the family. I believe it's still important to understand the basic symptoms and struggles that your child is coping with so you can provide the best support and change the situation. It can be challenging for parents and seasoned professionals to judge with precision how serious a problem in this area can be. The bottom line: try to understand and make a plan for supporting your child's problems in these areas, rather than sweeping them under the carpet.

found a mild learning disability in math, which was triggering stomachaches and even panicky feelings every time the class did "minute madness," in which they had to complete a certain number of addition or subtraction problems in sixty seconds. She began to compare herself negatively with the students sitting near her in the classroom—"I'm so stupid, I can never do this!"—even during reading, which was an area of strength for her. It appeared that Colleen was developing an anxiety disorder that could affect her reactions in a variety of social and academic situations.

By the time I saw Colleen in fourth grade to clarify some of her problems, she had gotten better in social situations and was getting appropriate accommodations in the classroom, which helped ease her anxiety episodes over schoolwork. However, two other distressing problems were developing: First, her mother had gotten a new job that required some out-of-town travel, and Colleen started worrying about her mother's safety every time she left. Second, Colleen began to lose confidence in her soccer ability, hesitating at key moments during games, feeling sick on the field, and doubting herself.

Fortunately, her parents recognized these familiar patterns, so they scheduled her for a few return visits to the same counselor who had helped her overcome the earlier tendency toward anxiety reactions. Working with the counselor again, Colleen learned some new anxiety-management strategies for the changing situations she faced as she got older.

Core Problems in Anxiety Disorders

Children and adolescents with anxiety disorders typically experience intense fear, worry, or uneasiness that can last for long periods and significantly affect their lives. If not treated early, anxiety disorders can lead to repeated school absences, problems with friends, low self-esteem, and substance abuse.

Research in this area can be difficult to do, since children's fears often change as they age. In general, experts suspect that a child's basic temperament may play a role in the development of recurrent excessive anxiety. For example, if your child tends to be shy and quiet in unfamiliar situations, she might be at risk for anxiety problems.

Your child's age is also important. It's perfectly normal for preschoolers to be afraid of the dark and monsters under the bed. It's normal in elementary school for children to worry about whether anyone will play with them at recess or whether they'll succeed on the one-minute math test. Likewise, many middle school kids are anxious about whom they'll sit with at the lunch table. You might want to watch for signs of anxiety disorders when your child is between ages six and eight, because during these years children typically become less afraid of the dark and imaginary creatures, and *more* anxious about school performance and social relationships.

We also know that children and adolescents are more likely to have an anxiety disorder if either parent has this problem, but we don't know how much of that is due to biology, environment, or a mixture of both. More data are needed to clarify how anxiety tendencies can be inherited.

General Treatment Overview

If you or your child's teacher have noticed anxiety symptoms in your child, you should consider asking the child's pediatrician or guidance counselor for a referral to a mental health professional. I'd suggest you look for someone who specializes in cognitive behavior therapy with children and teens, and who's used to working with families. If symptoms are extreme or haven't responded to good psychotherapy in the past, you might want to consult a psychiatrist to discuss antianxiety medications.

Lots of treatment methods are available for kids with anxiety disorders once an accurate diagnosis has been reached. Your child might benefit from cognitive behavior treatment, where he'd learn how to handle his fears by changing the way he thinks and behaves. Relaxation training and biofeedback techniques can help ease stress, tension, and anxiety. Other techniques such as modeling, imagining and visualizing, modifying self-talk, and challenging irrational beliefs can be effective. With all of these methods, children are first taught to recognize early signs of anxiety and then how to use coping techniques. Parent training and family therapy can be quite helpful, too.

If these methods don't work, you might want to consider antidepressant or antianxiety medication, because some kids with anxiety disorders benefit from a combination of these treatments.

In the next section, I'll discuss several important kinds of anxiety problems in more detail, including particular symptoms and possible causes. You'll see that these patterns overlap to a great extent; usually, a child experiences more than one type of anxiety pattern. The anecdotes I'll include will show you how the different types can occur together or evolve from one to another over time.

Generalized Anxiety Disorder

Generalized anxiety disorder (GAD) is just what it sounds like—a problem of excess unrealistic anxiety. Kids with this problem have extreme, unrealistic, nonstop worries about everyday life activities that last at least six months. In children and adolescents, GAD used to be called overanxious disorder of childhood (and some professionals still use this term). Children with this pattern experience much more chronic and excessive worry, along with physical symptoms of trembling, aches, sleeplessness, stomach upsets, dizziness, or irritability.

Their worries cascade thick and fast: "What if I don't get an A on that test? What if I don't score any baskets in the big game? I'm afraid I'm going to be late for homeroom!" You may also notice your child seems self-conscious, tense, and has a strong need for reassurance. She may complain about stomachaches or other discomforts that don't seem to have a physical cause.

This was what had happened to John, who appeared in my clinic with a fairly common combination of generalized anxiety in addition to a specific phobia. Ever since he was a baby, he'd tended to react fearfully to new people, animals, loud sounds, and car rides, although he could sometimes handle these situations calmly. For the first few days of each school year, he'd have trouble separating from his parents. He tended to respond better to warm teachers and withdrew from more formal or strict instructors. He'd experienced night terrors as a preschooler, and by the time he came for evaluation at age eleven, he was having regular nightmares. John's parents had tried to manage his frequent anxiety attacks over the years with the help of supportive teachers, until an incident during fifth grade aggravated his symptoms to the point that they sought professional help.

As a prank, his classmates tucked the class gerbil into John's lunch box a few minutes before lunch break. As expected, upon discovering the gerbil he reacted intensely—especially when the gerbil nipped his finger while escaping. The other children were delighted when John panicked and ran from the room. He was sent home for the rest of the day when he couldn't calm down for the afternoon lessons. Over the next few days, his previous wariness about animals developed into a full-blown phobia: He couldn't visit his aunt's house because of her cat, and he'd walk in the other direction if a dog barked. The class gerbil had to be moved to another room because he would hyperventilate and sweat in its presence.

In John's situation, we recommended a fairly standard treatment plan, which was coordinated by a child psychologist colleague. First, we began a carefully planned combination of individual play therapy and cognitive behavior therapy. Along with this, the psychologist coached John's parents on how to gradually reexpose him to situations with animals in which he had previously been comfortable. Supportive work by the guidance counselor with both John and his classmates helped him return to his previous level of comfort with furry animals during a relatively brief five-week period. His parents and his psychologist wisely decided to continue psychotherapy after that time to address his underlying long-term anxiety problems in a variety of ways.

Phobias

As you can see in John's situation, phobias often appear together with more general anxiety patterns and seem to increase as children grow older. Children with specific phobias suffer from an intense, unrealistic fear reaction to a specific object or situation, such as spiders, dogs, or attending school. The level of fear is usually inappropriate to the situation, and the child usually knows the fear is irrational. This fear can lead to the avoidance of common, everyday situations. The most common specific phobia in the general population is fear of animals—particularly dogs, snakes, insects, and mice. About 2 percent of eleven-year-old children are believed to have at least one phobia; that number rises to about 5 percent among fourteen- to sixteen-year-old teens. Social phobia, a fear of humiliating oneself in public, is one of the major phobias among adolescents.

Because kids with phobias try to avoid the objects and situations they fear, the disorder can greatly restrict their lives. Of course, mild discomfort about a situation or specific item or animal isn't a full-blown phobia. You should investigate if your child is developing a phobia if the fear interferes with your child's ability to play, go to school, socialize with friends, or live a normal life.

A child who has a particularly frightening or threatening experience with an animal or in certain situations may develop a specific phobia. For instance, a child who's been bitten by a vicious dog may come to fear all dogs, no matter how harmless or friendly. Witnessing a traumatic event in which others experience harm or extreme fear is another risk factor for specific phobia, as is repeated information or warnings about potentially dangerous situations or animals. It's also possible that your child can learn fears from others. For instance, if you respond with intense fear and anxiety whenever you see a harmless garden snake, your child could learn to respond the same way.

Treatment

Phobias are usually very treatable, and with proper care almost all phobia patients can completely overcome their fears. In fact, most children who get treated completely overcome their fears for the rest of their lives.

Cognitive behavior therapy is particularly effective and usually the first choice of treatment for phobias. During this type of behavior ther-

---

Emotional and Physical Reactions in Phobias

- feelings of panic, dread, horror, or terror
- automatic and uncontrollable reactions that seem to "take over" a child's thoughts
- rapid heartbeat, shortness of breath, stomach tightening or "butterflies," trembling, and an overwhelming desire to flee the situation— the physical reactions associated with extreme fear
- extreme measures taken to avoid the feared object or situation
- anticipatory anxiety (avoiding situations or objects that trigger a response of intense fear and anxiety)

apy, your child will meet with a trained therapist and confront the feared object or situation in a carefully planned, gradual way to learn to control the physical reactions of fear. First, your child will imagine the feared object or situation, then gradually begin to look at pictures depicting the object or situation. Finally, your child will actually experience the situation or come in contact with the feared object. By confronting rather than running away from the object of fear, the child gets used to it and can lose the terror, horror, panic, and dread.

Although behavioral therapy is the main method of treatment, case reports have documented improvement of symptoms with the use of certain SSRI antidepressants (such as Prozac) to control the panic experienced during a phobic situation, as well as the anxiety aroused by anticipation of that situation.

Post-Traumatic Stress Disorder

Some children who have been exposed to a traumatic event, such as a sexual or physical assault, a death, a car accident, or a natural disaster, may develop post-traumatic stress disorder (PTSD).

Symptoms

It's important to realize that children may not show exactly the same symptoms as adults, and young children may show few symptoms, in part because they aren't capable of verbally describing their feelings and experiences. Instead, young children may report more generalized fears such as fear of strangers or separation, sleep disturbances, and a preoccupation

---

Common Symptoms of PTSD

- "reliving" the traumatic event (such as with flashbacks and nightmares)
- avoidance behaviors (such as avoiding places related to the trauma)
- emotional numbing

with certain words or symbols. They might avoid situations that may or may not be related to the trauma. Because they don't typically have the verbal and conceptual skills to cope effectively with sudden stress, they look to family members for comfort. Some children in this situation may repeat the trauma during play or may regress; for instance, they may stop being toilet trained or become unexplainably more aggressive.

Preschoolers (through about age five) are particularly vulnerable to disruption of their previously secure world. Abandonment is a major fear in this age group, and children who have lost family members and even pets or toys will need special reassurance. You may notice thumb sucking, bed-wetting, fears of the dark or of animals, clinging, night terrors, loss of bladder or bowel control, constipation, speech problems or stuttering, or appetite changes.

Elementary-school-aged children may not experience visual flashbacks or amnesia, but they may recall events related to the trauma out of sequence. They also may form "omen" ideas, suggesting that there were warning signs that predicted the trauma. This can lead children to believe that if they pay enough attention, they'll be able to recognize future "warning signs." You may notice your school-aged child reenacting the trauma in play and drawings, compulsively repeating some aspect of the upsetting event.

Regressive behavior can occur at any age, but it's particularly common during preschool through elementary school. You may notice your child seems more irritable, whiny, or clingy. There may be aggressive behavior at home or school and competition with younger siblings for your attention. Your child may experience night terrors, nightmares, fear of the dark, and not want to go to school. She may seem uninterested in playing with her friends, losing interest or having trouble concentrating at school.

Peer reactions are especially significant in kids between the ages of eleven and thirteen, and your child may no longer be interested in being with his friends. Try to help your child understand that his feelings are appropriate. You may notice sleep or appetite problems, rebellion, or refusal to do chores. There may be school problems, such as fighting, withdrawal, loss of interest, or attention-seeking behavior. Your preteen may complain about physical problems such as vague aches, headaches, acne, or bowel problems.

Teenagers often experience the classic adult symptoms of PTSD, but they are also more likely than younger children or adults to become impulsive and aggressive. You may notice your teen complaining of headaches and tension, various psychosomatic symptoms such as rashes or bowel problems, and problems with appetite and sleep. Girls may begin having painful menstrual periods or stop menstruating completely. Your teen may seem more agitated or apathetic or may stop fighting with you over issues of parental control.

Not surprisingly, children and adolescents who have experienced traumatic events often develop other problems as well, such as fear, anxiety, depression, self-destructive behavior, feelings of isolation, poor self-esteem, difficulty in trusting others, and substance abuse. They may have trouble with friends and family, act out, and begin to do poorly in school.

Risk Factors

Three factors may increase the chance that a child will develop PTSD: the severity of the traumatic event, adults' reactions to the traumatic event, and how involved the child was in the traumatic event. The way your family members support each other and cope with the problem can also affect the severity of symptoms in your child, since studies show that children and teens with the most family support and least parental distress have fewer symptoms.

The type of trauma also influences the chances of developing PTSD. Traumas such as rape and assault are more likely to cause PTSD than other traumas—and the more traumatic events a child has experienced, the greater the chance of developing PTSD.

Sadly, traumatic events were at the heart of significant problems in the life of Anna, who had been adopted from an orphanage in Ukraine at age five. It soon became clear to her adoptive parents that she suffered with a serious mixture of PTSD symptoms, apparently reflecting sexual abuse during early childhood. Her situation was complicated by a condition called reactive attachment disorder, which interfered with her ability to form secure relationships with her warm adoptive parents.

Anna had spent her first two years living in poverty with her biological parents, and then her next three years in an understaffed Ukrainian orphanage. While no one knew much about those first two years, orphanage officials suspected she may have been sexually abused. Once Anna had moved into the orphanage, she would sometimes approach a male visitor and begin inappropriate sexual cuddling; at other times, she'd run away screaming in fear.

Since Anna hadn't gotten any psychological treatment in Ukraine, her reactions to men worsened once she came to the United States. These fears were particularly striking in light of her father's active, loving involvement and the supportive interest of several male relatives in the extended family. Her parents appropriately took her for psychotherapy right away. Over the next few months, her unique reactions to men were gradually replaced by a more settled reaction, but new problems arose that suggested more basic difficulties in forming emotional attachments. Anna had been abnormally compliant in the orphanage, but once adopted she became irrational and sometimes violent—screaming, hitting, breaking things, and biting. Sometimes she arbitrarily refused favorite foods or activities or gave flat, emotionless responses to her mother and older sister. At other times, she was demanding and clingy, with exclusive attachment to certain girls in her kindergarten class at her new school. She didn't seem to notice her friends' reactions when she became aggressive toward them.

Treatment

Although some resilient children's symptoms get better on their own, many others will continue to experience PTSD symptoms for years if not treated. Typically, cognitive behavior therapy is the most effective approach. This type of therapy begins by having the child discuss the traumatic event. Play therapy can be used to treat young children with PTSD who aren't able to deal with the trauma more directly. With the aid of games and drawings, the play therapist helps the child process traumatic memories. Relaxation and assertiveness training techniques are then taught as a way of managing anxiety. In addition, the child learns how to correct distorted thoughts related to the trauma.

Although there is some controversy about whether to expose children to the events that scare them, exposure-based treatments seem to be most relevant when memories or reminders distress the child. If exposure is used, the child can be exposed gradually and taught to relax while recalling the experiences. Through this procedure, the child learns not to be afraid of memories. This type of therapy also helps counteract a child's false beliefs, such as "I'm completely unsafe in the world."

Fortunately, Anna responded well to treatment. Psychological testing at that time showed she had strong nonverbal reasoning skills, and she learned English quickly. With her lively intellect, her response to intensive individual and family-oriented psychotherapy twice a week over the next two years was quite positive, and by age seven her attachment problems had mostly faded away.

Treatment is often paired with family therapy and parent education about PTSD symptoms and their effects, because it's as important for parents to understand the effects of PTSD in their child. In fact, research shows that the better the parents can cope with and support their child, the better their child will function. This is why it may be important for you to get treatment as well, so you can develop the necessary coping skills to help your children.

Obsessive-Compulsive Disorder

Everyone occasionally obsesses about some minor issue ("Did I turn off the iron? Did I lock the front door?") or experiences an eccentric need to perform an odd ritual or two. But kids with obsessive-compulsive disorder (OCD) have a far more relentless set of symptoms. They're plagued by persistent, recurring thoughts (obsessions) that reflect exaggerated anxiety or fears, such as being contaminated or behaving improperly. The obsessions may lead a child to perform a ritual or routine (compulsions), such as washing the hands, repeating phrases, or hoarding as a way of easing the anxiety caused by the obsession. About two in every one hundred teenagers struggle with OCD.

Symptoms

Children with OCD often worry that they're crazy or out of control because they know their behavior and thoughts aren't normal. In addition, they often don't feel well—either because of the general stress from their disorder or because of poor nutrition or lack of sleep. Many children with OCD are prone to stress-related ailments such as headaches and upset stomachs.

This disorder can appear in children as young as three, but more often it begins once kids are a bit older. Kids and adults usually have the same symptoms, although children often have more trouble describing their fears and experience frustration and problems with coping. Children with OCD also often suffer with additional anxiety disorders (such as panic disorder or social phobia), depression, disruptive behavior disorders (such as oppositional defiant disorder or attention-deficit/hyperactivity disorder), learning disorders, eating disorders, or tic disorders such as Tourette's syndrome. They can become so caught up in their obsessions and compulsions that they can no longer function at home or in school.

That's what happened to a client of mine I'll call Ashley, who in early childhood was already showing a short attention span. It took her forever to complete tasks around the house, and she became more meticulous and perfectionistic when she entered school. Specific obsessive-compulsive symptoms appeared more prominently by age ten, when she began to wash her hands endlessly and felt compelled to repeatedly touch certain objects. She apologized over and over for these actions. She often seemed to "zone out" in class or when being given instructions, struggled in following verbal instructions, and seemed to lack common sense. A psychiatrist diagnosed OCD along with some features of generalized anxiety, separation anxiety, subdued mood, and some evidence of withdrawal. Ashley was referred to us for neuropsychological evaluation because she also had a history of learning problems. At age three, she'd been placed in an early childhood exceptional education program with speech/language therapy and occupational therapy because of low-average receptive and expressive language skills. She'd struggled throughout her school career, especially in reading, writing, and math.

Cause

So far, experts haven't found a single, universal cause of OCD, but many cases appear to be related in part to a mixture of genetics, brain chemicals, and problems in brain communication.

Although experts haven't yet identified any specific genes for OCD, research suggests that heredity may play a role in some cases. Childhood-onset OCD tends to run in families (sometimes along with tic disorders). If you or your spouse has OCD, there's a slightly higher risk that your child will develop the condition, although the risk is still low.

Some experts believe that low levels of a brain chemical called serotonin are linked to OCD. Brain cells use serotonin to communicate with each other; symptoms improve when the person with OCD is given drugs that increase the brain concentration of serotonin (such as certain antidepressants, like Prozac). Brain scans also show that the brain cell circuits involved in OCD become normal after the person takes a serotonin-boosting medication or receives cognitive behavior psychotherapy.

Treatment

Most children with OCD improve with a combination treatment plan of SSRI antidepressants and a cognitive behavior treatment program—that's what helped Ashley. In particular, a type of behavioral therapy known as exposure and response prevention is useful in treating OCD. In this approach, a child is deliberately and voluntarily exposed to whatever triggers the obsessive thoughts, then is taught how to handle the anxiety and avoid performing the compulsive rituals. It's also essential that families work with the therapist and the child to learn how to manage the child's symptoms and participate effectively in behavioral and drug treatment.

Medication can be considered when children are experiencing significant OCD-related impairment or distress, and when cognitive behavior therapy is unavailable or isn't working well. Presently, only four anti-OCD medications have been approved by the U.S. Food and Drug Administration for use in children: clomipramine (Anafranil), fluoxetine (Prozac), fluvoxamine (Luvox), and sertraline (Zoloft). Doctors may still prescribe other available medications to children of any age that they deem appropriate, but many physicians prefer to use medication specifically approved for use in children.

Remaining Questions

Experts don't always agree about exactly how to use medication for children who are struggling with varying forms of anxiety. I firmly believe in trying psychosocial interventions first—except for a few extreme cases. I tell parents who want to give their children medication to ease their anxious distress, "*You're* the medicine."

When your child is in therapy, at some level, so are you. Whether you meet together as a family or participate in some form of parent training sessions, or you just consult with your child's therapist from time to time, your actions and feelings have a crucial impact on how your child learns to cope with the very human emotion of anxiety. Most important, you are sort of a cotherapist who should support the primary therapist's work. If you also have anxiety or related issues of your own, don't be embarrassed to face up to those issues and get some help for yourself. It could be the best thing you ever did for your child.

Second, the quality of the relationship between the therapist and the patient can be just as powerful as the particular therapy techniques. It's not that the therapy relationship is always cozy or comfortable, but there has to be *trust*, and there has to be a *good working relationship*. This is particularly true between the therapist and your child, but it also involves your own feelings about the therapist.

Third, a lot of the oppositional behavior and avoidance that children have can be rooted in anxiety, which may or may not be apparent on the surface. If you're dealing with one of the disruptive behavior patterns outlined in chapter 7, make sure to look closely for accompanying anxiety issues and deal with them, too.

Finally, not all children who worry develop physical symptoms or avoid situations, and their anxiety may not be serious enough to be diagnosed as formal anxiety disorder. But these milder types of anxiety can still make your child uncomfortable, so you may want to think about having your child get some therapy to help deal with that anxiety.

Worried or Sad?

Many children with anxiety also show problems with mood, such as excessive sadness, reduced self-esteem, critical thinking, or withdrawal. In fact, the anxiety patterns outlined in this chapter are closely related to the mood problems I'll talk about in the next chapter. Effective treatments also overlap to a significant degree.

The symptoms in both of these chapters fall into the category of "internalizing" problems—those that seem to affect a child's "inside" life as much or even more than the "externalizing" problems caused by disruptive behavior disorders.

If the specific anxiety patterns outlined in this chapter don't exactly describe your child, but he or she seems to feel troubled inside in different ways, you may want to read about the closely related mood problems in the next chapter.

10

Mood Difficulties: Depression and Bipolar Disorder

KIM WAS an introspective, sensitive teenager who struggled in school with a mild reading disability and an unrelenting feeling of unhappiness. "Life is all gray," she told her mother. "Everything seems foggy and dull. I can't think, and I can't concentrate."

It had been years ago—really, as long as she could remember—since the "gray fog" had descended, shrouding her life with a lack of happiness. Finally, as a senior in high school, Kim recognized her symptoms in a psychology textbook and asked her mom for a referral to a psychologist. After a few months of family and individual psychotherapy and a brief course of antidepressants, Kim reports that the gray fog has faded away and her depression is gone. "She's like a different person," her mother reports. "She's smiling and happy now. She's stopped being argumentative, she's doing better in school, and she even likes to read!"

Just about everybody feels down in the dumps now and then, including kids. Fleeting unhappiness may occur when your child flunks a test, breaks up with a date, or loses a ball game. The profound mourning following the loss of a beloved grandparent might last several months or more—again, in some situations this may be completely normal.

But a key difference between sad feelings and a clinical depression is that sad feelings go away within a reasonable time. Depression does not. Even mild depression—which is what Kim struggled with—can blunt day-to-day experiences, turning life into an endless, joyless slog. As it worsens, depression can interfere with eating, sleep, school, friends, self-image, and attitude. It can lead to alcohol or drug use, and, occasionally, suicide attempts. What's worse, kids who suffer from depression won't just "snap out of it." Untreated, these feelings can last for weeks, months, or years.

As a parent—especially of a teenager—you may expect your child to be plagued by some of these low feelings. But if your child is depressed for weeks and months on end, you should think about consulting a mental health expert. This problem really isn't that unusual—some experts say as many as one in every thirty-three children (and *one in eight* teens) may be depressed. Yet sadly, up to two-thirds of children with depression don't get the help they need, according to the National Mental Health Association. The actual statistics vary, depending on the length, severity, and nature of the mood problems. More conservative research-based estimates suggest that major depression affects 1 percent of preschoolers, 2 to 3 percent of elementary-school-aged children, and 6 to 8 percent of adolescents. Once a young person has experienced an episode of major depression, he or she is at risk of experiencing another episode of depression within the next five years.

Children with attention problems, learning disorders, or conduct disorders are at especially high risk for depression. Although in early to middle childhood boys and girls are at equal risk for depression, as they enter puberty, the risk to girls rises. Teen girls carry twice the risk of depression as do boys.

In this chapter, you'll learn about different degrees of depression, including dysthymia (a mild form of depression, which is what Kim had) and major depression, as well as a related condition known as bipolar disorder (formerly called manic depression). We'll also discuss milder symptoms of depression that aren't as severe, and that usually crop up in response to a stressful situation; mental health experts call this "adjustment disorder with depressed mood," or "adjustment disorder with mixed emotional features" if both mood and anxiety problems are prominent.

Mild Depression

Parents often dismiss mild persistent depression—what experts call dysthymia—in children and teens as simply a phase or a kind of bad behavior. That's just what Kim's parents did, because they didn't realize that ignoring this persistent low mood can lead to severe depression or substance abuse if it's not treated appropriately. This less severe, yet typically more chronic form of depression can be diagnosed when a child or teen feels depressed for at least a year and also has at least two other symptoms of a major depression. (You'll learn more about these specific symptoms later in this chapter.) Dysthymia or dysthymic disorder may occur along with any of the other patterns that I cover in this book. In particular, I've seen many children with undiagnosed or undertreated learning disabilities who've fallen into an ongoing sense of helplessness as a kind of defense. They feel that nothing they do with their schoolwork ever seems quite good enough.

This was the case with Gary, who had been in a funk for more than a year when his dyslexia was finally identified in sixth grade. He was bright, so his reading and writing struggles had been missed as he scrambled to compensate year after year. Testing helped clarify this pattern. A half dozen counseling sessions and encouragement from his parents helped him regain his spark. As he began to understand his learning difficulty, he mastered ways to cope, such as listening to most of his reading material on tape.

Gary's situation shows that clear, careful evaluation and well-designed treatment can prevent mood problems from festering, so if you suspect that your child is depressed, you should visit a mental health specialist right away for a comprehensive evaluation and appropriate treatment.

Major Depression

Major depression is just what it sounds like—severe or intense symptoms that many children aren't able to explain or understand. (It's also important to remember that children with major depression often have anxiety, conduct disorders, ADHD, substance abuse issues, or other problems at the same time.) Sadly, as many as 7 percent of adolescents who develop major depressive disorder may commit suicide, which is why you should take your child's depressed mood seriously.

Amy's downward depression spiral began with an episode of bulimia during her sophomore year of high school. With counseling she began to improve, but the next summer her problems returned. Isolated from friends, she started sleeping too much and became quite critical of herself. Her thoughts gradually became more distorted, and she convinced herself that no one liked her—despite her siblings' genuine love and a large group of close friends who kept asking her to go out with them during the summer. After a few weeks of this, she took an overdose of her brother's arthritis pain medication and ended up in the emergency room. Amy's depression responded to more intensive counseling and medication, and she gradually returned to her former more healthy lifestyle.

What Causes Depression?

There are many potential causes of depression, including both psychological and physical triggers of bereavement, poverty, chronic stress, negative life events, and abuse. Many psychologists believe that the root of depression lies in unrealistic and distorted thinking patterns—in fact, many depressed children have markedly different thinking patterns than do those who aren't depressed.

Every child who struggles with depression arrived at this point by a combination of genetic makeup and a mixture of helpful or less helpful life experiences. Stress (such as in Gary's case) or communication mix-ups (such as Amy's distorted messages) matter a lot. In the end, I think it's going to be a lot harder and take a lot longer to figure out the psychological factors that determine who gets depressed and who doesn't, even though we already have many reliable clues from studying stress and learned helplessness. We shouldn't assume that the exciting clues coming from brain research are more important than influences from experience.

Brain Chemistry

At the same time, the physical roots of depression can be found in the nerve cells of the brain. When the levels of some message-carrying brain chemicals drop, messages can't cross the gaps between brain cells and communication in the brain slows down. The most important messenger chemicals related to depression are serotonin, norepinephrine, and dopamine. When the levels of these chemicals drop, you get depressed, and probably vice versa drugs that boost the levels of these chemicals can relieve depression.

Although serotonin, norepinephrine, and dopamine are of vital importance in the development of depression, scientists suspect that it's probably not a simple cause-and-effect relationship. The brain's biochemical pathways for emotion and mood are just too complex. While it may be possible to directly relieve depression by increasing the availability of serotonin in certain brain systems, for example, it might be that the level of this particular chemical triggers yet-undiscovered changes in other neurotransmitter systems, and that those changes are really responsible for easing depression.

Genetics

Children who develop major depression also are more likely to have a family history of the disorder than are patients with adolescent- or adult-onset depression. However, don't assume that this means it's "all in the genes." Many parents feel guilty that they've "given" their kids an inherited problem when a child is afflicted with the same struggles the parent had growing up. Your mood problems, if you have them, can have an important impact on your children, and it's difficult in any given case to estimate what might be due to genes or what might be due to family interaction. Even if heredity does appear likely in a particular case, I often find myself explaining to parents that we're responsible for our behavior but certainly not for our genes, so it doesn't make sense to feel guilty about transmitting depression to your child. Regretful, perhaps, but not guilty.

Symptoms

The most important symptom of depression is a sad or irritable mood that lasts for days or weeks at a time, often leading to a loss of interest in activities. In addition, a range of other symptoms can be clues to depression—most kids won't have them all, but every depressed child will have some of them. Depression may cause a range of vague, nonspecific *physical* problems such as headaches, muscle aches, stomachaches, or tiredness. The child may gain or lose weight, or have trouble sleeping. Problems at school may appear, including frequent absences, plummeting grades, or lack of concentration on schoolwork. Social relationships typically suffer; your child may seem uninterested in being with friends or develop problems with relationships. There may be some emotional problems: your child may feel agitated or lethargic, worthless or guilty, with outbursts of irritability or crying. The mood difficulties may lead to more dramatic behavior, such as threatening to run away from home or talking about suicide.

As I mentioned in the last chapter, many children experience anxiety and mood problems at the same time. Still, there are some important differences between the two. A good way to think of the difference between anxiety and depression is that anxiety is related to feeling scared and too revved up, whereas depression is related to feeling sad and not revved up enough. Kids struggling with anxiety tend to avoid anxiety-provoking situations; kids who are depressed tend to withdraw. As a result—and to highlight the differences between anxiety and depression—some of the treatments for anxiety try to reduce the emotional "overexcitement," whereas kids who are depressed often need to become more energized or active.

Diagnosing Depression

Diagnosing depression in kids can be tricky because early symptoms are sometimes hard to detect or may be attributed to other causes. I believe that the most important tools in discovering mood problems in children and adolescents combine careful interviewing and detailed review of their behavior. When school or medical professionals suspect that a child or teen may be depressed, they sometimes use questionnaires to screen for this problem (see box). If your child's scores on one of these tests suggests depression, you and your child should have a comprehensive evaluation by a mental health professional.

Questionnaires to Screen for Depression

- Children's Depression Inventory (CDI) (for ages seven to seventeen)
- Beck Depression Inventory (BDI) (for older teens)
- Center for Epidemiologic Studies Depression (CES-D) Scale

Treatment

A good diagnosis followed by an effective treatment plan is critical, particularly in more serious cases of depression in which suicide can become a risk. It's important to realize how serious depression can be, because suicide is the second leading cause of death among adolescents, killing five teens a day in the United States. But it doesn't have to be this way, since at least 80 percent of youngsters who committed suicide *were never treated for their depression.*

The good news is that once depression is properly diagnosed, your child will probably respond quickly to treatment, which I think should always involve psychotherapy and/or family therapy, occasionally adding antidepressants in severe or persistent cases.

Psychotherapy

Certain types of short-term psychotherapy—especially cognitive behavior therapy (CBT)—can clearly work well in easing depression in children and adolescents. CBT is based on the idea that people with depression have distorted ways of thinking about themselves, the world, and their future. CBT focuses on changing these distortions over a brief time.

In Gary's situation, for example, the therapist worked with him to list possible reasons for his reading problems, then discussed why each one made more or less sense. Gary's first reason for his reading problem was "I'm stupid." Eventually, his therapist helped him realize that in fact he had reading problems because "My brain wiring makes me learn differently."

With careful coaching and support from her therapists, Amy straightened out her thinking about her friends by sitting down and talking to them directly.

Another important part of psychotherapy helps to ease depression by changing the child's relationships with other people. Because the quality of a patient's relationship with the therapist is vital, many therapists take an "interpersonal" approach to treatment. For example, Amy's therapist carefully discussed Amy's misperception that the therapist was disappointed with her during their first few meetings together. Second, family therapy can improve your child's depressed mood by improving how people communicate, act, and feel toward each other. This can help build both independence and intimacy among family members.

A number of studies has shown that CBT eases depression in nearly 65 percent of cases—higher than either traditional supportive therapy or family therapy—and does so more quickly. However, thorough reviews of many studies of psychological treatment for depression have not found one method consistently better than another. More research is needed into what methods are most powerful in which situations.

Once your child begins to improve, remember that it's sometimes important to continue psychotherapy for several months to help your child and your family cope with the aftereffects of the depression, reinforce better ways of dealing with stress, and help you understand how your child's thoughts and behaviors could contribute to a relapse.

Medication

Research clearly demonstrates that antidepressant medications can be effective treatments for depression in adults, often when combined with psychotherapy. Using medication to treat depression in children and adolescents, however, has caused quite a bit of controversy. Many doctors have been understandably reluctant to treat young people with medications because, until fairly recently, little evidence was available about how safe these drugs are in children and how well they work.

In most cases of mild depression, I believe the first step should be psychotherapy alone. However, when depression just doesn't respond to therapy as soon as the psychiatrist and therapist think it should have—which could be a matter of weeks or months—a trial of antidepressant medication could be recommended for a specified time, along with therapy and behavioral interventions at home and at school.

As we learned earlier in this chapter, when the levels of serotonin and other brain chemicals are too low, messages can't cross the gaps between brain cells, and communication in the brain slows down. SSRIs boost the levels of these chemicals and relieve depression.

In the last few years studies with children and adolescents show some of the newer antidepressant medications can help in the short-term treatment of severe and persistent depression in young people (see box for the list of these drugs).

Although not all SSRIs have specifically been approved for use in young people, all of them have been prescribed for children as an "off label" use. Although all SSRIs seem to work approximately equally well in general, each drug has a profile all its own—and certain people will respond much better to one than to another.

Unfortunately, there has not been much research showing how these drugs affect children over the long run. Some experts worry about side effects of these drugs; some boost a child's energy, which some experts worry could lead a child to act on thoughts of suicide. Others worry about

---

Selective Serotonin Reuptake Inhibitor (SSRI) Antidepressants

- Prozac (fluoxetine)
- Celexa (citalopram HBr)
- Luvox (fluvoxamine)
- Zoloft (sertraline)
- Paxil (paroxetine)

possible effects that might only turn up years later—especially since younger children are still developing physically and mentally in ways that could be affected by antidepressants. If your doctor recommends a medication, you should fully discuss the risks and reasons for treatment with the psychiatrist who is prescribing the drug.

In 2004, the National Institute of Mental Health released its results from a large study comparing the long-term effectiveness of Prozac, CBT, and combination treatments for depression in teens. The study showed that combining Prozac and CBT produced the best success rate in treating depression in adolescents—71 percent of the kids had improved at the end of twelve weeks. With medication alone, 61 percent improved; 44 percent improved with CBT alone.

Adjustment Disorder with Depressed Mood

Sometimes a child may experience depression after a stressful event. This pattern is sometimes called reactive depression, or adjustment disorder with depressed mood, and includes symptoms similar to other depressive disorders but that are often more short-lived. Several other types of adjustment disorders include:

- patterns with prominent anxiety features
- a mixture of anxiety and depressive symptoms
- reduction of work productivity
- acting-out behaviors

Current NIMH Depression Studies

NIMH is currently funding two other studies involving adolescents with depression: Treatment of Resistant Depression in Adolescents (TORDIA) and Treatment of Adolescent Suicide Attempters (TASA). For more information about these two studies, you can visit www.nimh.nih.gov/studies/index.cfm or www.clinicaltrials.gov.

As a parent, you should realize that these diagnoses may apply if your child has "a little of" the other main problems that I reviewed in the previous chapters.

Symptoms

Kids who are having an adjustment disorder with depressed mood may become sad, cry a lot, lose interest in normal activities, or isolate themselves. In some cases, the mood reaction can lead them to act out against the rules of family, school, or society—skipping school, fighting, or being reckless. Others with an adjustment disorder may start doing poorly in school or develop trouble in close, personal relationships. Teens are particularly vulnerable to developing an adjustment disorder with depressed mood.

Adjustment reactions can be triggered when there's a lifestyle change for a kid who already has other problems, such as a learning disorder or ADHD. For example, if your child has ADHD and then starts at a new school or suddenly gets harder homework assignments as he moves into high school, you might notice the onset of an adjustment reaction.

Diagnosis

A mental health professional can try to help you tell the difference between a "phase" and an adjustment disorder by taking a careful personal history, focusing on details surrounding stressful events in your child's life. Usually symptoms of an adjustment disorder develop within three months of the beginning of the problem. An adjustment disorder usually lasts no longer than three to six months, but it may persist if your child suffers from chronic stress.

Treatment

Psychotherapy can help lessen symptoms before they become disabling. Because of the relationship between the symptoms and a specific type of stress, the therapist may place more emphasis on fixing the problem that caused the stress in the first place. For example, if your child's depression was triggered by a new blast of severe teasing at school, you'll probably want to work intensively with school staff to stop your child from being bullied—before considering more dramatic solutions such as changing schools or starting medication. Often, children get depressed in reaction to stress when they don't think there's a solution to their problem. In such cases, helping your child find a reasonable solution is a key part of treatment.

Bipolar Disorder

Once called manic depression, this pattern involves alternating periods of depression and manic highs that can sometimes be severe enough or disruptive enough to land a child in the hospital. Children who are experiencing a manic phase may be overly elated, irritable, paranoid, or hyperactive. They may engage in previously uncharacteristic risky behaviors, talk loudly or quickly, change topics too quickly, refuse to be interrupted, and go for days without rest. Attention can flit constantly from one thing to the next, and you may notice increased sexual thoughts, feelings, or behaviors, or the use of explicit sexual language. Your child may be agitated and act without considering the risks.

After days or weeks of feeling all-powerful, the child can suddenly crash to earth in a severe depression, feeling defeated and doomed. To children in this phase, the world that yesterday was bright and full of promise is today a bleak, gray disaster. Between 20 to 40 percent of adolescents with major depression go on to develop bipolar disorder within five years after depression begins. Although rare in young children, bipolar disorder has recently been identified more often in both children and adolescents.

Symptoms

Bipolar disorder may begin with either manic, depressive, or mixed manic and depressive symptoms. When the illness begins before or soon after puberty, it's often characterized by continuous, rapid-cycling, irritable symptoms that may occur along with disruptive behavior disorders such as ADHD or conduct disorder. On the other hand, later adolescent-onset bipolar disorder often begins suddenly, often with a manic episode, followed by a pattern of relatively stable periods between episodes. There is also less likelihood of having ADHD or CD in those with later-onset bipolar disorder.

Cause

Bipolar disorder appears to be related to a biochemical imbalance in the brain that usually responds best to a combined treatment plan of medication and psychotherapy. While there is strong evidence that this condition has a genetic component, just because one of your children has the disease doesn't mean the others will necessarily follow the same path. Evidence suggests that bipolar disorder beginning in childhood or early adolescence may be a different, possibly more serious form of the illness.

Diagnosis

If your child has any of these bipolar symptoms or appears to be depressed and also has severe ADHD-like symptoms, with temper outbursts and mood swings, a psychiatrist or psychologist with experience in bipolar disorder should be consulted—especially if there is a family history of the illness.

Treatment

Treatment of children and adolescents diagnosed with bipolar disorder is based mainly on experience with adults, since as yet there is limited data with children on mood-stabilizing medications such as lithium or valproate. Researchers are currently evaluating both drug and therapy treatments for bipolar disorder in young people. With any of these drugs, the prescribing physician *must* monitor your child closely and provide continual follow-up to make sure side effects are not a problem. You should also realize that using antidepressants to treat depression in a person who has bipolar disorder may trigger additional manic symptoms if the drug is taken without a mood stabilizer, such as lithium or valproate. In addition, using stimulant medications to treat ADHD or ADHD-like symptoms in a child or adolescent with bipolar disorder may worsen manic symptoms.

It can be hard to determine which young patients will become manic, but there is a greater risk among those with a family history of bipolar disorder. If manic symptoms develop or markedly worsen during antidepressant or stimulant use, you should consult a child psychiatrist to consider bipolar disorder.

Remaining Questions

At least in some geographic areas, some professionals have at some times overdiagnosed some of the disorders that I talk about in this book, as enthusiasm about a new or revised diagnosis builds. One could argue that this happened with ADHD during the last decade, and with Asperger's syndrome during this decade. I'm afraid bipolar disorder may be at risk for being overdiagnosed in some situations now. This doesn't mean you shouldn't carefully investigate the possibility if the question arises—but I emphasize *carefully*. When it comes to treatment, I generally prefer to go with psychosocial interventions first with most children who have mood problems, as well as anxiety issues, except for some severe cases.

As I write this book, we're still evaluating the scientific evidence regarding the risk that some depressed kids may turn suicidal thinking into suicide attempts after taking antidepressant medication. Caution is in order, but I wouldn't advise throwing the baby out with the bathwater. This type of concern is clearly the responsibility of the prescribing physician, but to be safe, you should closely monitor your child's whereabouts and activities during medication start-up in these situations.

11

Rarer, Complicating, and Controversial Diagnoses

CHARLIE'S MOTHER FIRST NOTICED her son's unusual behavior when he was about eighteen months old, when he suddenly stopped taking naps and sleeping at night. Although he didn't normally cry much, when he did fall asleep, he'd often wake up screaming. He'd have episodes of holding his pacifier tightly and shaking it vigorously in front of his face while making guttural noises. He was obsessed with the TV show *Wheel of Fortune* and would stand beside the TV, pretending to spin the wheel, shaking his hands in front of his face as he squealed.

Charlie's pediatrician suspected a possible autistic spectrum disorder because of these early patterns, so his parents enrolled him in an early childhood special education program. Unfortunately, the picture got more complicated as time passed. Charlie became more physically aggressive and violent during kindergarten, banging his head on the wall, biting, and hitting family and friends. He'd sometimes sit still with a fearful look on his face, eventually admitting at age six that during these times he was frightened by visions of dead people. Since then, he's had repeated visual hallucinations of dead people and bugs. He talks to objects and says he communicates with aliens. He creates and hoards small constructions with cans and wires that he says he uses as antennae to receive information from outer space, or as safety devices to protect his eyes from the lights in the sky.

Charlie continues to have trouble sleeping and unstable moods. He has grandiose ideas, telling his mother and teachers that he knows more then they do and that he has special knowledge that he can't share. He has lots of energy, speaking quickly, skipping words or stuttering, so that his conversation is hard to follow. Although generally sweet and affectionate, he continues to have frequent aggressive episodes.

For many years doctors couldn't agree on how to describe his basic problems. When he was three, Charlie had been diagnosed with ADHD. Two years later he was hospitalized for psychiatric treatment after chasing his mother with a knife and stabbing his forearm with a needle, after which he was diagnosed with bipolar disorder. During his hospitalization, he improved slightly on medication. By the time a colleague of mine saw him at age seven, the complexity and quality of his disordered thinking, his relatively few mood problems, and the classic paranoid quality of his hallucinations and delusions led her to diagnose Charlie with the rare condition of childhood schizophrenia.

Some psychiatric disorders like this aren't common in children, which is why I've included them here in one general chapter. They are still important to consider, if only because they are sometimes confused with other more common problems.

In the next part of this chapter, I'll discuss a few examples of these rare childhood disorders, including childhood schizophrenia, Tourette's syndrome, and Rett disorder. Please keep in mind that this isn't intended to be an exhaustive list of the rarer problems that you may encounter—it's just a small sample. Later, I'll briefly review other types of problems and issues that sometimes need to be considered.

Schizophrenia

As you saw in Charlie's case, childhood schizophrenia is a rare but serious disorder that causes strange thinking, abnormal feelings, and unusual behavior. It's an uncommon psychiatric illness in children under age twelve, and it's hard to recognize in its early phases. When schizophrenia does develop in childhood, it usually begins between the ages of seven and thirteen. It's far more common to see this condition begin during the teenage years, when it is found in about three out of every one thousand teens. Most cases of schizophrenia emerge in late adolescence or early adulthood, however, eventually affecting about one out of a hundred people.

Symptoms

The behavior of children and teens with schizophrenia may be different from that of adult patients with this illness. Most of these children show delays in language and other functions well before their symptoms of hallucinations, delusions, and disordered thinking appear. In the first years of life, about 30 percent of these children have temporary symptoms of a pervasive developmental disorder, such as rocking or arm flapping. There may be uneven motor development, such as unusual methods of crawling.

Early Symptoms of Schizophrenia in Children

- trouble telling the difference between dreams and reality (this is still normal during late preschool years and even for some early elementary children)
- visual or auditory hallucinations
- confused thinking
- vivid and bizarre thoughts and ideas
- extreme moodiness (but depression and/or mania may indicate psychosis along with a mood disorder, rather than schizophrenia)
- peculiar behavior
- feelings of persecution
- extremely immature behavior
- severe anxiety and fearfulness
- confusing TV or movies with reality
- severe problems in making and keeping friends

However, the behavior of children with this illness may change over time. As in Charlie's case, schizophrenic psychosis usually develops gradually in children, without the sudden psychotic "break" with reality that sometimes occurs in adolescents and adults. Children may begin talking about strange fears and ideas, clinging to parents, or saying things that don't make sense. Children who used to enjoy relationships with others may become more shy or withdrawn. In fact, children with schizophrenia typically appear to be emotionless—neither their voice nor facial expressions change in response to emotional situations. Events that would normally make children laugh or cry may produce no response.

Cause

Experts presume that schizophrenia may be linked to chemical abnormalities in the brain. What exactly causes these abnormalities is still being studied, although there seems to be an inherited vulnerability. It is *not* caused by poor parenting or poor childhood conditions.

Diagnosis

There's no simple blood test or brain scan that can diagnose schizophrenia. Instead, a doctor bases the diagnosis on a thorough assessment of the child's symptoms, psychological tests, and lack of evidence of any other underlying condition, such as drug abuse or a brain tumor.

Treatment

As of yet, we can't cure schizophrenia, but it's usually possible to reduce or control symptoms. Children with schizophrenia may need a combination of medication and individual therapy, family therapy, and specialized programs. Unfortunately, children can be more susceptible than adults to the side effects of traditional antipsychotic drugs such as haloperidol: tremors, slowed movements, and movement disorders. Newer antipsychotic drugs (such as risperidone) may be safer.

Children should be referred to a child and adolescent psychiatrist who is specifically trained and skilled at evaluating, diagnosing, and treating children with psychotic disorders. Children with schizophrenia may need to be hospitalized when the symptoms worsen, so that drug doses can be adjusted.

Tourette's Syndrome

Tourette's syndrome (sometimes called Tourette's disorder) is a neurological condition that causes repetitive motor and vocal tics. It typically begins in childhood and is much more common in boys than girls. The most common motor tics involve the eyelids, eyebrows, and other facial or neck muscles; arms, shoulders, and legs are sometimes involved. Vocal "tics" may include grunting, throat clearing, coughing, or cursing. The tics usually fluctuate, varying between nonexistent to such constant activity that some patients have trouble functioning at all.

Up to 20 or 30 percent of children in the general population have transient tics at some point, and a smaller number have ongoing tics. Tourette's syndrome is much more common than it was once thought to be and is the most complex and severe type of tic disorder.

Andy was a patient of mine whose early medical and developmental history were essentially normal, except for early hearing problems due to fluid in his middle ears. A bright boy and good student, he had two loving parents who both worked in health-related fields. At about age seven, Andy began repetitively blinking his eyes, grimacing, and opening his jaws, along with coughs, sniffs, gulps, and deep-throated growls. These movements and vocalizations ebbed and flowed; some disappeared and were replaced by others. They often got worse when Andy felt anxious or stressed. He was diagnosed with Tourette's syndrome at age nine, but medication wasn't recommended at first because the tics were mild. However, his neurologist referred him to me for a neuropsychological evaluation because Andy also showed classic ADHD signs along with some obsessive-compulsive symptoms. He was impulsive, disorganized, and had trouble paying attention in class. Eventually a brief trial of Ritalin was tried, but when it worsened his tics, he later showed modest improvement with a different drug, Strattera. My neuropsychological evaluation found no evidence of learning disabilities or other mental processing problems beyond what could be accounted for by his ADHD.

Andy has also shown slight obsessive-compulsive symptoms since his tics emerged, including a tendency to check that doors are locked at night and an overfocused interest in whales. These weren't severe enough to diagnose an actual obsessive-compulsive disorder, which often occurs along with tic disorders. And although Andy tended to be unaware of other people's feelings, he was still interested in people and had a couple of close friends, so we felt sure he wasn't autistic.

Core Problems

Common simple tics include eye blinking, shoulder jerking, picking movements, grunting, sniffing, and barking. Complex tics include facial grimacing, arm flapping, coprolalia (use of obscene words), and repeating words (either one's own, or someone else's words or phrases).

The type, location, frequency, and severity of tics often change over time. In some cases, symptoms may disappear for weeks or even months. Although there is an involuntary quality to tics, most kids can control their symptoms at least briefly, and sometimes for hours at a time. However, suppressing tics often simply postpones more severe outbursts later on, since the impulse to express tics is ultimately irresistible. Anxiety, stress, and fatigue can intensify the tics, but tics usually diminish during sleep or when the person is focused on an activity. Some drugs (particularly stimulants or cocaine) tend to make tics worse.

In many cases, tics are the worst between ages nine and eleven, but between 5 and 10 percent of children continue to have unchanged or worsening symptoms in adolescence and adulthood. In this group, tics will probably continue for many years.

Obsessions, compulsions, impulsive behavior, and mood swings—much like Andy showed—are also common. Children with chronic tic disorders also have higher risk for ADHD and other behavior problems.

Cause

An abnormal metabolism of brain chemicals called dopamine and serotonin is linked to Tourette's syndrome, which is genetically transmitted. Parents have a 50 percent chance of passing this genetic material on to each child. Girls with the gene pattern have a 70 percent chance of having symptoms, but boys with the same gene pattern are much more likely to experience symptoms.

Diagnosis

An accurate diagnosis is the single most important component in managing Tourette's syndrome and other tic disorders. To be diagnosed with the full syndrome, a child must experience multiple motor tics as well as one or more vocal tics for more than one year. These don't need to occur all at once, but in general the tics may occur many times a day in brief, intense groupings, nearly every day.

Your child's doctor will want to rule out any secondary causes of tic disorders. This basic workup is usually appropriate in a child with a gradual onset of symptoms, a progressively worsening series of tics, and a family history of tics or obsessive-compulsive disorder.

A complete physical examination, with specific attention to the neurologic exam, is important. Your child's thyroid-stimulating hormone (TSH) level should be measured, since tics can occur together with hyperthyroidism. A throat culture should be checked for group A beta-hemolytic streptococcus bacteria, especially if symptoms get worse after ear or throat infections. However, the evidence of strep infection with a single occurrence of worsening tics is not enough to make a diagnosis of streptococcus-induced, autoimmune-caused Tourette's syndrome.

Differences Between Tics and Other Movement Disorders

Tics are a movement disorder that occurs suddenly during normal activity. Other movement disorders are quite different:

- Chorea—a pattern of nonrepetitive irregular movements
- Stereotypy—constant, repetitive behaviors performed for no obvious reason
- Dystonias—a slow, constant repetitive behavior

An electroencephalogram (EEG) is useful only if there is a problem distinguishing tics from epilepsy. Similarly, brain imaging studies don't usually contribute much to a diagnosis, and the importance of other tests depends on symptoms. For example, a urine drug screen for cocaine and stimulants might be helpful in a teenager who suddenly develops tics and inappropriate behavior, to rule out substance abuse.

Treatment

Particularly in mild cases, educating other people in your child's life is the most important thing you can do. Everyone should understand that the child can't completely suppress the tics, so the best thing to do is ignore them. Some children with mild tics benefit from counseling to help them adapt their movements into everyday life activities. For children with more frequent or severe symptoms, the best way to manage tics is to join a positive reinforcement program aimed at boosting social and academic skills and reducing negative behavior.

In addition, medications that affect brain levels of dopamine can help, although there is a risk of side effects. The goal in tic control is to use the lowest dosage that will improve the child's function to an acceptable level. Often, this requires only modest levels of tic reduction. Some of the most common drug treatments to manage tics are haloperidol (Haldol), pimozide (Orap), risperidone (Risperdal), and clonidine (Catapres).

Many children with Tourette's syndrome have other conditions that may need to be treated. Treatment of ADHD in children who also have Tourette's has been controversial because of reports that stimulants can hasten the onset or increase the severity of tics. However, this doesn't mean that stimulant treatment in children with significant ADHD symptoms is never appropriate to try. (And Strattera, the new nonstimulant medication for ADHD, may be an alternative.)

Rett Syndrome

This rare, progressive neurological disorder occurs in girls and produces autistic-like behavior, learning disabilities, poor muscle tone, purposeless hand movements, lessened ability to express feelings, poor eye contact, a lag in brain and head growth, walking abnormalities, and seizures. It's also called Rett disorder and is officially included as one of the five disorders under the umbrella term *pervasive developmental disorders* (or *autism spectrum disorders*) as listed in the *DSM-IV-TR*.

The syndrome, which involves a faulty X chromosome, appears in about one out of every ten thousand to fifteen thousand live female births. Symptoms usually begin in early childhood, between the ages of six to eighteen months. Experts believe that while boys can get Rett syndrome, in boys the condition is fatal (usually before birth). This is because girls have two X chromosomes, only one of which is active in any particular cell—so only about half the cells in a girl's nervous system will actually be using the defective Rett syndrome gene. Because boys have a single X chromosome, all of their cells must use the faulty version of the gene, which experts believe results in fatal defects.

Core Problems

Rett syndrome appears early. The child develops normally for the first months of life until about six to eighteen months of age, when she begins to gradually deteriorate mentally and physically. Generally, she loses communication skills and purposeful use of her hands. Some children have already begun to use single words and word combinations when they begin losing their speaking ability. Soon, stereotyped hand movements and slowed head growth become apparent.

As the damage to the nervous system worsens, the child may begin to have trouble walking or crawling. Most girls affected with Rett syndrome don't crawl with the normal pattern, but may "bottom scoot" without using their hands. While some girls begin walking independently, others show significant delay or inability to walk independently. Some begin walking and then lose this skill, while others continue to walk throughout life. Still others don't walk until late childhood or adolescence.

One of the most striking symptoms is loss of conscious control of the hands, leading to compulsive hand-wringing. Although rarely fatal in girls, Rett syndrome nevertheless causes permanent impairment.

A girl's problems may include severe seizures, which tend to become less intense in later adolescence. Disorganized breathing patterns may also appear, improving with age. Mild to severe scoliosis (curvature of the spine) is a prominent feature. Apraxia (the inability to program the body to perform motor movements) is a fundamental and severely handicapping aspect of the condition that can interfere with every body movement, including eye gaze and speech.

Cause

Researchers now generally agree that Rett syndrome is a chronic developmental disorder rather than a progressive, degenerative disorder. In October 1999, scientists discovered a genetic mutation on the X chromosome linked to Rett syndrome found in up to 75 percent of Rett cases. The gene produces part of a switch that shuts off production of as-yet-unidentified proteins. Experts suspect that overproduction of some proteins might cause the nervous system deterioration characteristic of the disease. Discovery of the gene will help unravel the steps of the disease process and could eventually lead to drugs to lessen the damage.

Diagnosis

Due to both apraxia and lack of verbal communication skills, an accurate assessment of intelligence is usually difficult. Most traditional testing methods require use of the hands and/or speech, which may be very limited for the girl with Rett. Diagnosing the disorder before age four or five years was sometimes tricky in the past, but the discovery of the genetic mutation should lead to a genetic test to improve the accuracy of early diagnosis. Rett has sometimes been mistaken for autism, cerebral palsy, or nonspecific developmental delay.

Treatment

There is no cure for Rett syndrome, but there are several treatment options, including interventions outlined for the learning disorders and autistic-like behavior patterns that may occur. Some children may require special nutritional programs to keep weight on.

Prognosis

Predicting how severe Rett syndrome will be isn't easy, but in spite of the severe problems that this condition causes, most girls with Rett syndrome survive at least into their forties. Girls and women with Rett can continue to learn and enjoy family and friends well into middle age and beyond, and they can live a full life, with engaging personalities as they participate in social, school, and fun activities. However, sudden, unexplained death can occur, possibly from brain-stem problems that interfere with breathing.

Complicating and Controversial Diagnoses

It's important to acknowledge that your child's behavior may require extra evaluation and treatment if you notice complicating problems, such as substance abuse (alcohol or other drugs), eating disorders (such as bulimia and anorexia nervosa), response to abuse or neglect (particularly reactive attachment disorder), and personality disorders (including borderline or schizoid). If your child has one or more of these additional problems, it is usually important to supplement the general evaluation and treatment approaches outlined above with team members who specialize in these areas.

In addition, a number of other neurological and genetic conditions can accompany, trigger, or worsen the main type of problems in this book. Some examples might include cerebral palsy, traumatic brain injury, epilepsy, hydrocephalus, neurofibromatosis, fragile X syndrome, and many others.

Then there are a number of emerging or proposed diagnoses that you may have heard of, but which I believe need more research before they should be considered well-defined enough to explain major portions of children's problems. These include:

- sensory integration disorder
- auditory processing disorders
- dysfunction of eye movements

Along with many other scientifically minded professionals, I believe there hasn't been enough sound research for these to stand alone as important explanations for a child's problems, although they may illustrate symptoms or even ongoing patterns. This isn't to deny that basic problems in hearing, vision, and oversensitivity can matter a lot. But typically, I find that when children come in for evaluations, some combination of the validated, established concepts that I discuss in the previous chapters are almost always enough to explain the child's struggles and to point toward appropriate treatment. For those rare times when the main concepts covered in this book just don't fit, I don't think we should just turn to the controversial categories. In my opinion, it's more prudent to simply say "I don't know" or "Our field can't explain every situation or variation" than to resort to proposed diagnoses that haven't yet been well studied. I also believe that most of the treatments associated with these controversial diagnoses haven't been studied enough to determine whether they are *specifically* effective, or whether it's *general* professional attention, hopeful encouragement, refocusing of attention, and reinforcement of behavior patterns that are improving the behavior.

Sensory Integration Dysfunction

Even though progress is being made in measuring differences among the sensory responses of individuals and in relating these patterns to well-established psychological and developmental disorders, questions remain about the importance of the basic sensory processing problems in a child's behavior, emotions, and learning patterns. In other words, differences between sensory processing that are sometimes examined by professionals such as occupational therapists may just as likely be the *result* of psychological issues as a *cause* of psychological issues.

Auditory Processing Disorders or
Central Auditory Processing Disorders

Some proponents of these concepts concern me because they eagerly jump forward in their theories and treatments before completing important scientific studies. Some proponents go so far as to deny the relevance of scientific testing methods. Even though theory in this area has led to the development of intervention methods with some demonstrated effectiveness (such as the Fast ForWord program), active debate continues as to what it is about these methods that seems to work.

Dysfunctional Eye Movements

Problems in this area include eye tracking of moving objects or print on a page, and the way the two eyes work together. Major professional organizations in ophthalmology, pediatrics, and learning disabilities have repeatedly pointed out that evidence for the effectiveness of proposed treatment methods for these problems is weak. Furthermore, treating eye movement problems is clearly not enough to cure important problems such as reading disabilities. The problems that children with nonverbal learning disorders have with spatial and visual-perceptual skills involve higher centers in the brain—not simply eye movements.

Other Ideas

As far as I'm concerned, research has also disproven some older theories as to the cause of children's problems—but still these theories linger in the popular press. These discredited theories include the division of "visual learners" versus "auditory learners," the idea that sugar or artificial ingredients in diet can cause ADHD, and the idea that reading disabilities are often caused by visual-perceptual problems such as poor right-left orientation or visual shape discrimination.

Epilogue

NOW THAT YOU'VE MADE IT through the book, let's return to the Appalachian Trail—the story that I told you in the preface. One year, my wife and I (and the dogs) decided to hike our way to one of our kids' college graduation. Part of the trail passed right through his small college town in the mountains, so we combined our walk in the woods with the family celebration. As we came off the trail into town, after a particularly hard week of muddy trails and biting blackflies, we needed directions to make our way the last few blocks to the college campus. You might imagine that we looked (and smelled!) quite a sight: spattered pants and boots, unwashed hair, and two dead-tired dogs. (By the way, is this how you sometimes think you look as a parent?)

Just then, three college students drove up and parked at the trailhead, intending to head into the hills for a day hike. They cheerfully (but from a distance!) gave us the directions we needed.

The next day before the graduation ceremony, we learned from our son that the three young women we'd met the day before were actually his friends. At a party the night we arrived, he was commenting that his parents had hiked into town on the "AT." The three women—perhaps impressed by our athletic ambition, but perhaps something else—were quite struck by the story, and one exclaimed, "Wow! They're hard-core old people!"

Could we have been getting a touch of respect from the kids?

Now that you've read in this book about figuring out your child's patterns, I want to encourage you to go ahead and be "hard-core parents," no matter how tired you get or how it makes you look. Earn the respect you deserve for your efforts. Get your map, keep on going despite the mud and flies, and push through the exhaustion. It's your choice. It's lots of miles, but you can make it.

It's my sincere hope that by now you've gotten a much better idea not just of what *might* be wrong with your child, but what concrete steps you can take right now to address your child's problems. I can imagine how lost, anxious, or frustrated you probably were when you first started reading. By now, you should have some solid ideas on where to turn for help, how to get a diagnosis, what treatments are available, and how to start understanding your child's challenging issues.

Maybe you've gotten lucky. After reading this book, filling out the charts and checklists, and talking to the experts, you may be clear about what's going on with your child. You might have a straightforward direction in which to head. If that's the case—terrific!

However, if the map still doesn't seem clear, don't despair. Some kids don't show a clear-cut pattern of one sort or another on the surface. Instead, it may require more digging. Your child may show parts of a pattern fairly clearly—and so you start working with that and keep mapping. Remember that even the best experts shouldn't rush to diagnose a problem. Development unfolds over time, and lots of changes can occur in your child's behavior—especially in younger kids. For example, most experts agree that it's not usually reliable to diagnose autism in a one-year-old. And it would be premature to say a five-year-old has dyslexia, because at this age kids are only in the beginning stages of reading. A cautious professional might conclude there are "features of" or a "risk of" a particular diagnosis at a young age, rather than jump to a conclusion too early.

For your child's sake, please don't get stuck or throw up your hands if you don't have a textbook case of dyslexia, depression, or autistic disorder. That's just the way many kids are made, with "a little of this and a little of that." They don't always fit into categories all the time, and so you work with what you've got.

It may be that your child doesn't have a diagnosable disorder, but instead shows clear-cut tendencies toward or borderline features of one of the disorders I outlined in the book. That's good in two ways. First, now you understand the problem and you know what your options are for treatment. For instance, if your child seems to have a mild case of ADHD that probably doesn't call for medication, you'd almost always need to try behavioral management. Second, if a child has *tendencies* toward a particular problem or disability—has important but borderline features of a disorder—this can give you hope that you've got a milder problem on your hands.

This was the case with Joseph. When I first evaluated him during second grade, we confirmed his psychologist's suspicion that he had a mild, "subclinical" degree of ADHD, along with weaknesses in verbal learning skills that represented features of a mixed receptive and expressive language disorder. This map of his problems helped his family choose a positive series of interventions for him over the years, including behavior management to boost his organization and attention, extra help from the learning center at his parochial grade school, and therapy at the speech/hearing clinic staffed by speech pathology graduate students at a local university. His parents later made a strategic switch to the public middle school where he could get further speech/language therapy and extra help in specially designed study halls for students who were struggling but didn't have full-blown learning disabilities. His pediatrician eventually prescribed medication to enhance his attention to schoolwork, and the family scheduled some counseling sessions with a social worker when Joseph had physical anxiety symptoms such as aches and pains from time to time during seventh grade.

A follow-up evaluation during eighth grade pinpointed a need for extra tutoring in reading comprehension and written expression, which Joseph's parents arranged with a previous teacher who had strong rapport with him. By high school, he was hanging in there academically with a minimum of continuing speech/language consultation and was successfully involved in a top-rank gymnastics team to counterbalance the low-level ongoing frustration with the academic demands of his challenging suburban school. Joseph is a perfect example of how paying attention to mild or borderline issues can make a significant impact on a child's life.

Then there was Jessica, whom you may recall from chapter 8. Jessica worked with her family, a variety of professionals in and out of school, and most importantly with her own self-image to cope with the social problems associated with her diagnosis of Asperger's syndrome. With this support, she did well in school and got admitted to a fine small liberal arts college. She and her parents were helped tremendously by having a clear picture of what her disorder meant, and how she could use her above-average intelligence to keep moving forward in school and in her community. She may never have a wide circle of friends, but her ability to maintain relationships with a few close buddies has made her life rich and rewarding.

These examples show how much can be gained by working closely with experts in and out of school, and supporting your child to the best of your ability. As parents, you know your child better than anyone else—so keep drawing a clearer map if things don't seem to be working as well as they should! This is what Karen's parents did in the following example.

Karen had been enrolled in a learning disabilities program throughout most of her elementary and middle school years. Not until she hit the demands of her large regional high school, however, did she start getting really discouraged. She began fighting with teachers over the IEP accommodations she was supposed to get and made some poor choices about friends. Her parents quickly realized that her gentle spirit and long-term conscientious work ethic were simply not being nurtured in the new school environment, so by October of her freshman year they consulted a psychologist to figure out what to do.

A thorough neuropsychological evaluation recommended by the psychologist pinpointed the depth of Karen's dyslexia at that time, but we also concluded that her school had probably placed too much emphasis on accommodations and compensations earlier in her school career, without asking for enough "rolling up the sleeves" to work on basic reading remediation. Now, the combination of psychotherapy consultation and testing evaluation gave her parents the information they needed to go back and negotiate with the school to intensify her program, spending more time on basic language arts instruction using research-based methods, and communicating more thoroughly to her regular classroom teachers about what needed to be done. Karen has now overcome a depressive episode and is moving forward in both school skills and social/emotional health.

You've Just Begun . . .

The parents of kids like Joseph, Jessica, and Karen aren't any different from you. They started out confused, frustrated, and/or scared—but they knew that something should be done for their child, and they were all determined not to stop until they had answers. If they could do it, so can you, no matter how daunting the journey may seem at the outset.

"Okay, I'll put in the time and energy," you say, "but what about the expenses?" Sometimes existing institutions (especially the schools) just aren't able or willing to assume the costs of the interventions that you've decided your child needs. Deciding where to cut corners, what to do yourself, what to barter for, and what to spend precious family resources on are extra tough decisions. They deserve careful, committed thought, keeping two things in mind:

First, many interventions are important investments in your child's future. They may not have entertainment value or material value, but they're things you can reasonably expect will help your child. They are worth paying for.

Second, some of the interventions—such as psychotherapy for anxiety problems—require a certain number of sessions a month. Any less than that, and your kid just won't benefit. As you make difficult financial decisions, you need to understand that you shouldn't "water down" the treatment too much just to save money. That's like taking too small a dose of Tylenol for your headache. You *say* you're taking Tylenol, but you really aren't.

If cost is an issue, you may be able to find reduced-cost options at university-based graduate student clinics, teaching hospitals, organizations staffed by volunteers, or places in the community with sliding-scale fee structures. There are philanthropic organizations that will underwrite the cost of some of these interventions for some children, such as the dyslexia learning centers sponsored in some cities by Masonic lodges.

I trust that over the course of this book you've discovered at least some of the what, why, how, where, and when that's associated with your child's challenging learning struggles, behaviors, or emotions. I hope you've gotten a clearer idea of how to pursue a better understanding of what's going on with your particular situation, and how to use that knowledge to work with health and educational professionals to get the best diagnosis and treatment for your child. With this knowledge, I hope I've helped you realize that you can help your child achieve his birthright—a happy, fulfilling, successful life. Keep on hiking!

Glossary

abstraction   The ability to relate ideas or understand concepts at a higher level than the literal or concrete meaning.

accommodations   Techniques and materials that allow a child with a learning disability or other problem to complete school tasks more easily and effectively. Examples of accommodations include giving a child a spell-checker, tape recorder, or extra time to complete a test.

achievement test   A test that measures the extent to which a child has learned particular information or mastered certain skills.

aptitude test   A test that measures a child's ability to learn and the likelihood of achieving success in schoolwork.

articulation   The production of speech sounds resulting from the movements of the lips, jaw, and tongue as they modify the flow of air.

assistive technology   Equipment that enhances the ability of students to be more efficient and successful. This might include computer grammar or spell-checkers, an overhead projector used by a teacher, or books on tape.

attention span   The length of time an individual can concentrate on a task without being distracted or losing interest.

auditory discrimination   The ability to detect differences in sounds. This may include the ability to detect the differences between the noises made by a train and a car, or detecting the differences made by the sounds of letters, such as between *p* and *b*.

auditory figure-ground   The ability to pay attention to one sound in the midst of background noise (such as hearing the teacher's voice amid classroom noise).

auditory memory   The ability to retain information that one hears. Auditory memory may involve short-term or long-term memory, such as recalling information presented just a few moments or hours earlier. Auditory memory may also involve sequential memory, such as recalling a series of information in proper order (such as the alphabet).

behavior modification   A technique intended to change a person's behavior by rewarding desirable actions and ignoring or presenting negative consequences for undesirable behavior.

central nervous system (CNS)   The brain and spinal cord.

child study committee   A group of education experts in a school designed to handle referrals of students suspected of being handicapped. Committees typically include at least four people, including the school principal or a person chosen by the principal, the child's teacher or teachers, specialists, and the referring individual. Often parents are also part of the committee.

cognition   The process of knowing—of recognizing, interpreting, judging, and reasoning. Perception is considered a part of cognition by some experts, but not by others.

cognitive   The process of knowing in the broadest sense, including perception, memory, and judgment.

cognitive deficit   A perceptual, memory, or conceptual problem that interferes with learning.

cognitive retraining   Developing or relearning the processes involved in thinking.

cognitive style   A person's typical approach to learning activities and problem solving. For example, some people carefully analyze each task, deciding what must be done and in what order, whereas another might impulsively react to tasks in a haphazard manner.

confidential file   File of an individual student maintained by the school that contains a variety of teacher evaluations conducted to determine whether a child is handicapped, as well as any other information related to special education placement. Parents have the right to inspect the file and have copies of any information contained in it.

coping skills   The ability to deal with problems and difficulties by attempting to overcome them or accept them.

cumulative file   General file maintained by the school for any child enrolled in the school. Parents have a right to inspect the file and have copies of any information contained in it.

developmental lag A delay in some aspect of physical or mental development.

discrimination The ability to discern fine differences among stimuli, whether visual, auditory, tactile, and so on.

distractibility The shifting of attention from a task to sounds, sights, or other stimuli in the environment.

dyscalculia Problems understanding or using mathematical symbols or functions needed to succeed in arithmetic. A child with dyscalculia may be able to read and write but has trouble performing mathematical calculations.

dysgraphia Trouble producing legible handwriting at an age-appropriate speed. Some definitions of dysgraphia also include difficulty composing written output.

dysnomia Difficulty in remembering names or recalling appropriate words necessary for oral or written language.

dyspraxia Problems performing fine motor acts such as using a pencil, buttoning a coat, or using a zipper. A person with dyspraxia has difficulty producing and sequencing the movements necessary to perform these kinds of tasks.

early intervention program A program designed to help developmentally delayed infants and preschool children so as to help prevent problems as the children get older.

echolalia Repetition of words or phrases.

educational consultant/diagnostician An individual who may be familiar with school curricula and requirements at various grade levels and may or may not have a background in learning disabilities. This person may conduct educational evaluations.

educational evaluation An assessment of a child's performance to determine whether a child is handicapped. Although the specific content of an educational evaluation is not specified by law, the evaluation typically includes a battery of tests and classroom observation, together with an analysis of classwork, designed to determine the current achievement levels in reading, math, spelling, and so on. Perceptual abilities and learning style may also be evaluated.

emotional lability Rapid and drastic changes in emotions (such as laughing, crying, and anger), often without apparent reason.

expressive language Communication through writing, speaking, and/or gestures.

eye-hand coordination The ability of the eyes and hands to work together to complete a task. Drawing, throwing a ball, or writing would all be examples of activities requiring eye-hand coordination.

far point copying The ability to write information copied from a distance, such as taking notes from material presented on a blackboard at the front of the classroom.

figure-ground discrimination   The ability to identify important information from the surrounding environment, such as picking out one word from among others on a crowded page.

fine motor skills   The ability to use small muscles for precise tasks, such as writing neatly, tying bows, zipping a zipper, playing Pick Up sticks, or typing.

frustration tolerance   The ability to deal with frustrating events in daily life or challenging mental tasks without becoming angry or aggressive.

gross motor skills   The ability to use large muscles for activities requiring strength and balance, such as running, jumping, or kicking a ball.

hyperactivity   Disorganized, disruptive behavior characterized by constant or excessive movement. A hyperactive child usually has trouble focusing on one task for a long period and may react more intensely to a situation than would a nonhyperactive child.

hyperkinesis   Another term for hyperactivity.

hypoactivity   Underactivity. A hypoactive child may appear to lack energy and seem to be in a daze.

IEP   See INDIVIDUALIZED EDUCATION PLAN (program).

IEP committee   A group of educators and concerned individuals who write the individualized education plan (IEP) for a student identified by the school's eligibility committee as handicapped. Members of the IEP committee typically include the child's teacher, another school employee qualified in special education, the child's parent, the student (if appropriate), and any other interested individuals whom the school or the parents choose.

impulsivity   Reacting to a situation without considering the risks or consequences.

individualized education plan (IEP)   A written educational prescription developed for each child with a learning disability. School districts are required by law to develop these plans in cooperation with parents.

learning disability   Disability involved in understanding or using language, manifested in impaired listening, thinking, talking, reading, writing, or arithmetic skills, according to U.S. federal legislation. This includes perceptual handicaps, brain injury, minimal brain dysfunction, and developmental aphasia.

locus of control   The tendency to attribute success or failure either to internal factors (such as effort) or to external factors (such as chance). Children with learning disabilities tend to blame failure on themselves (internal locus of control) and success on luck (external locus of control), leading to frustration and passivity.

mainstreaming   Placing a child with special educational needs into regular classrooms for at least a part of the child's day. Many experts believe mainstreaming is beneficial both to the special child and also to the nonhandi-capped fellow students. The term *inclusion* is similar to *mainstreaming*.

mental age   The age for which a score on a mental ability test is average or normal. The term is most appropriately used in the early years, when mental growth is rapid.

near point copying   Writing while copying from material close to the student. Copying information from a textbook or from note cards is an example of near point copying.

neuropsychological examination   A series of tasks that allow observation of performance presumed to be related to brain function.

perseveration   Repeating words, motions, or tasks that are no longer appropriate or useful, even if they were previously useful. A child who persever-ates often has trouble shifting to a new task and instead continues working on an old task long after classmates have stopped.

phonics approach   A method of teaching reading and spelling that empha-sizes learning the sounds that individual letters and combinations of let-ters make in a word. In the phonics approach, the child sounds out individual letters or letter combinations and then blends them to form a word, as a way of decoding words. Many school districts include both the phonics and whole language approaches in their elementary school read-ing courses.

psychomotor   Pertaining to the motor effects of psychological processes. Psy-chomotor tests are tests of motor skills that depend on sensory or percep-tual motor coordination.

receptive language (decoding)   Language that is received by an individual. Listening and reading are two examples of receptive language.

resource room   A place where a special education student goes for specified periods of time regularly to receive educational support.

sensorimotor   The relationship between sensation and movement (sometimes spelled *sensory-motor*).

sensory acuity   The ability to respond to sensation at normal levels of inten-sity.

sight words   Words a child can recognize on sight without the deliberate use of word-attack skills.

spatial relationships   A child's ability to perceive the relationships between objects, including shapes, distances, and directions.

special education   Instruction specifically designed for handicapped children.

specific language disability   A severe problem in some aspect of listening, speaking, reading, writing, or spelling in a child whose skills in the other ar-eas are age appropriate.

specific learning disability   The official term used in federal legislation to refer to problems in certain areas of learning, rather than in all areas of learning.

tactile   The sensation of touch; the ability to receive and interpret stimuli through contact with the skin.

visual discrimination   The ability to detect similarities or differences in material presented visually, such as the ability to discriminate *o* from *c*, *m* from *n*, or a circle from an oval.

visual figure-ground   The ability to focus on the foreground of material presented visually, rather than on material in the background. Children who have trouble with the visual figure-ground may find it hard to keep their place while reading and may find a crowded page of print or illustrations confusing.

visual memory   The ability to retain information presented visually, usually implying spatial information rather than verbal information or information in words. This may involve short-term memory (recalling details only a few seconds old), long-term memory (recalling information presented more than a minute before), or sequential memory (remembering a series of items in correct order).

visual motor   The ability to translate information received visually into a motor response. Children with visual motor problems may have poor handwriting, for example.

word-attack skills   The ability to analyze reading words phonetically to identify what the word sounds like.

word recognition   The ability to read or pronounce a word, either deliberately using word-attack skills or immediately by sight. Word recognition does not necessarily imply understanding what the word means.

Appendix A
For More Information . . .

There are many, many helpful books and Web sites for parents about specific problem areas that I've reviewed in the previous chapters. I've selected a few to highlight here, with notes describing why I like these particular choices. In fact, a good number of the ideas in this book relate back to the material presented in more detail in these valuable sources.

Learning

Adams, M. J., et al. *Phonemic Awareness in Young Children: A Classroom Curriculum.* Baltimore: Brookes Publishing, 1997.

This and other similar books provide good descriptions, examples, and exercises for phonological processing, the core deficit in dyslexia. While most of these programs have been designed for general instruction and prevention in the kindergarten and first-grade classrooms, the recommendations can easily be adapted for older children who are still struggling with reading decoding.

Shaywitz, Sally. *Overcoming Dyslexia: A New and Complete Science-Based Program for Overcoming Reading Problems at Any Level.* New York: Knopf, 2003.

This is an outstanding presentation representing the "state of the science" on reading disabilities, loaded with specific discussions of interventions. However, I believe the research on the specifics of brain processing in dyslexia is still ongoing, and that her proposal that one out of five children should be diagnosed with dyslexia may be debated further and eventually revised.

Spear-Swerling, Louise, and Robert Sternberg. *Off Track: When Poor Readers Become "Learning Disabled."* Boulder, CO: Westview Press, 1997.

This book focuses on a well-supported understanding about how reading develops, and how getting "off track" at various steps along the way leads to different kinds of problems that need different treatments. This book cuts through debates on hotly debated issues such as phonics vs. whole language instruction. It offers good explanations of the steps to mastering good reading and different interventions reflecting the fact that "one size does not fit all."

Thompson, Sue. *Source for Nonverbal Learning Disorders.* East Moline, IL: LinguiSystems, 1997.

Although a number of more recent books have been published on this topic, the late Sue Thompson was a forward-thinking pioneer in putting "flesh on the bones" of the basic principles for intervention with NLD that had been outlined on the basis of research by the pediatric neuropsychologist Dr. Byron Rourke and colleagues. Be aware that few of the intervention suggestions for NLD have been subjected to rigorous research, so these recommendations should be taken as *likely to help* rather than *proven effective*. Beware also of the pessimism about risks for long-term adjustment of children with NLD in Thompson's and Rourke's writings, particularly with those children who show some but not all of the core symptoms.

ADHD/Disruptive Behaviors

Barkley, Russell. *Taking Charge of ADHD: The Complete, Authoritative Guide for Parents.* New York: Guilford Press, 2000.

Barkley's clear, parent-friendly style, extensive research-based knowledge about ADHD, and specific behavior management directions for a wide variety of situations make this book a valuable starting point for active reading by any parent or teacher working with a child with ADHD. The behavioral program outlined in this book forms the backbone of the parent training program that we teach in our clinic. Sections on medication are balanced and scientifically based. There is significant overlap between the recommendations in this book and Barkley's books on oppositional defiant disorder, but I think the ADHD version is more to the point. I also think that the behavior management approach ought to be supplemented or substituted with a strong family psychotherapy element for working with children who have ODD without ADHD.

> Forehand, Rex, and Nicholas Long. *Parenting the Strong-Willed Child, Revised and Updated Edition: The Clinically Proven Five-Week Program for Parents of Two- to Six-Year-Olds.* New York: McGraw-Hill, 2002.

The authors' decades of careful research on behavioral interventions for children with disruptive behavior disorders is aptly reflected in this parenting guide.

> Hallowell, Edward M., and John J. Ratey. *Driven to Distraction: Recognizing and Coping with Attention Deficit Disorder from Childhood Through Adulthood.* New York: Touchstone, 1995.

This popular book is parent-friendly and educational and provides vivid stories, in part because its authors are health professionals who have ADD. It's now available on audio CD in both full and abridged versions.

> Nadeau, Kathleen G. *The Survival Guide for College Students with ADD or LD.* Washington, DC: Magination Press, 1994.

This book supplies practical ideas for your older child as he or she proceeds to greater independence.

Autistic Spectrum

> Attwood, Tony. *Asperger's Syndrome: A Guide for Parents and Professionals.* London: Taylor & Francis Group, 1997.

This Australian psychologist's work for more than two decades with children with Asperger's disorder gave him a pragmatic wisdom that he communicates well in both this popular book and in his speaking presentations. The book is well-balanced and discusses a broad range of issues that children with mild forms of pervasive developmental disorders (PDD) face, with many practical suggestions.

> Klass, Perri, and Eileen Costello. *Quirky Kids: Understanding and Helping Your Child Who Doesn't Fit In—When to Worry and When Not to Worry.* New York: Ballantine, 2003.

This book sensitively acknowledges and illustrates the wide spectrum of children with basic social or related deficits, above and beyond those who actually receive diagnoses of autism, Asperger's disorder, or PDD. The discussion of different types of professionals who can evaluate and treat children's problems in chapter 2 is quite good, even for parents who have children with other types of problems.

Powers, Michael, with Janet Poland. *Asperger Syndrome and Your Child: A Parent's Guide.* New York: HarperResource, 2003.

Full of warmth and humor, many touching stories about children, and practical suggestions, this very readable book is a good introduction for parents who've just learned their child has Asperger's disorder.

Siegel, Bryna. *The World of the Autistic Child: Understanding and Treating Autistic Spectrum Disorders.* London: Oxford University Press, 1998.

The author's depth of understanding has made this a classic in helping other people understand what it's like to cope with autism.

Anxiety and Mood Disorders

Seligman, Martin E. *The Optimistic Child: Proven Program to Safeguard Children from Depression and Build Lifelong Resilience.* New York: Harper-Collins, 1996.

This preventive, positive approach to mood problems is based on extensive research and sound psychological theory.

Spence, Sue, Vanessa Cobham, Ann Wignall, and Ronald M. Rapee. *Helping Your Anxious Child: A Step-by-Step Guide for Parents.* Oakland, CA: New Harbinger Publications, 2000.

This book is written with clear sequences of strategies to try. In the areas of anxiety and mood, sometimes logical sequences don't work the way they're planned, so don't hesitate to consult with professionals if your child doesn't respond exactly as expected to the good ideas that you read here.

Special Education Programs

Twatchman-Cullen, Diane, and Jennifer Twachtman-Reilly. *How Well Does Your IEP Measure Up? Quality Indicators for Effective Service Delivery.* Higganum, CT: Starfish Specialty Publications, 2002.

This is one of many books that give parents ideas on how to work with schools in writing good Individualized Education Programs. Now that the 2004 revision of IDEA has been passed, some of the details in books like this will need to be updated.

Other Related Issues

Blackburn, Lynn Bennett. *Growing Up with Epilepsy: A Practical Guide for Parents.* New York: Demos Medical Publications, 2003.

This sensitive, insightful, up-to-date book helps cut through a complex topic, with ample attention to psychological and educational issues as well as medical factors.

Dornbush, Marilyn P., and Sheryl K. Pruitt. *Teaching the Tiger: A Handbook for Individuals Involved in the Education of Students with Attention Deficit Disorders, Tourette Syndrome or Obsessive-Compulsive Disorder.* Duarte, CA: Hope Press, 1995.

Psychological Treatments

The following books, three of which are published by the American Psychological Association, are written for professionals, but they are worth reading if you really want to check out what therapy approaches are backed by solid research. Be prepared for some serious reading and thoughtful commentary by the authors. Topics include most of the main problems that I've discussed in this book, plus common difficulties such as temper tantrums and sleep, and (in the last book) important research on different approaches to play therapy.

Christophersen, Edward R., and Susan L. Mortweet. *Treatments That Work with Children: Empirically Supported Strategies for Managing Childhood Problems.* Washington, DC: American Psychological Association, 2001.

Hibbs, Euthymia D., and Peter S. Jensen. *Psychosocial Treatments for Child and Adolescent Disorders: Empirically Based Strategies for Clinical Practice, Second Edition.* Washington, DC: American Psychological Association, 1996.

Jacobson, John W., Richard M. Foxx, and James A. Mulick, eds. *Controversial Therapies for Developmental Disabilities.* New York: Lawrence Earlbaum Associates, 2004.

Reddy, Linda A., Tara M. Files-Hall, and Charles E. Schaeffer. *Empirically Based Play Interventions for Children.* Washington, DC: American Psychological Association, 2005.

Appendix B
Helpful Organizations and Associations

Agoraphobia
(see PHOBIAS)

Anxiety Disorders

Anxiety Disorders Association of America
11900 Parklawn Drive #100
Rockville, MD 20852-2624
(301) 231-9350
E-mail: AnxDis@aol.com
www.adaa.org

Anxiety Disorders Association of Canada
Association Canadienne des Troubles Anxieux
P.O. Box 461, Station "D"
Scarborough, Ontario M1R 5B8
Canada
(888) 223-2252
E-mail: contactus@anxietycanada.ca
www.anxietycanada.ca

The Anxiety Panic Internet Resource
www.algy.com/anxiety/index.shtml

Childhood Anxiety Network
www.childhoodanxietynetwork.org

National Phobics Society
Zion Community Resource Centre
339 Stretford Road, Hulme
Manchester M15 4ZY
England
Phone: 0870 7700 456
www.phobics-society.org.uk

notMYkid.org
33 W. Indian School Road
Phoenix, AZ 85013-3205
(602) 652-0163
www.notmykid.org

The Panic Anxiety Disorder Association of South Australia
PADA Inc.
P.O. Box 83
Fullarton 5063
South Australia
Phone: (08) 8227 1044
Fax: (08) 8227 1266
E-mail: pada@chariot.net.au
www.panicanxietydisorder.org.au

Aphasia

Aphasia Hope Foundation (AHF)
2436 W. 137th Street
Leawood, KS 66224
(913) 402-8306; (866) 449-5804
www.aphasiahope.org

National Aphasia Association
156 Fifth Avenue, Suite 707
New York, NY 10010
(800) 922-4622
www.aphasia.org

Apraxia

Childhood Apraxia of Speech Association of North America (CASANA)
1151 Freeport Road, #243
Pittsburgh, PA 15238
(412) 767-6589

Apraxia-Kids Web Site
Referral helpline: (412) 343-7102
www.apraxia-kids.org

Asperger's Syndrome

Asperger's Disorder Home Page
www.aspergers.com

Asperger Syndrome Coalition of the United States
P.O. Box 351268
Jacksonville, FL 32235
(866) 4-ASPRGR
www.asperger.org

Dr. Tony Attwood's Web Site
www.tonyattwood.com.au

Online Asperger Syndrome Information and Support Web Site (OASIS)
www.udel.edu/bkirby/asperger

Ataxia

Ataxia-Telangiectasia Children's Project
668 S. Military Trail
Deerfield Beach, FL 33442
(800) 5-HELP-A-T
www.atcp.org

The National Ataxia Foundation
2600 Fernbrook Lane, Suite 119
Minneapolis, MN 55477
(612) 553-0020
www.ataxia.org

Attention-Deficit/Hyperactivity Disorder

ADHD Canada
Web site only
www.adhdcanada.ca

Attention Deficit Disorder
Web site only
www.ADD.Idsite.com

Attention Deficit Information Network, Inc.
475 Hillside Avenue
Needham, MA 02194
(781) 455-9895
www.addinfonetwork.com

Camps for Children and Adults with Attention Deficit Disorder
499 N.W. Seventieth Avenue, Suite 101
Plantation, FL 33317
(954) 587-3700

Challenging Behaviour Foundation
32 Twydall Lane
Gillingham, Kent ME8 6HX
United Kingdom
Phone: 01634 838739
E-mail: info@thecbf.org.uk
www.thecbf.org.uk

**Children and Adults with Attention-Deficit/Hyperactivity
Disorder (CHADD)**
8181 Professional Place, Suite 201
Landover, MD 20785
(301) 306-7070; (800) 233-4050 (to request information packet)
E-mail: national@chadd.org
www.chadd.org

National Attention Deficit Disorder Association
P.O. Box 1303
Northbrook, IL 60065-1303
E-mail: mail@add.org
www.add.org

notMYkid.org
33 W. Indian School Road
Phoenix, AZ 85013-3205
(602) 652-0163
www.notmykid.org

One ADD Place
Web site only
www.greatconnect.com/oneaddplace

Autism

Autism Network International
P.O. Box 448
Syracuse, NY 13210
(315) 476-2462
www.ani.autistics.org

Autism Research Institute
4111182 Adams Avenue
San Diego, CA 92116
(619) 281-7165
www.autism-society.org

Autism Society of America
7910 Woodmont Avenue, Suite 650
Bethesda, MD 20814-3015
(800) 3AUTISM, ext. 150; (301) 657-0881
www.autism-society.org

Cure Autism Now (CAN)
5455 Wilshire Boulevard, Suite 715
Los Angeles, CA 90036
(323) 549-0500; (888) 828-8476
www.cureautismnow.org

Families for Early Autism Treatment
P.O. Box 255722
Sacramento, CA 95865
www.feat.org

National Alliance for Autism Research
414 Wall Street, Research Park
Princeton, NJ 08540
(888) 777-NAAR; (609) 430-9160
www.babydoc.home.pipeline.com/naar/naar.htm

National Autistic Society
393 City Road
London, EC1V 1NG
United Kingdom
Phone: (0)20 7833 2299
www.nas.org.uk

Bipolar Disorder

Depression and Bipolar Support Alliance
730 N. Franklin Street, Suite 501
Chicago, Illinois 60610
(800) 826-3632; (312) 642-0049
www.dbsalliance.org

Manic Depression Fellowship
Castle Works
21 St. George's Road
London SE1 6ES
United Kingdom
Phone: 08456 340 540
www.bipolar.about.com/gi/dynamic/offsite.htm?site=http%3A%2F%2Fwww
.mdf.org.uk%2F

Bulimia
(see EATING DISORDERS)

Cerebral Palsy

United Cerebral Palsy Association
1522 K Street NW, Suite 1112
Washington, DC 20005
(800) 872-5827; (202) 776-0406
www.ucpa.org

Depression

Depression and Bipolar Support Alliance
730 N. Franklin Street, Suite 501
Chicago, Illinois 60610
(800) 826-3632; (312) 642-0049
www.dbsalliance.org

National Depressive & Manic-Depressive Association, Canada—DMDA Canada, Inc.
41000 Notre Dame Avenue
Winnipeg, Manitoba R3G 2J6
Canada
(204) 786-0987

Developmental Disabilities
(see also DOWN SYNDROME; FRAGILE X SYNDROME)

American Association of University Affiliated Programs for Persons with Developmental Disabilities
8630 Fenton Street, Suite 410
Silver Spring, MD 20910
(301) 588-8252
www.aauap.org

American Association on Mental Retardation
444 N. Capitol Street NW, Suite 846
Washington, DC 20001
(800) 424-3688; (202) 387-1968
www.aamr.org

The Arc
(formerly Association for Retarded Citizens of the U.S.)
500 E. Border Street, Suite 300
Arlington, TX 76010
(800) 433-5255; (817) 261-6003
www.thearc.org

Association of University Centers on Disabilities (AUCD)
10 Wayne Avenue, Suite 920
Silver Spring, MD 20910
(301) 588-8252
www.aucd.org

Clearinghouse on Disability Information
Office of Special Education and Rehabilitative Services (OSERS)
Communication and Media Support Services (CMSS)
U.S. Department of Education
550 Twelfth Street SW, Room 5133
Washington, DC 20004
(202) 245-7303; TTY: (202) 205-5637
www.ed.gov/about/offices/list/osers/index.html

Council for Exceptional Children (CEC)
1110 N. Glebe Road, Suite 300
Arlington, VA 22201
(703) 620-3660; (800) 224-6830; toll-free TTY: (866) 915-5000
www.cec.sped.org

Federation for Children with Special Needs
1135 Tremont Street, Suite 420
Boston, MA 02120
(617) 236-7210; (800) 331-0688
www.fcsn.org

National Association of State Directors of Special Education, Inc. (NASDSE)
1800 Diagonal Road, Suite 320
Alexandria, VA 22314
(703) 519-3800; TTY: (703) 519-7008
www.nasdse.org

National Dissemination Center for Children with Disabilities (NICHCY)
P.O. Box 1492
Washington, DC 20013-1492
(202) 884-8200; (800) 695-0285
www.nichcy.org

National Fragile X Foundation
P.O. Box 190488
San Francisco, CA 94119
(800) 688-8765
www.fragilex.org

National Information Center for Children and Youth with Disabilities
P.O. Box 1492
Washington, DC 20013
(800) 695-0285 (voice/TTY); (202) 884-8200 (voice/TTY)—phones answered
live 9:30 a.m. to 6:30 p.m. EST
www.nichcy.org

National Institute for People with Disabilities
460 W. Thirty-forth Street
New York, NY 10001
(212) 563-7474
www.yai.org

National Institute on Disability and Rehabilitative Research
Switzer Building
330 C Street SW, Suite 3060 MES
Washington, DC 20202
(202) 205-8134
www.ed.gov/offices/OSERS/NIDRR/nidrr.html

Office of Special Education and Rehabilitation Services
Switzer Building
330 C Street SW, Suite 3006
Washington, DC 20202
(202) 205-5465
www.ed.gov/offices/OSERS

Office of Special Education Programs
Switzer Building
330 C Street SW, Suite 3086
Washington, DC 20202
(202) 205-5507

Parents Helping Parents: The Parent-Directed Family Resource Center for Children with Special Needs
3041 Olcott Street
Santa Clara, CA 95054
(408) 727-5775
www.php.com

Rehabilitation Services Administration
Switzer Building
330 C Street SW, Suite 3026
Washington, DC 20202
(202) 205-5482
www.ed.gov/offices/OSERS/RSA/rsa.html

Special Olympics International
1325 G Street NW, Suite 500
Washington, DC 20005
(202) 628-3630
www.specialolympics.org

Voice of the Retarded
5005 Newport Drive, Suite 108
Rolling Meadows, IL 60008
(847) 253-6020

Wisconsin Department of Public Instruction Special Education Web Site
www.dpi.state.wi.us/dlsea/een/index.html
(Check your state for it's own special education Web site.)

Disability Information

American Association of People with Disabilities
1819 H Street NW, Suite 330
Washington, DC 20006
(800) 840-8844; (800) 235-7125
www.aapd-dc.org

Association for the Severely Handicapped
29 W. Susquehanna Avenue, Suite 210
Baltimore, MD 21204
(410) 828-8274
www.tash.org

Association on Higher Education and Disability (AHEAD)
University of Massachusetts/Boston
100 Morrissey Boulevard
Boston, MA 02125-3393
(617) 287-3880
www.ahead.org
International, multicultural organization of professionals committed to full participation in higher education for persons with disabilities.

Children's Defense Fund
25 E Street NW
Washington, DC 20001
(202) 628-8787
www.childrensdefense.org

Clearinghouse on Disability Information
Office of Special Education and Rehabilitative Services
Room 3132, Switzer Building
330 C Street SW
Washington, DC 20202-2524
(202) 205-8241 (voice/TTY)

Commission on Mental and Physical Disability Law
American Bar Association
740 Fifteenth Street NW
Washington, DC 20005
(202) 662-1570
www.abanet.org/disability/home.html

Council for Exceptional Children (CEC)
1920 Association Drive
Reston, VA 20191-1589
(703) 620-3660 (voice); (703) 264-9446 (TTY)
E-mail: cec@cec.sped.org
www.cec.sped.org/home.htm

Disability Rights Education and Defense Fund, Inc.
2212 Sixth Street
Berkeley, CA 94710
(510) 644-2555
www.dredf.org

Disability Statistics Rehabilitation, Research and Training Center
3333 California Street, Room 340
University of California at San Francisco
San Francisco, CA 94118
(415) 502-5210 (voice); (415) 502-5217 (TTY)
E-mail: distats@itsa.ucsf.edu
www.dsc.ucsf.edu

ERIC Clearinghouse on Disabilities and Gifted Education
Council for Exceptional Children (CEC)
1920 Association Drive
Reston, VA 20191-1589
(800) 328-0272 (voice/TTY); (703) 264-9449 (TTY)
E-mail: ericec@cec.sped.org
www.cec.sped.org/ericec.htm

Family Center for Technology and Disabilities
Academy for Educational Development (AED)
1825 Connecticut Avenue NW, Seventh Floor
Washington, DC 20009-5721
(202) 884-8068
www.fctd.info

Family Resource Center on Disabilities
20 E. Jackson Boulevard, Room 900
Chicago, IL 60604
(800) 952-4199 (voice/TTY; toll-free in Illinois only)
(312) 939-3513 (voice); (312) 939-3519 (TTY)

Family Village
(A global community of disability-related resources)
Waisman Center
University of Wisconsin–Madison
1500 Highland Avenue
Madison, WI 53705-2280
www.familyvillage.wisc.edu

National Association of Protection and Advocacy Systems
900 Second Street NE, Suite 211
Washington, DC 20002
(202) 408-9514
www.protectionandadvocacy.com/napas.htm

National Clearinghouse on Women and Girls with Disabilities
114 E. Thirty-second Street, Suite 701
New York, NY 10016
(212) 725-1803
www.onisland.com/eec

National Easter Seal Society
230 W. Monroe Street, Suite 1800
Chicago, IL 60606
(800) 221-6827; (312) 726-6200
www.easter-seals.org

National Information Center for Children and Youth with Disabilities
1875 Connecticut Avenue, Eighth Floor
Washington, DC 20009
(800) 695-0285
www.aed.org/nichcy

National Institute on Disability and Rehabilitative Research
Switzer Building
330 C Street SW, Suite 3060 MES
Washington, DC 20202
(202) 205-8134
www.ed.gov/offices/OSERS/NIDRR/nidrr.html

National Library Service for the Blind and Physically Handicapped
500 E. Remington Road, Suite 200
Schaumburg, IL 60173
(800) 331-2020; (800) 221-3004; (708) 843-2020

National Maternal and Child Health Clearinghouse
2070 Chain Bridge Road, Suite 450
Vienna, VA 22182-2536
(703) 821-8955, ext. 254 or 265
E-mail: nmchc@circsol.com
Publications available in Spanish; Spanish speaker on staff

National Mental Health Association
1021 Prince Street
Alexandria, VA 22314-2971
(800) 969-6642; (703) 684-7722; (800) 433-5959 (TTY)
E-mail: nmhainfo@aol.com
www.nmha.org

National Organization on Disability
910 Sixteenth Street NW, Suite 600
Washington, DC 20006
(202) 293-5960
www.nod.org

National Parent Network on Disabilities
1130 Seventeenth Street NW, Suite 400
Washington, DC 20036
(202) 463-2299 (voice/TTY)
E-mail: npnd@cs.com
www.npnd.org

Parents Helping Parents: The Parent-Directed Family Resource Center for Children with Special Needs
3041 Olcott Street
Santa Clara, CA 95054
(408) 727-5775
Publications available in Spanish; Spanish speaker on staff
E-mail: info@php.com
www.php.com

Protection and Advocacy
100 Howe Avenue, Suite 185-N
Sacramento, CA 95825
(800) 776-5746
www.pai-ca.org

Sibling Support Project
Children's Hospital and Medical Center
P.O. Box 5371 CL-09
Seattle, WA 98105
(206) 368-0371
www.chmc.org/department/sibsupp/default.htm

TASH
(formerly the Association for Persons with Severe Handicaps)
29 W. Susquehanna Avenue, Suite 210
Baltimore, MD 21204
(410) 828-8274 (voice); (410) 828-1306 (TTY)
E-mail: info@tash.org
www.tash.org

World Institute on Disability
510 Sixteenth Street, Suite 100
Oakland, CA 94612
(510) 763-4100
www.wid.org

Down Syndrome
(see also DEVELOPMENTAL DISABILITIES)

Canadian Down Syndrome Society
811 Fourteenth Street NW
Calgary, Alberta T2N 2A4
Canada
(403) 270-8500; (800) 883-5608
E-mail: dsinfo@cdss.ca
www.cdss.ca

Down's Syndrome Association
Langdon Down Centre
2a Langdon Park
Teddington TW11 9PS
United Kingdom
Phone: 0845 230 0372
E-mail: info@downs-syndrome.org.uk
www.downs-syndrome.org.uk

International Resource Center for Down Syndrome
1621 Euclid Avenue, Suite 514
Cleveland, OH 44115
(216) 621-5858; (800) 899-3039

National Down Syndrome Congress
1605 Chantilly Drive NE, Suite 250
Atlanta, GA 30324
(800) 232-NDSC; (404) 633-1555

National Down Syndrome Society
666 Broadway, Suite 810
New York, NY 10012
(800) 221-4602; (212) 460-9330
www.ndss.org

Dyslexia
(see also LEARNING DISABILITIES)

British Dyslexia Association
98 London Road
Reading RG1 5AU
United Kingdom
Phone: 0118 966 2677
E-mail: admin@bda-dyslexia.demon.co.uk
www.bda-dyslexia.org.uk/main/home/index.asp

Dyslexia Research Institute (DRI)
5746 Centerville Road
Tallahassee, FL 32309
(850) 893-2216
www.dyslexia-add.org

Hello Friend/Ennis William Cosby Foundation
Ennis William Cosby Foundation
P.O. Box 4061
Santa Monica, CA 90411
www.hellofriend.org

International Dyslexia Association
(formerly the Orton Dyslexia Society)
Chester Building #382
8600 LaSalle Road
Baltimore, MD 21286-2044
(800) 222-3123; (410) 296-0232
E-mail: info@interdys.org
www.interdys.org

Learning Disabilities Association
4156 Library Road
Pittsburgh, PA 15234
(412) 341-1515
www.ldanatl.org

The Learning Disabilities Association of Canada
323 Chapel Street
Ottawa, Ontario K1N 7Z2
Canada
(613) 238-5721
E-mail: information@ldac-taac.ca
www.ldac-taac.ca/english/links.htm

National Center for Learning Disabilities
381 Park Avenue South, Suite 1401
New York, NY 10016
(212) 545-7510; toll-free (888) 575-7373
www.ncld.org

Recording for the Blind and Dyslexic
The Anne T. Macdonald Center
20 Roszel Road
Princeton, NJ 08540
(800) 221-4792; (609) 452-0606
E-mail: custserv@rfbd.org
www.rfbd.org

Eating Disorders

Eating Disorders Association
103 Prince of Wales Road
Norwich NR1 1DW
United Kingdom
Phone: 0870 770 3256
www.edauk.com

National Association of Anorexia Nervosa and Associated Disorders
P.O. Box 7
Highland Park, IL 60035
(847) 831-3438
www.anad.org

National Eating Disorders Association
(formerly Eating Disorders Awareness and Prevention)
603 Stewart Street, Suite 803
Seattle, WA 98101
(800) 931-2237; (206) 382-3587
www.nationaleatingdisorders.org

Education/Special Education

American Council on Rural Special Education (ACRES)
Kansas State University
2323 Anderson Avenue, Suite 226
Manhattan, KS 66502
(785) 532-2737
E-mail: acres@ksu.edu
www.ksu.edu/acres

American Therapeutic Recreation Association
P.O. Box 15215
Hattiesburg, MS 39404-5215
(800) 553-0304; (601) 264-3413
E-mail: atra@atra-tr.org
www.atra-tr.org

Department of Education
400 Maryland Avenue SW
Washington, DC 20202
(800) USA-LEARN
www.ed.gov

Head Start Bureau
Administration on Children, Youth and Families
U.S. Department of Health & Human Services
P.O. Box 1182
Washington, DC 20013
www.acf.dhhs.gov/programs/hsb

HEATH Resource Center (National Clearinghouse on Postsecondary Education for Individuals with Disabilities)
One Dupont Circle NW, Suite 800
Washington, DC 20036-1193
(800) 544-3284; (202) 939-9320 (voice/TTY)
E-mail: heath@ace.nche.edu
www.acenet.edu/Programs/HEATH/home.html

National Association for the Education of Young Children (NAEYC)
1509 Sixteenth Street NW
Washington, DC 20036
(800) 424-2460

National Association of Private Schools for Exceptional Children (NAPSEC)
1522 K Street NW, Suite 1032
Washington, DC 20005
(202) 408-3338
E-mail: napsec@aol.com
www.napsec.com

National Clearinghouse on Careers and Professions Related to Early Intervention and Education for Children with Disabilities
Council for Exceptional Children
1920 Association Drive
Reston, VA 20191-1589
(800) 641-7824; (703) 264-9474 (voice); (703) 264-9480 (TTY)
E-mail: ncpse@cec.sped.org
www.special-ed-careers.org

National Head Start Association
1651 Prince Street
Alexandria, VA 22314
(703) 739-0875
www.nhsa.org

National Health Information Center
P.O. Box 1133
Washington, DC 20013-1133
(800) 336-4797; (301) 565-4167
E-mail: nhicinfo@health.org
nhic-nt.health.org

Office of Civil Rights
U.S. Department of Education, OCR
330 C Street SW, Suite 5000
Washington, DC 20202-1100
(202) 205-5413
www.ed.gov/offices/OCR

Office of Educational Research and Improvement
555 New Jersey Avenue NW
Washington, DC 20208
(202) 219-1385
www.ed.gov/offices/OERI

Office of Special Education and Rehabilitation Services
Switzer Building
330 C Street SW, Suite 3006
Washington, DC 20202
(202) 205-5465
www.ed.gov/offices/OSERS

Office of Special Education Programs
Switzer Building
330 C Street SW, Suite 3086
Washington, DC 20202
(202) 205-5507

Parent Advocacy Coalition for Educational Rights
4826 Chicago Avenue South
Minneapolis, MN 55417
(612) 827-2966
www.pacer.org

Epilepsy

American Epilepsy Society
342 N. Main Street
West Hartford, CT 06117-2507
(860) 586-7505
www.aesnet.org

Epilepsy Foundation—National Office
4351 Garden City Drive, Fifth Floor
Landover, MD 20785-4941
(800) 332-1000; (301) 459-3700
Publications available in Spanish; Spanish speaker on staff
E-mail: postmaster@efa.org
www.efa.org

Epilepsy International
www.epiworld.com

Family Support

Canadian Parents Dot Com
Web site only
www.canadianparents.com

Family Resource Center on Disabilities
20 E. Jackson Boulevard, Room 900
Chicago, IL 60604
(800) 952-4199 (voice/TTY; toll-free in Illinois only);
(312) 939-3513 (voice); (312) 939-3519 (TTY)

Family Voices
(A national coalition speaking for children with special health care needs)
P.O. Box 769
Algodones, NM 87001
(888) 835-5669; (505) 867-2368
E-mail: kidshealth@familyvoices.org
www.familyvoices.org

Federation of Families for Children's Mental Health
1021 Prince Street
Alexandria, VA 22314-2971
E-mail: ffcmh@ffcmh.com
www.ffcmh.org

Research and Training Center on Family Support and Children's Mental Health
Portland State University
P.O. Box 751
Portland, OR 97207-0751
(800) 628-1696; (503) 725-4040 (voice); (503) 725-4165 (TTY)
E-mail: caplane@rri.pdx.edu
www.rtc.pdx.edu

Fragile X Syndrome

National Fragile X Foundation
1441 York Street, Suite 303
Denver, CO 80206
(800) 688-8765; (303) 333-6155
E-mail: natlfx@sprintmail.com
www.nfxf.org

General

American Academy of Pediatrics (AAP)
141 Northwest Point Boulevard
Elk Grove Village, IL 60007-1098
(847) 434-4000
www.aap.org

Australian Psychological Society
Level 11
257 Collins Street
Melbourne VIC 8009
Australia
Phone: (03) 8662 3300; toll-free: 1-800 333 497
E-mail: contactus@psychology.org.au
www.psychology.org.au

British Psychological Society
St Andrews House
48 Princess Road East
Leicester LE1 7DR
United Kingdom
Phone: 0116 254 9568
E-mail: enquiry@bps.org.uk
www.bps.org.uk/home-page.cfm

Canadian Psychological Association
141 Laurier Avenue West, Suite 702
Ottawa, Ontario K1P 5J3
Canada
(888) 472-0657; (613) 237-2144
E-mail: cpa@cpa.ca
www.cpa.ca

European Federation of Psychologists' Associations
www.efpa.be/start.php

German Psychological Society
Deutsche Gesellschaft für Psychologie
www.dgps.de

International Neuropsychological Society
Western State Hospital
P.O. Box 2500
Staunton, VA 24402-2500
(540) 332-8391
E-mail: bmarcopulos@ilc-ins.org
www.ilc-ins.org

International Union of Psychological Science
web@iupsys.org

Italian Psychological Society
(Società Italiana di Psicologia)
Via Tagliamento 76
00198
Roma
Italia
Phone: 06 8845136
E-mail: sipsit@tin.it
www.sips.it/index.html?includi=home

New Zealand Psychological Society
P.O. Box 4092
Wellington
New Zealand
Phone: 0064 4 473 4884
www.psychology.org.nz

World Health Organization
Avenue Appia 20
1211 Geneva 27
Switzerland
Phone: (+41 22) 791 21 11

Genetics

Alliance of Genetic Support Groups
4301 Connecticut NW, Suite 404
Washington, DC 20008
(800) 336-4363; (202) 966-5557
E-mail: info@geneticalliance.org
www.geneticalliance.org

Gifted Children

American Association for Gifted Children at Duke University
Box 90270
Durham, NC 27708-0270
(919) 783-6152
www.aagc.org

ERIC Clearinghouse on Disabilities and Gifted Education
Council for Exceptional Children (CEC)
1110 N. Glebe Road, Suite 300
Arlington, VA 22201-5704
(800) 328-0272 (voice/TTY)
www.ericec.org

Hyperlexia

American Hyperlexia Association
479 Spring Road
Elmhurst, IL 60126
(708) 530-8551
www.hyperlexia.org

Canadian Hyperlexia Association
300 John Street, Box 87673
Thornhill, Ontario L3T 7R3
Canada
(905) 886-9163
E-mail: cha@ican.net
home.ican.net/~cha

Independent Living

Research and Training Center on Independent Living
University of Kansas
4089 Dole Building
Lawrence, KS 66045-2930
(785) 864-4095 (voice/TTY)
E-mail: rtcil@kuhub.cc.ukansas.edu
www.lsi.ukans.edu/rtcil/catalog1.htm

Lead Poisoning

The Environmental Protection Agency
Safe Drinking Water Hotline
(800) 426-4791
For information on laboratories certified to test for lead in water.

The National Center for Lead-Safe Housing
205 American City Building
Columbia, MD 21044
(410) 964-1230
For information about lead in housing.

The National Lead Information Center
8601 Georgia Avenue, Suite 503
Silver Spring, MD 20910
(800) 424-5323; (800) LEAD-FYI (1-800-532-3394)
www.epa.gov/lead/nlic.htm

Learning Disabilities

British Institute of Learning Disabilities
Green Street
Kidderminster, Worcestershire DY10 1JL
United Kingdom
www.bild.org.uk

Council for Exceptional Children and the Division for Learning Disabilities
1920 Association Drive
Reston, VA 22091-1589
(800) 328-0272; (703) 620-3660
Council for Exceptional Children: www.cec.sped.org
Division for Learning Disabilities: www.dldcec.org

Council for Learning Disabilities
P.O. Box 40303
Overland Park, KS 66204
(913) 492-2546
www.cldinternational.org

Federation for Children with Special Needs
1135 Tremont Street, Suite 420
Boston, MA 02120
(617) 236-7210; (800) 331-0688
www.fcsn.org

Foundation for People with Learning Disabilities
Sea Containers House
20 Upper Ground
London SE1 9QB
United Kingdom
Phone: 020 7803 1100
www.learningdisabilities.org.uk/index.cfm

LD On-Line
Web site only
www.ldonline.org

Learning Disabilities Association of America (LDA)
(formerly ACLD)
4156 Library Road
Pittsburgh, PA 15234
(888) 300-6710; (412) 341-1515; (412) 341-8077
Publications available in Spanish
E-mail: vldanatl@usaor.ne
www.ldanatl.org

The Learning Disabilities Association of Canada
323 Chapel Street
Ottawa, Ontario K1N 7Z2
Canada
(613) 238-5721
E-mail: information@ldac-taac.ca
www.ldac-taac.ca/english/links.htm

Learning Resources Network
1550 Hayes Drive
Manhattan, KS 66502
(800) 678-5376
www.lern.org

National Center for Learning Disabilities (NCLD)
381 Park Avenue South, Suite 1401
New York, NY 10016
(212) 545-7510; (888) 575-7373
www.ncld.org

Nonverbal Learning Disorder on the Web
Web site only
www.NLDontheweb.org

Nonverbal Learning Disorders Association
2446 Albany Avenue
West Hartford, CT 06117
(860) 570-0217
www.nlda.org

Schwab Foundation for Learning
1650 South Amphlett Boulevard, Suite 300
San Mateo, CA 94402
(800) 230-0988
www.schwablearning.org

Specific Learning Difficulties of South Australia
298 Portrush Road
Kensington 5068
South Australia
Phone: 08 8431 1655
E-mail: info@speld-sa.org.au
www.speld-sa.org.au

Manic Depression
(see BIPOLAR DISORDER)

Mental Health/Mental Illness

The American Academy of Child and Adolescent Psychiatry
3615 Wisconsin Avenue NW
Washington, DC 20016-3007
(202) 966-7300
www.aacap.org

American Psychiatric Association
1000 Wilson Boulevard, Suite 1825
Arlington, VA 22209-3901
(703) 907-7300
www.psych.org

American Psychological Association
750 First Street NE
Washington, DC 20002-4242
(800) 374-2721; (202) 336-5510
www.apa.org

Canadian Mental Health Association
8 King Street East, Suite 810
Toronto, Ontario M5C 1B5
Canada
(416) 484-7750
www.cmha.ca/bins/index.asp

Center for Mental Health Services
5600 Fishers Lane, Room 17-99
Rockville, MD 20857
www.mentalhealth.org

Federation of Families for Children's Mental Health
1101 King Street, Suite 420
Alexandria, VA 22314
(703) 684-7710
www.ffcmh.org

National Alliance for the Mentally Ill (NAMI)
200 N. Glebe Road, Suite 1015
Arlington, VA 22203-3754
(800) 950-NAMI; (703) 524-7600; (703) 516-7991 (TTY)
E-mail: namiofc@aol.com
www.nami.org

National Association for the Dually Diagnosed (NADD)
132 Fair Street
Kingston, NY 12401
(800) 331-5362; (845) 331-4336
www.thenadd.org

National Institute of Mental Health (NIMH)
5600 Fishers Lane
Rockville, MD 20857
(301) 443-4513
www.nimh.nih.gov

Mental Retardation
(see also DEVELOPMENTAL DISABILITIES; DOWN SYNDROME; FRAGILE X SYNDROME)

The Arc
(formerly the Association for Retarded Citizens of the U.S.)
500 E. Border Street, Suite 300
Arlington, TX 76010
(800) 433-5255; (817) 261-6003 (voice); (817) 277-0553 (TTY)
E-mail: thearc@metronet.com
www.thearc.org/welcome.html

International Resource Center for Down Syndrome
Keith Building
1621 Euclid Avenue, Suite 514
Cleveland, OH 44115
(216) 621-5858; (800) 899-3039 (toll-free in Ohio only)
E-mail: hf854@cleveland.freenet.edu

National Down Syndrome Congress
1605 Chantilly Drive, Suite 250
Atlanta, GA 30324
(800) 232-6372; (404) 633-1555
Pamphlet available in Spanish
E-mail: NDSCcenter@aol.com
www.carol.net/~ndsc

National Down Syndrome Society
666 Broadway, Eighth Floor
New York, NY 10012-2317
(800) 221-4602; (212) 460-9330
E-mail: info@ndss.org
www.ndss.org

Special Olympics International
1325 G Street NW, Suite 500
Washington, DC 20005
(202) 628-3630
Publications available in Spanish and French
Spanish and French speakers on staff
E-mail: specialolympics@msn.com
www.specialolympics.org

Nonverbal Learning Disorder

Nonverbal Learning Disorder on the Web
Web site only
www.NLDontheweb.org

Nonverbal Learning Disorders Association
2446 Albany Avenue
West Hartford, CT 06117
(860) 570-0217
www.nlda.org

Obsessive-Compulsive Disorder

Childhood Anxiety Network
www.childhoodanxietynetwork.org

O.C. Foundation, Inc.
676 State Street
New Haven, CT 06511
(203) 401-2070
E-mail: info@ocfoundation.org
www.ocfoundation.org

Oppositional Defiant Disorder

notMYkid.org
33 W. Indian School Road
Phoenix, AZ 85013-3205
(602) 652-0163
www.notmykid.org

Panic Disorder

Childhood Anxiety Network
www.childhoodanxietynetwork.org

National Phobics Society
Zion Community Resource Centre
339 Stretford Road
Hulme, Manchester M15 4ZY
England
Phone: 0870 7700 456
www.phobics-society.org.uk

Parenting

Center on Positive Behavioral Interventions and Supports
1761 Alder Street
1235 University of Oregon
Eugene, OR 97403-5262
(541) 346-2505
www.pbis.org

MUMS, National Parent-to-Parent Network
150 Custer Court
Green Bay, WI 54301-1243
(920) 336-5333; (877) 336-5333 (parents only)
www.netnet.net/mums

Zero to Three
(formerly National Center for Clinical Infant Programs)
2000 M Street NW, Suite 200
Washington, DC 20036
(800) 899-4301 (for publications); (202) 638-1144
www.zerotothree.org

Phobias

Agoraphobia in Australia
www.agoraphobiaaustralia.org

Anxiety Disorders Association of America
11900 Parklawn Drive #100
Rockville, MD 20852-2624
(301) 231-9350
E-mail: AnxDis@aol.com
www.adaa.org

Childhood Anxiety Network
www.childhoodanxietynetwork.org

National Phobics Society
Zion Community Resource Centre
339 Stretford Road
Hulme, Manchester M15 4ZY
England
Phone: 0870 7700 456
www.phobics-society.org.uk

Post-Traumatic Stress Disorder

Anxiety Disorders Association of America
11900 Parklawn Drive #100
Rockville, MD 20852-2624
(301) 231-9350
E-mail: AnxDis@aol.com
www.adaa.org

Childhood Anxiety Network
www.childhoodanxietynetwork.org

European Society for Traumatic Stress Studies
Web site only
E-mail: secretariat@estss.org
www.estss.org

National Center for PTSD
VA Medical Center (116D)
215 N. Main Street
White River Junction, VT 05009
(802) 296-6300
www.ncptsd.org

PTSD Alliance
(877) 507-PTSD (toll-free)
www.ptsdalliance.org/home2.html

Rehabilitation

National Rehabilitation Information Center (NARIC)
8455 Colesville Road, Suite 935
Silver Spring, MD 20910-3319
(800) 346-2742; (301) 588-9284 (voice); (301) 495-5626 (TTY)
Spanish speaker on staff
www.naric.com/naric

Rehabilitation Research and Training Center on Positive Behavioral Support
13301 Bruce B. Downs Boulevard
Tampa, FL 33612
(813) 974-4612

Rett Syndrome

International Rett Syndrome Association
9121 Piscataway Road, Suite 2B
Clinton, MD 20735-2561
(800) 818-7388; (301) 856-3334
E-mail: irsa@rettsyndrome.org
www.rettsyndrome.org

Rett Syndrome Research Foundation (RSRF)
4600 Devitt Drive
Cincinnati, OH 45246
(513) 874-3020
www.rsrf.org

Schizophrenia

Schizophrenia.com Web Site
Schizophrenia.com

World Fellowship for Schizophrenia and Allied Disorders
124 Merton Street, Suite 507
Toronto, Ontario M4S 2Z2
Canada
(416) 961-2855; fax: (416) 961-1948
E-mail: info@world-schizophrenia.org
www.world-schizophrenia.org

Sensory Integration Dysfunction

Childhood Anxiety Network
www.childhoodanxietynetwork.org

OT Kids, Inc.
www.alaska.net/~otkids

Speech/Language Problems

American Speech-Language-Hearing Association (ASHA)
10801 Rockville Pike
Rockville, MD 20852
(800) 638-8255 (voice/TTY); (301) 897-5700 (voice/TTY)
E-mail: actioncenter@asha.org
www.asha.org

National Black Association for Speech-Language and Hearing (NBASLH)
P.O. Box 61328
Charleston, SC 29419
(843) 574-6441
www.nbaslh.org

National Stuttering Project
5100 E. La Palma Avenue, Suite 208
Anaheim Hills, CA 92807
(800) 364-1677; (714) 693-7480
E-mail: nspmail@aol.com
www.nspstutter.org

Speak Easy International Foundation, Inc. (SEIF)
233 Concord Drive
Paramus, NJ 07652
(201) 262-0895
www.speak-easy.org

Stuttering Foundation of America
3100 Walnut Grove Road #603
P.O. Box 11749
Memphis, TN 38111
(800) 992-9392
E-mail: stuttersfa@aol.com
www.stuttersfa.org

Stuttering

National Center for Stuttering
200 E. Thirty-third Street, Suite 17C
New York, NY 10016
(800) 221-2483
www.stuttering.com

National Stuttering Association (NSA)
119 W. Fortieth Street, Fourteenth Floor
New York, NY 10018
(212) 944-4050; (800) 937-8888
www.westutter.org

Speak Easy International Foundation, Inc. (SEIF)
233 Concord Drive
Paramus, NJ 07652
(201) 262-0895
www.speak-easy.org

Stuttering Foundation of America (SFA)
3100 Walnut Grove Road, Suite 603
Memphis, TN 38111
(901) 452-7343; (800) 992-9392
www.stutteringhelp.org
www.tartamudez.org (Spanish)

The Stuttering Home Page
www.stutteringhomepage.com

Suicide

American Association of Suicidology
5221 Wisconsin Avenue NW
Washington, DC 20015
(202) 237-2280
www.suicidology.org

Australia's National Youth Suicide Prevention Strategy Communications Project
300 Queen Street
Melbourne, Victoria 3000
Australia
Phone: (03) 9214 7888
www.aifs.gov.au/ysp

Canadian Association for Suicide Prevention (CASP)
c/o The Support Network
301 11456 Jasper Avenue
Edmonton, Alberta T5K 0M1
Canada
(780) 482-0198
E-mail: casp@suicideprevention.ca
www.suicideprevention.ca

Canadian Kids' Help Phone
National, toll-free, twenty-four-hour, bilingual child and youth telephone counseling service and Web site
(800) 668-6868
www.kidshelp.sympatico.ca

notMYkid.org
33 W. Indian School Road
Phoenix, AZ 85013-3205
(602) 652-0163
www.notmykid.org

The Samaritans
The Upper Mill
Kingston Road
Ewell, Surrey KT17 2AF
United Kingdom
Phone: 020 8394 8300
E-mail: admin@samaritans.org
www.samaritans.org.uk

Yellow Ribbon International
P.O. Box 644
Westminster, CO 80036-0644
(303) 429-3530
E-mail: ask4help@yellowribbon.org
www.yellowribbon.org

Technology

Alliance for Technology Access
2175 E. Francisco Boulevard, Suite L
San Rafael, CA 94901
(800) 455-7970; (415) 455-4575 (voice); (415) 455-0491 (TTY)
E-mail: atainfo@ataccess.org
www.ataccess.org

Center for Universal Design
North Carolina State University School of Design
Box 8613
Raleigh, NC 27695-8613
(800) 647-6777; (919) 515-3082 (voice/TTY)
E-mail: cahd@ncsu.edu
www.design.ncsu.edu/cud

RESNA (Rehabilitation Engineering and Assistive Technology Society of North America)
1700 N. Moore Street, Suite 1540
Arlington, VA 22209-1903
(703) 524-6686 (voice); (703) 524-6639 (TTY)
E-mail: natloffice@resna.org
www.resna.org

Technical Assistance Alliance for Parent Centers (the Alliance)
PACER Center
4826 Chicago Avenue South
Minneapolis, MN 55417-1098
(888) 248-0822; (612) 827-2966; (612) 827-7770 (TTY)
Spanish speaker on staff
E-mail: alliance@taalliance.org
www.taalliance.org

Tourette's Syndrome

Tourette Syndrome Association
4240 Bell Boulevard
Bayside, NY 11361
(800) 237-0717; (718) 224-2999
E-mail: tourette@ix.netcom.com
www.tsa-usa.org

References

Adams, M. J., et al. *Phonemic Awareness in Young Children: A Classroom Curriculum.* Baltimore: Brookes Publishing, 1997.

Agner, K. D. "Diagnosis and treatment of bipolar disorder in children and adolescents." *Journal of Clinical Psychiatry* 65 (suppl. 15) (2004): 30–34.

Ahn, M. S., and J. A. Frazier. "Diagnostic and treatment issues in childhood-onset bipolar disorder." *Essential Psychopharmacology* 6, no. 1 (2004): 25–44.

Akshoomoff, N., K. Pierce, and E. Courchesne. "The neurobiological basis of autism from a developmental perspective." *Development and Psychopathology* 14 (2002): 613–34.

Alerian, A. J. "Use of selective serotonin reuptake inhibitors in childhood depression." *Lancet* 364, no. 9435 (August 21, 2004): 660–61.

Aman, M. G. "Management of hyperactivity and other acting-out problems in patients with autism spectrum disorder." *Seminars in Pediatric Neurology* 11, no. 3 (2004): 225–28.

American Academy of Pediatrics Committee on Children with Disabilities. "The pediatrician's role in the diagnosis and management of autistic spectrum disorder in children." *Pediatrics* 107, no. 5 (2001): 1221–26.

American Psychiatric Association. *Diagnostic and Statistical Manual of Mental Disorders: DSM-IV-TR* (fourth edition, text revision). Washington, DC: American Psychiatric Association, 2000.

Arnold, L. E. "Treatment alternatives for attention-deficit/hyperactivity disorder." In P. J. Jensen and J. Cooper, eds. *Attention-Deficit/Hyperactivity Disorder: State of the Science and Best Practices*. Kingston, NJ: Civic Research Institute, 2002.

Attwood, Tony. *Asperger's Syndrome: A Guide for Parents and Professionals*. London: Taylor & Francis Group, 1997.

Autism Society of America. "Biomedical and Dietary Treatments" (fact sheet). Bethesda, MD: Autism Society of America, 2003. Available from www.autism-society.org/site/PageServer?pagename=BiomedicalDietary Treatments.

Baird, G., T. Charman, S. Baron-Cohen, et al. "A screening instrument for autism at 18 months of age: A 6-year follow-up study." *Journal of the American Academy of Child and Adolescent Psychiatry* 39 (2000): 694–702.

Barkley, R. A. *Attention Deficit Hyperactivity Disorder: A Handbook for Diagnosis and Treatment*. 2nd ed. New York: Guilford Press, 1998.

———. *Taking Charge of ADHD: The Complete, Authoritative Guide for Parents*. New York: Guilford Press, 2000.

Baumgaertel, A. "Alternative and controversial treatments for attention-deficit/hyperactivity disorder." *Pediatric Clinics of North America* 46 (1999): 977–92.

Berument, S. K., M. Rutter, C. Lord, A. Pickles, and A. Bailey. "Autism screening questionnaire: Diagnostic validity." *British Journal of Psychiatry* 175 (1999): 444–51.

Birmaher, B., N. D. Ryan, D. E. Williamson, et al. "Childhood and adolescent depression: A review of the past 10 years. Part 1." *Journal of the American Academy of Child and Adolescent Psychiatry* 35, no. 11 (1996): 1427–39.

Brent, D. A. "Antidepressants and pediatric depression—the risk of doing nothing." *New England Journal of Medicine* 351, no. 16 (October 14, 2004): 1598–601.

Brent, D. A., M. Oquendo, B. Birmaher, et al. "Familial transmission of mood disorders: Convergence and divergence with transmission of suicidal behavior." *Journal of the American Academy of Child and Adolescent Psychiatry* 43, no. 10 (October 2004): 1259–66.

Brown, J., P. Cohen, J. G. Johnson, et al. "Childhood abuse and neglect: Specificity of effects on adolescent and young adult depression and suicidality." *Journal of the American Academy of Child and Adolescent Psychiatry* 38, no. 12 (1999): 1490–96.

Burke, Jeffrey D., Rolf Loeber, and Boris Birmaher. "Oppositional Defiant Disorder and Conduct Disorder: A Review of the Past 10 Years, Part II." *Journal of the American Academy of Child and Adolescent Psychiatry* 41, no. 11 (November 2002): 1275–93.

Chabot, R. J., and G. Serfontein. "Quantitative electroencephalographic profiles of children with attention deficit disorder." *Biological Psychiatry* 40 (1996): 951–63.

CHADD. "Children and Adults with Attention-Deficit/Hyperactivity Disorder," CHADD Fact Sheet #5. July 2001. www.chadd.org/fs/fs5.htm.

Christophersen, Edward R., and Susan L. Mortweet. *Treatments That Work with Children: Empirically Supported Strategies for Managing Childhood Problems.* Washington, DC: American Psychological Association, 2001.

Committee for Education and the Workforce Web site. Final IDEA bill. http://edworkforce.house.gov/issues/108th/education/idea/conferencereport/confrept.htm.

Committee on Children with Disabilities, American Academy of Pediatrics. "Technical report: The pediatrician's role in the diagnosis and management of autistic spectrum disorder in children." *Pediatrics* 107, no. 5 (2001): 1–18.

Connor, D. F., and R. J. Steingard. "New formulations of stimulants for attention-deficit hyperactivity disorder: Therapeutic potential." *CNS Drugs* 18, no. 14 (2004): 1011–30.

Council for Exceptional Children's Summary of Significant Issues in IDEA 2004. www.cec.sped.org/pp/IDEA_120204.pdf.

Courchesne, E., R. Carper, and N. Akshoomoff. "Evidence of brain overgrowth in the first year of life in autism." *Journal of the American Medical Association* 290, no. 3 (2003): 337–44.

Dery, M., J. Toupin, R. Pauze, and P. Verlaan. "Frequency of mental health disorders in a sample of elementary school students receiving special educational services for behavioural difficulties." *Canadian Journal of Psychiatry* 49, no. 11 (November 2004): 769–75.

Dugdale, A. "Rationale for psychostimulants in ADHD." *Britism Medical Journal* 330, no. 7482 (January 8, 2005): 95.

Ehlers, S., C. Gillberg, and L. Wing. "A screening questionnaire for Asperger syndrome and other high-functioning autism spectrum disorders in school age children." *Journal of Autism and Developmental Disorders* 29, no. 2 (1999): 129–41.

Eli Lilly Web site. Strattera. www.strattera.com/index.jsp.

El-Sayed, E., J. O. Larsson, H. E. Persson, et al. "Altered cortical activity in children with attention-deficit/hyperactivity disorder during attentional load task." *Journal of the American Academy of Child and Adolescent Psychiatry* 41 (2002): 811–19.

FDA consumer information Web site. Strattera. www.fda.gov/cder/consumerinfo/druginfo/strattera.htm.

Filipek, P. A., P. J. Accardo, G. T. Baranek, et al. "The screening and diagnosis of autism spectrum disorders." *Journal of Autism and Developmental Disorders* 29, no. 2 (1999): 439–84.

Filipek, P. A., P. J. Accardo, S. Ashwal, et al. "Practice parameter: Screening and diagnosis of autism." *Neurology* 55 (2000): 468–79.

Foley, D. L., A. Pickles, H. M. Maes, et al. "Course and short-term outcomes of separation anxiety disorder in a community sample of twins." *Journal of the American Academy of Child and Adolescent Psychiatry* 43, no. 9 (September 2004): 1107–14.

Food and Drug Administration. Cylert letter. www.fda.gov/medwatch/safety/1999/cylert.htm.

Forehand, Rex, and Nicholas Long. *Parenting the Strong-Willed Child, Revised and Updated Edition: The Clinically Proven Five-Week Program for Parents of Two- to Six-Year-Olds.* New York: McGraw-Hill, 2002.

Fuchs, T., N. Birbaumer, W. Lutzenberger, J. H. Gruzelier, et al. "Neurofeedback treatment for attention-deficit/hyperactivity disorder in children: A comparison with methylphenidate." *Applied Psychophysiology and Biofeedback* 28 (2003): 1–12.

Gross, D., L. Fogg, C. Garvey, and W. Julion. "Behavior problems in young children: An analysis of cross-informant agreements and disagreements." *Research in Nursing and Health* 27, no. 6 (December 2004): 413–25.

Hallowell, Edward M., and John J. Ratey. *Driven to Distraction: Recognizing and Coping with Attention Deficit Disorder from Childhood Through Adulthood.* New York: Touchstone, 1995.

Hayes, D. "Recent developments in antidepressant therapy in special populations." *American Journal of Managed Care* 10 (6 suppl.)(July 2004): S179–85.

Hibbs, Euthymia D., and Peter S. Jensen. *Psychosocial Treatments for Child and Adolescent Disorders: Empirically Based Strategies for Clinical Practice.* 2nd ed. Washington, DC: American Psychological Association, 1996.

Hviid, A., M. Stellfeld, J. Wohlfahrt, and M. Melbye. "Association between thimerosal-containing vaccine and autism." *Journal of the American Medical Association* 290, no. 13 (2003): 1763–66.

Jacobson, John W., Richard M. Foxx, and James A. Mulick, eds. *Controversial Therapies for Developmental Disabilities.* New York: Lawrence Earlbaum Associates, 2004.

King, Robert A., et al. "Practice parameters for the assessment and treatment of children and adolescents with obsessive-compulsive disorder." *Journal of the American Academy of Child and Adolescent Psychiatry* 37 (10 suppl.)(1998).

Klass, Perri, and Eileen Costello. *Quirky Kids: Understanding and Helping Your Child Who Doesn't Fit In—When to Worry and When Not to Worry.* New York: Ballantine, 2003.

Klein, D. F. "SSRIs in children and suicide." *Science* 305, no. 5689 (September 3, 2004): 1401.

Korvatska, E., J. Van de Water, T. F. Anders, and M. E. Gershwin. "Genetic and immunologic considerations in autism." *Neurobiology of Disease* 9 (2002): 107–25.

Kratochvil, C. J., L. L. Greenhill, J. S. March, et al. "The role of stimulants in the treatment of preschool children with attention-deficit hyperactivity disorder." *CNS Drugs* 18, no. 14 (2004): 957–66. Review.

Kurtz, S. M. "Treating ADHD in schools." *School Nurse News* 21, no. 5 (November 2004): 29–33.

Lerner, J. W. *Learning Disabilities: Theories, Diagnosis, and Teaching Strategies.* 8th ed. Boston, MA: Houghton Mifflin, 2002.

Lewinsohn, P. M., D. N. Klein, and J. R. Seely. "Bipolar disorders in a community sample of older adolescents: Prevalence, phenomenology, comorbidity, and course." *Journal of the American Academy of Child and Adolescent Psychiatry* 34, no. 4 (1995): 454–63.

Lewinsohn, P. M., P. Rohde, and J. R. Seeley. "Major depressive disorder in older adolescents: Prevalence, risk factors, and clinical implications." *Clinical Psychology Review* 18, no. 7 (1998): 765–94.

Loeber, Rolf, Jeffrey Burke, Benjamin Lahey, et al. "Oppositional Defiant and Conduct Disorder: A Review of the Past 10 Years, Part I." *Journal of the American Academy of Child and Adolescent Psychiatry* 39, no. 12 (December 2000): 1468–84.

Loo, S. K. "EEG and neurofeedback findings in ADHD." *ADHD Report* 11 (2003): 1–6.

Loo, S. K., C. Hopfer, P. D. Teale, and M. L. Reite. "EEG Correlates of Methylphenidate Response in ADHD: Association with Cognitive and Behavioral Measures." *Journal of Clinical Neurophysiology* 21, no. 6 (November/December 2004): 457–64.

Lord, C., S. Risi, L. Lambrecht, et al. "The autism diagnostic observation schedule-generic: A standard measure of social and communication deficits associated with the spectrum of autism." *Journal of Autism and Developmental Disorders* 30, no. 3 (2000): 205–30.

Louters, L. L. "Don't overlook childhood depression." *Journal of the American Academy of Physician's Assistants* 17, no. 9 (September 2004): 18–24. Review.

Lovaas, O. I. "Behavioral treatment and normal educational and intellectual functioning in young autistic children." *Journal of Consulting and Clinical Psychology* 55 (1987): 3–9.

Malhotra, S., and N. Gupta. "Childhood disintegrative disorder." *Journal of Autism and Developmental Disorders* 29, no. 6 (1999): 491–98.

McCarthy, J., D. Arrese, A. McGlashan, et al. "Sustained attention and visual processing speed in children and adolescents with bipolar disorder and other psychiatric disorders." *Psychology Reports* 95, no. 1 (August 2004): 39–47.

McDougle, C. J. "Methylphenidate an effective treatment for ADHD?" *Journal of Autism and Developmental Disorders* 34, no. 5 (October 2004): 593–94.

McDougle, C. J., K. A. Stigler, and D. J. Posey. "Treatment of aggression in children and adolescents with autism and conduct disorder." *Journal of Clinical Psychiatry* 64 (suppl. 4) (2003): 16–25.

McEachin, J. J., T. Smith, and O. I. Lovaas. "Long-term outcome for children with autism who received early intensive behavioral treatment." *American Journal on Mental Retardation* 97 (1993): 359–72.

Mercer, C. D., and A. R. Mercer. *Teaching Students with Learning Problems.* 6th ed. New York: Prentice Hall College, 2001.

Merikangas, K. R., and N. C. Low. "The epidemiology of mood disorders." *Current Psychiatry Reports* 6, no. 6 (December 2004): 411–21.

Monastra, V. J., D. M. Monastra, and S. George. "The effects of stimulant therapy, EEG biofeedback and parenting style on the primary symptoms of attention-deficit/hyperactivity disorder." *Applied Psychophysiology and Biofeedback* 27 (2001): 231–49.

Monroe, S. M., P. Rohde, J. R. Seeley, et al. "Life events and depression in adolescence: Relationship loss as a prospective risk factor for first onset of major depressive disorder." *Journal of Abnormal Psychology* 108, no. 4 (1999): 606–14.

MTA Cooperative Group. "A 14-month randomized clinical trial of treatment strategies for attention deficit hyperactivity disorder." *Archives of General Psychiatry* 56, no. 12 (1999).

Murray, M. L., C. S. de Vries, and I. C. Wong. "A drug utilization study of antidepressants in children and adolescents using the General Practice Research Database." *Archives of Disease in Childhood* 89, no. 12 (December 2004): 1098–102.

Nadeau, Kathleen G. *The Survival Guide for College Students with ADD or LD.* Washington, DC: Magination Press, 1994.

National Association of School Psychologists. Committee Reports (IDEA changes). U.S. House of Representatives Report 108–77. www.nasponline .org/advocacy/IDEAHouseReport.pdf.

———. IDEA Information Page. www.nasponline.org/advocacy/IDEAinformation.html.

———. Legislative Updates. nasponline.org/advocacy/index.html#legupdates.

———. U.S. Senate Report 108–185. www.nasponline.org/advocacy/IDEACommittee.pdf.

National Dissemination Center for Children with Disabilities. Asperger's Disorder. April 1, 2004. www.nichcy.org/resources/asperger.asp.

————. Autistic Disorder. April 1, 2004. www.nichcy.org/resources/autism.asp.

————. Childhood Disintegrative Disorder. April 2, 2004. www.nichcy.org/resources/disintegrative.asp.

————. PDD-NOS. April 1, 2004. www.nichcy.org/resources/pddnos.asp.

National Mental Health Association. "Children's Mental Health Statistics." www.nmha.org/children/prevent/stats.cfm. 2005.

Newman, T. B. "A black-box warning for antidepressants in children?" *New England Journal of Medicine* 351, no. 16 (October 2004): 1595–98.

Pelham, W. E., T. Wheeler, and A. Chronis. "Empirically supported psychosocial treatments for attention deficit hyperactivity disorder." *Journal of Clinical Child Psychology* 27 (1998): 190–205.

Pelletier, P. M., S. A. Ahmad, and B. P. Rourke. "Classification rules for basic phonological processing disabilities and nonverbal learning disabilities: Formulation and external validity." *Child Neuropsychology* 7 (2001): 84–98.

Pennington, B. F. *The Development of Psychopathology: Nature and Nurture.* New York: Guilford Press, 2002.

————. *Diagnosing Learning Disorders: A Neuropsychological Framework.* New York: Guilford Press, 1991.

Petti, V. L., S. L. Voelker, D. L. Shore, and S. E. Hayman-Abello. "Perception of nonverbal emotion cues by children with nonverbal learning disabilities." *Journal of Developmental and Physical Disabilities* 15 (2003): 23–26.

Powers, M. D., ed. *Children with Autism: A Parent's Guide.* 2nd ed. Bethesda, MD: Woodbine House, 2000.

Powers, Michael, with Janet Poland. *Asperger Syndrome and Your Child: A Parent's Guide.* New York: HarperResource, 2003.

President's Commission on Excellence in Special Education. *A New Era: Revitalizing Special Education for Children and Their Families.* Washington, DC: 2002. www.ed.gov/inits/commissionsboards/whspecialeducation/reports/index.html.

Reddy, Linda A., Tara M. Files-Hall, and Charles E. Schaeffer. *Empirically Based Play Interventions for Children.* Washington, DC: American Psychological Association, 2005.

Research Units on Pediatric Psychopharmacology Network. "Risperidone in children with autism and serious behavioral problems." *New England Journal of Medicine* 347, no. 5 (2002): 314–21.

Ris, Douglas. *The syndrome of nonverbal learning disabilities (NLD): A critical analysis.* 2004 AACN Workshops, Workshop #5. June 10–12, 2004.

Robbins, D. I., D. Fein, M. I. Barton, and J. A. Green. "The modified checklist for autism in toddlers: An initial study investigating the early detection of autism and pervasive developmental disorders." *Journal of Autism and Developmental Disorders* 31, no. 2 (2001): 149–51.

Rourke, Byron P., ed. *Syndrome of Nonverbal Learning Disabilities.* New York: Guilford Press, 1995.

Schaffer, D., P. Fisher, M. K. Dulkan, et al. "The NIMH Diagnostic Interview Schedule for Children Version 2.3 (DISC-2.3): Description, acceptability, prevalence rates and performance in the MECA study." *Journal of the American Academy of Child and Adolescent Psychiatry* 35, no. 7 (1996): 865–77.

Seligman, Martin E. *The Optimistic Child: Proven Program to Safeguard Children from Depression and Build Lifelong Resilience.* New York: Harper, 1996.

Shaywitz, Sally. *Overcoming Dyslexia: A New and Complete Science-Based Program for Overcoming Reading Problems at Any Level.* New York: Knopf, 2003.

Siegel, Bryna. *The World of the Autistic Child: Understanding and Treating Autistic Spectrum Disorders.* London: Oxford University Press, 1998.

Spear-Swerling, L., and R. J. Sternberg. *Off-Track: When Poor Readers Become Learning Disabled.* Boulder, CO: Westview, 1996.

Spence, Sue, Vanessa Cobham, Ann Wignall, and Ronald M. Rapee. *Helping Your Anxious Child: A Step-By-Step Guide for Parents.*

Spencer, T., J. Biederman, and T. Wilens. "Attention-deficit/hyperactivity disorder and comorbidity." *Pediatric Clinics of North America* 46, no. 5 (1999): 915–27.

Stone, W. L., E. E. Coonrod, and O. Y. Ousley. "Brief report: Screening tool for autism in two-year-olds (STAT): Development and preliminary data." *Journal of Autism and Developmental Disorders* 30, no. 6 (2000): 607–12.

Swanson, J. M., K. McBurnett, et al. "Effect of stimulant medication on children with attention deficit disorder: A review of reviews." *Exceptional Children* 60 (1993): 154–62.

Tadevosyan-Leyfer, O., M. Dowd, R. Mankoski, B. Winklosky. et al. "A principal components analysis of the autism diagnostic interview-revised." *Journal of the American Academy of Child and Adolescent Psychiatry* 42, no. 7 (2003): 864–72.

Tan, M., and R. Appleton. "Attention deficit and hyperactivity disorder, methylphenidate, and epilepsy." *Archives of Disease in Childhood* 90, no. 1 (January 2005): 57–59.

Thompson, Sue. "Nonverbal learning disorders." LDOnline (1996), www.ldon line.org/ld_indepth/general_info/nld.html.

———. "Nonverbal learning disorders revisited in 1997." LDOnline (1997), www.ldonline.org/ld_indepth/general_info/nld.html.

Timimi, S. "Rethinking childhood depression." *British Medical Journal* 329, no. 7479 (December 11, 2004): 1394–96.

Turkington, Carol A. *Making the Antidepressant Decision.* Chicago: Lowell House, 2001.

Turkington, Carol A., and Joseph R. Harris. *The Encyclopedia of Learning Disabilities.* New York: Facts on File, 2005.

U.S. Department of Health and Human Services, Substance Abuse and Mental Health Services Administration (SAMHSA), National Mental Health Information Service, Center for Mental Health Services. "Children's Mental Health Facts: Children and Adolescents with Anxiety Disorders." April 2003. www.mentalhealth.org/publications/allpubs/CA-0007/default.asp.

Vellutino, Frank R., Jack M. Fletcher, Margaret J. Snowling, and Donna M. Scanlon. "Specific reading disability (dyslexia): What have we learned in the past four decades?" *Journal of Child Psychology and Psychiatry* 45 no. 1 (2004): 2–40.

Vitiello, B., and P. Jensen. "Medication development and testing in children and adolescents." *Archives of General Psychiatry* 54 (1997): 871–76.

Volkmar, F. R. "Childhood disintegrative disorder: Issues for *DSM-IV.*" *Journal of Autism and Developmental Disorders* 22 (1999): 625–42.

Volkmar, F., A. Klin, W. Marans, and D. Cohen. "Childhood disintegrative disorder." In D. Cohen and F. Volkmar, eds., *Handbook of Autism and Pervasive Developmental Disorders,* 2nd ed., 60–93. New York: Wiley, 1997.

Volkmar, Fred R., Catherine Lord, Anthony Bailey, Robert T. Schultz, and Ami Klin. "Autism and pervasive developmental disorders." *Journal of Child Psychology and Psychiatry* 45, no. 1 (2004): 135–70.

Weissman, M. M., S. Wolk, R. B. Goldstein, et al. "Depressed adolescents grown up." *Journal of the American Medical Association* 281 (1999): 1701–13.

Wong, I. C., F. M. Besag, P. J. Santosh, and M. L. Murray. "Use of selective serotonin reuptake inhibitors in children and adolescents." *Drug Safety* 27, no. 13 (2004): 991–1000.

Zalsman, G., O. Pumeranz, G. Peretz, et al. "Attention patterns in children with attention deficit disorder with or without hyperactivity." *Scientific World Journal* 3 (November 13, 2003): 1093–1107.

Index

brain chemistry (*continued*)
in obsessive-compulsive
disorder, 206
in schizophrenia, 226
in Tourette's syndrome, 228
brain injury, 67
attention-deficit/hyperactivity
disorder and, 148–49
conduct disorder and, 162
fine motor disability and, 130
nonverbal learning disabilities
and, 125
traumatic, 48, 149, 233
bulimia, 212, 233
bullying, 162, 163

carbamazepine (Tegretol), 188
Catapres (clonidine), 153, 230
Celexa (citalopram HBr), 217
Centers for Disease Control
(CDC), 170
Center for Epidemiologic Studies
Depression (CES-D) Scale,
215
central auditory processing
disorders, 234–35
cerebral palsy, 60–61, 69, 233
helpful organizations and
associations for, 260
Checklist of Autism in Toddlers
(CHAT), 180
checklists, 23–25, 28–33, 157
Child Behavior Checklist, 28, 95
Childhood Asperger Syndrome
Test (CAST), 181
Children and Adults with
Attention-Deficit Disorder
(CHAAD), 155
Children's Depression Inventory
(CDI), 215
child study teams, 43–46, 56
chorea, 229
citalopram HBr (Celexa), 217
Clinical Evaluation of Language
Fundamentals, 95
clomipramine (Anafranil), 206

clonidine (Catapres), 153, 230
cognitive ability, testing of, 95
cognitive behavior therapy (CBT),
75–76, 78
for anxiety disorders, 196, 198
for depression, 215–16, 218
for obsessive-compulsive
disorder, 206
for phobias, 199–200
for post-traumatic stress
disorder, 203
cognitive disabilities, 97, 136
see also mental retardation
complex tasks, breaking down, 151
Comprehensive Test of
Phonological Processing, 95
Concerta (methylphenidate), 152
conduct disorder, 14, 155, 160–63
bipolar disorder and, 220
depression and, 210, 212
Continuous Performance Tasks,
95
coordination disorder, 10–11,
129–31
core deficits or problems, 6
in anxiety disorders, 195–96
in attention-deficit/hyperactivity
disorder, 143, 146–47
in autistic spectrum disorders,
171–73
in conduct disorder, 160–62
in coordination disorders,
129–30
in developmental speech and
language disorders, 126–27
in dyslexia, 118–19
in nonverbal learning
disabilities, 122–24
in oppositional-defiant disorder,
158–59
in Rett syndrome, 231–32
in Tourette's syndrome, 228
Cylert (pemoline), 153

daily living skills, 185
deaf-blindness, 47

IQ tests (*continued*)
  dyslexia and, 117, 119
  learning disabilities and, 102–4,
    110, 124
irrational beliefs, challenging, 196

Judgment of Line Orientation, 95

labels, 7–8
language disorders, 9–11, 101,
    126–29, 138
  autistic spectrum disorders and,
    173, 174
  checklist for, 30
  core deficits in, 126–27
  diagnosis of, 127
  helpful organizations and
    associations for, 287–88
  and learning second language,
    55
  special education for, 48, 71
  tests for, 95, 103
  treatment of, 60, 129
lead poisoning, information sources
    on, 278
learned helplessness, 212
learning disabilities (LDs), 5, 6,
    8–12, 67, 102, 105–41
  academic, 115–22
  adjustment disorder with
    depressed mood and, 219
  anxiety and, 17, 195
  assessment of, 113–14
  attention-deficit/hyperactivity
    disorder and, 14, 21, 145–46
  autism and, 60
  below-average intelligence and,
    131–38
  books on, 249–250
  clues signaling, 111–12
  coordination disorders, 129–31
  definitions of, 109–10
  depression and, 20, 210
  developmental speech and
    language disorders, 126–29
  extra help for, 11–12

helpful organizations and
    associations for, 279–81
learning problems versus,
    106–8
nonverbal, 122–26
obsessive-compulsive disorder
    and, 205
oppositional-defiant disorder
    and, 157
parental reactions to, 105, 106
patterns underlying, 138
school's responsibility in,
    112–13
special education for, 47–54, 57,
    71, 115
testing for, 86, 102–3
Web site for, 141
*see also specific learning
    disabilities*
listening comprehension problems,
    116, 138
lithium, 221
Lovaas, Ivar, 185
Luvox (fluvoxamine), 206, 217

manic depression, *see* bipolar
    disorder
math difficulties and disabilities, 9,
    11, 85–87
  anxiety and, 195
  calculation problems, 116,
    138
  clues signaling, 111
  dyslexia and, 117
  reasoning problems, 116, 138
  testing for, 97, 102–3
mean, 98
measles-mumps-rubella (MMR)
    vaccine, 177
Medicaid, 83
medical insurance, 81–82
medications, 80
  for anxiety disorders, 196
  for attention-deficit/
    hyperactivity disorder, 63–64,
    87, 146, 148, 150–54, 166